A COLD WAR FIGHTER PILOT
IN PEACETIME AND WAR

DEREK J. SHARP

FONTHILL

This book is dedicated to my brave dear friends and comrades who perished in the service of Her Majesty Queen Elizabeth II doing what they did best: flying their beloved aeroplanes.

Fonthill Media Language Policy

Fonthill Media publishes in the international English language market. One language edition is published worldwide. As there are minor differences in spelling and presentation, especially with regard to American English and British English, a policy is necessary to define which form of English to use. The Fonthill Policy is to use the form of English native to the author. Derek J. Sharp was born and educated in High Wycombe; therefore British English has been adopted in this publication.

Fonthill Media Limited
Fonthill Media LLC
www.fonthillmedia.com
office@fonthillmedia.com

First published in the United Kingdom and the United States of America 2019

British Library Cataloguing in Publication Data:
A catalogue record for this book is available from the British Library

Copyright © Derek J. Sharp 2019

ISBN 978-1-78155-737-2

Typeset in 10pt on 13pt Sabon
Printed and bound in England

Preface

It was a bomber's moon on the night of 25 June 1943. Clear skies and light winds made perfect flying conditions for Lancaster R5740 of No. 44 Squadron, airborne from sleepy RAF Dunholme Lodge in Lincolnshire. Its target was the synthetic petrol plant at Gelsenkirchen in the heavy industrial area of the Ruhr, known affectionately to crews as 'Happy Valley'. Its captain was Plt Off. Derek Sharp. Tragically, this was to be the crew's last sortie. Thirty aircraft failed to return from that raid and R5740, together with all its crew, vanished without a trace.

Fast forward some fifty years to yet another war and yet another pilot of a four-engined aircraft was flying intrepidly into an area of lethal skies—into yet another 'flak alley'. The captain was also called Derek Sharp, but this time the flak, though far less intense, was far more deadly. Far below his huge aeroplane, an incredibly sophisticated missile was launched and its target was Derek Mk 2.

During the Second World War, more than 55,000 Bomber Command aircrew lost their lives. Plt Off. Sharp was just one statistic. I was born not long afterwards and named after Derek Minden Sharp, who was in fact my uncle. I have had an incredibly charmed life and it has been suggested that possibly he has played some part in my survival.

This book was originally supposed to carry the title '*Blunty's Bumper Book of War Stories*', for it is in part a selection of incidents that have happened to me (or were caused by me) in both peace and war. However, something fairly mysterious happened during the time I was writing this book, which caused me to change the title. You will learn why if you read on.

There is a beautiful ABBA song, which ends with the lyrics: 'I close my eyes and my twilight images go by all too soon, like an angel passing through my room'.

Now, all too soon, I am also in the twilight of my life. However, though dimmer than it used to be, I still can capture many images in my mind's eye. It has also been suggested that a guardian angel may well have played a significant part in my life. Unquestionably, I have had a few perilous escapes. So maybe an angel has sat on my wing tip ever since I learnt to fly. One event, more than any other, remains crystal clear in my memory: the events of 15 February 1983, a day that changed my life forever. Now I look back on my life and wonder at times what would have been. Would I have made the highest office, as some of my close contemporaries did? Would I have had so much fun? Perhaps I would have died later in the First Gulf War, as some of my chums did? Whatever, that day it was said that an angel really did pass through my room. Indeed, perhaps she actually always sits on my wing whenever danger draws near.

Acknowledgements

Naturally, I would like to thank my father for joining the Royal Air Force in 1918, for if I had not been brought up on a 'marriage patch' at an RAF airfield, I might not have fallen in love with aeroplanes. Secondly, I must pay tribute to the plethora of qualified flying instructors (QFIs) who had the patience and skill to be able to turn a rough-and-ready slow learner into quite a reasonable aviator. I perversely might pay tribute to Donald Duck for meeting me on 15 February 1983, changing my life and thus opening many new doors for me. Finally, of course, I must pay enormous tribute to my soulmate, wife, and fellow pilot, Su Khoo, who not only played a significant part in the production of this book, both in layout, photography, and proofreading, but also accompanied me in flight on many of our later adventures.

A selfie of Su Khoo, aviation photographer. (*Su Khoo*)

Contents

1

In the Beginning

I have always had a burning passion for flying ever since, at the tender age of four, I looked up into a clear blue Suffolk sky and marvelled as Meteor jet fighters screamed across the airfield where I lived. Today, some sixty-eight years later, that passion burns just as strongly.

I suppose I would like to be known as an ex-fighter pilot. For sure, the first half of my extensive flying career was as an attack pilot. The very broad brush of being a fighter pilot encompasses a myriad of different tasks and roles. There is the interceptor pilot, known today as an 'air superiority pilot', the very stuff that Battle of Britain pilots were made of. We then have the attack pilots, also known as the 'mud movers', who support the Army on the battlefield. This is known as 'close air support'. They take out the tanks and other armoured vehicles and I was later to join a squadron whose emblem was indeed a can opener used to open tin cans! Then we have the vast range of bomber pilots who, though not true fighter pilots, do operate anything from large multi-crew aircraft to single-seat low-level attack. Their targets are various, but can include railways, airfields, and communications facilities.

I started as an attack pilot, but was also trained to shoot other aircraft down. Was I successful? Did I ever? You will have to read on to find out, but let us start with the present.

Yesterday, on a beautiful crisp winter's morning, I once again took to the sky. This is what I wrote after that magical flight:

> I could say that I was up with the lark, but I would be wrong.
> I arose long before any bird thought about early tasty worms.
> By dawn's early light, I was chatting to the Met Chappie and collecting Notams.
> Then, having managed to suss out how to open the massive hangar door (I was alone),
> I dragged my beautiful Steed out into the chilly morning air,
> Just as an enormous golden globe rose over the eastern horizon.
> After a short check that the controls were arranged in an eye-catching and pleasing manner,
> I started the engine, brutally disturbing the uncanny silence of that crisp January morn.
> Subsequently, having ensured that my engine was warm enough to carry me aloft,
> I opened up to full power and sailed heavenwards into a still calm sun-kissed sky.
> High above the frost and early morning mist.
> High above mortal man.

What joy!

No one but I disturbed the chilly air that frosty morn.

Apart from Angels, I must have been the only soul aloft.

What spirituality!

How ethereal it all seemed.

I don't think I have ever seen the Cotswolds look so beautiful.

It reminded me so much of the poem 'High Flight':

'Oh, I have slipped the surly bonds of earth/And danced the skies on laughter silvered wings.'

It reminded me also why I so love this part of our green and pleasant land. It really was one of those most perfect occasions. But I get ahead of myself. There is still much to tell. So much more.

The very first time I took to the air in an aerial machine on my own was actually an accident. On a balmy day in July 1960, on the playing fields of a well-known grammar school close to Bomber Command Headquarters, I was catapulted into the atmosphere in the school's single-seat glider. Unfortunately, or fortunately, depending on which way you look at it, the supervisor had omitted to fit the lift spoilers to the wing, which were necessary to prevent an *ab initio* student from actually flying. Hence, rather unexpectedly, my primitive craft and I soared to the dizzy height of 5 feet, landing shortly afterwards on the First XI cricket pitch, in the middle of an important match. Suffice to say, this did little to impress the team and the sight of a very young Bluntie being chased off the playing field by a horde of irate sixth formers waving cricket bats was a sight to behold. I can remember that auspicious event as if it were yesterday. However, it would be several years later before I ascended the heavens again on my own—that time in one of Her Majesty's finest Jet Provosts.

Many years and, indeed, zillions of miles later, I often crossed the mighty oceans late at night. In an effort to keep my flight deck crew awake, I would tell tales of derring-do and disasters that had befallen me over the years. Eventually, as many a tale contained the four elements of a good story—namely interest, knowledge, pathos, and humour—several co-pilots suggested I put pen to paper.

I make no apology that a few of my yarns have previously been published in house journals. Chances are that you will never have even heard of those magazines and thus not read the articles. More importantly, the majority of my adventures have never been published before because I did not want to be incarcerated at Her Majesty's pleasure. Now maybe I do not care anymore! Many incidents have been trawled from the depths of my memory, though it is interesting to note that several have come to me in dreams. Maybe someone jogged my subconscious memory. Who knows?

Interestingly, my flying career has always been touched by miraculous escapes and I have evaded the jaws of death several times. Though I will mention some examples, none better is the tale of my appointment with a mallard duck in February 1983. How I survived that incident will never truly be known; nevertheless, it has been suggested more than once that I have had an angel flying formation with me, keeping me safe. Though this theory is totally preposterous, some of my adventures cannot be explained away just by reason and logic. Indeed, even to this day, I have a fridge magnet with the inscription 'Never drive faster than your Guardian Angel can fly'. Wise words indeed; pity I often ignore them.

Anyway, here are my thoughts.

2
Early Days

I was born at 7 a.m. on Tuesday 23 October 1945, the first son of a RAF warrant officer. As far as I know (for we never met), his father (my grandfather) had been a captain in the Royal Lancashire Fusiliers. Apparently, I am distantly related to Ernest Shackleton, the famous Antarctic explorer, and, incidentally, I am also related to an American axe murder (though thankfully not by blood). Perhaps therefore it was inevitable that I would eventually seek a career in the Her Majesty's Armed Forces. My father lived for the RAF, as he had joined at the dawn of its inception and had been mentioned in dispatches for heroism in the Second World War. Regrettably, he had been forced to retire when my mother refused to accompany him on posting to Hong Kong after the war.

My father was an archetypal parent of his generation. The sharing of the children's upbringing was not for him. He was a very private man, though I am told that his men loved him. Sadly, though, towards the end of their lives, neither of my parents loved each other. Though they never divorced and lived in the same house, they never spoke. I am sure that was partly due to the war. They married and my father more or less immediately went off to war, only to return some six years later. No wonder they never got on. Mind you, I am not so sure my mother had much of a significant hand in my development either. She was the typical professional nurse, wedded to her profession, and it was almost certainly left to my elder sister, Gillian, to see to the day-to-day needs of my younger twin brothers and myself.

Regrettably, too, I knew nothing of my paternal grandfather, an officer in the Royal Lancashire Fusiliers, or indeed of the exploits of his son and my namesake, Plt Off. Derek Minden Sharp. I do know that my grandfather joined the Army in the twilight of the nineteenth century, having had to change his name to 'Sharp' (his mother's maiden name) as his father was of Irish descent and thus might have encountered a problem with his admission. My grandfather spent much of his career overseas, mainly in India, but my father was born within spitting distance of Farnborough airfield, one of the very first aviation sites. When he joined the RAF, this greatly disappointed my grandfather, who no doubt wanted his son to join his old regiment. Nevertheless, my father enjoyed an illustrious military career, at a time when the RAF was emerging from its embryonic birth. How I wish I could have served at that time. What adventures I would have had! I suppose my father must have inadvertently influenced me in my selection of my own career, which turned out somewhat satisfactorily, as you, dear reader, will find out.

The author's father and his men in front of a Lancaster, *c.* 1945. (*Author's collection*)

Times just after the Second World War were harsh and food rationing was still in force. We lived in RAF married quarters at RAF Stradishall in Suffolk (now a prison camp). We had no central heating and the modern conveniences that we all enjoy today were perhaps only seen in science fiction films. Maybe the conditions we lived under moulded my character, for the winter on 1946–47 was the coldest for fifty years. That severe, relentless winter will be long remembered as one of our most legendary, and Suffolk got much of the worst of it. I even remember the snow coming up to my bedroom window it was so deep. Even the Thames froze over.

My first introduction to aviation was quite early on and rather unusual. Aircrew are required to perform several survival drills at regular intervals throughout the year. Normally they are performed in a local swimming pool, though sometimes at sea. My first experience of this 'fun' event came earlier for me than most. During the balmy summer of '47, my father brought home a multi-seat life raft from the safety equipment section and proceeded to cut the protective top canopy off. Having filled it with water, my sister and I now had the perfect swimming pool. I do not recall logging that event as a serious safety equipment procedure, and it would be some forty more years before I again endured the delights of a multi-seat life raft, and even then it would be in the inclement waters of the Southwest Approaches and not my front garden. It would also not end with me toddling back into the family kitchen for hot milk and biscuits, but by being dragged unceremoniously out of an icy sea by air-sea rescue helicopter. No milk and biscuits for me then, but I suppose my spirits were possibly elevated by the traditional tot of rum.

Consequently, flying has always been in my blood from birth, and perhaps a guardian angel has always been there to catch me when I fell. I suppose the first time I 'took to the air' on my own was early in 1949 when I was just four years old. While fooling around, I fell out of an upstairs window. My angel that day realised it had work to do and amazingly I suffered no ill effects. Perhaps, luckily, I landed on my head!

The next time was late in 1954. Gillian had given me a 'hand-me-down' bicycle. True to my intrepid and adventurous nature, I decided that I should immediately take a ride up the main A40 trunk road. It was not too busy in those quiet days of 1954, but busy enough. It was not long before I encountered a right turn and I did just that, turn right. No signals, no messing around. Unfortunately, the lady driving the motorcar behind me was not terribly alert, and though she should have suspected that a nine-year-old boy, wobbling down the main road on a bicycle far too big for him, might do something rather silly, she ploughed on regardless. I turned across her bow and she hit me broadside on, sending me flying through the air. I fractured my left leg in two places. It would not be the last time I broke my bones. What happened to the lady driver, I know not, but I did end up in the casualty department at High Wycombe War Memorial Hospital. Interestingly, this was not long after my mother, who was the nursing sister in charge in A&E, had come on duty.

More broken bones were in store for me later in childhood, but despite those accidents, the desire to fly never left me. Though I failed to persuade my father to take me flying during those tender years, the sight and sound of Spitfires, Lancasters, and Meteors patrolling the skies above our married quarter at that Suffolk air base obviously left an indelible mark on my character, for I always knew that I wanted to fly. Nothing else would suffice and as soon as I had my chance I joined the Combined Cadet Force at my grammar school, RGS High Wycombe. It was here where I incurred the wrath of the First XI cricket team.

The author in a Grasshopper glider identical to one from schooldays. (*Su Khoo*)

Before that, I had already realised that a life of academia was definitely not for me. School was merely a means to an end to enable me to reach for the sky. I had a very modest education, firstly at a Roman Catholic primary school where nuns taught me. I am not sure if the standard of education was any good, but the food was terrible. I failed my 11+ examination to enable me to gain entrance to the local grammar school, which perhaps might have ruined my later chances of gaining a commission in the Armed Forces. Luckily, however, following two years at secondary modern school, I passed the entrance examination at 13+ and went to the RGS just a few years later than my contemporaries. Perhaps that is why I failed to excel at academics, but fortuitously I gained sufficient A-levels to join the RAF.

It was as a member of the Combined Cadet Force at the RGS that I enjoyed my first 'proper' flight. On a Thursday afternoon, late in summer, the sight, sound, and incredible experience of lifting off from Mother Earth in a pre-war Avro Anson of the Metropolitan Communication Squadron based at Booker Airfield is still today indelibly engraved in my memory. I recall clearly sitting on the left side of that ancient aircraft watching the extraordinarily amazing sight of the ground fall away from the Anson. It was as though my aircraft was fixed in space and it was indeed the earth that moved.

Chipmunk air experience flying followed at regular intervals throughout my formative years, invariably from White Waltham aerodrome near Maidenhead. I would cycle the 20 or so miles there on a Saturday or Sunday just for a half-hour trip. Little was I to know that less than seven or so years later, at that same airfield, I myself would be the pilot in command, giving air cadets their own thrilling first taste of aviation. Some sixty years later, I was still teaching air cadets the basics of airmanship.

It was during my time with the cadet force that the flying bug really took hold. Though passenger trips were OK, it was the introduction to gliding that really inspired. Now I was to actually take control of a real flying machine. After my painful experience with the Grasshopper adventure, culminating in the production of a deep furrow across the First X1 cricket pitch, I progressed onwards and upwards to larger and more capable flying machines. A gliding course at RAF Halton earned me my 'A & B certificates', the equivalent of my glider pilot's wings. Later, during my RAF flying course, I joined the local gliding club and soared to even greater heights. My final flight was on 20 March 1966, when I climbed to 7,200 feet in a Swallow, remaining aloft for some eighty-six minutes. This was all without an engine! Sadly, I was never to fly an aeroplane without an engine ever again; though later I used my earlier skills to good effect when the engine unexpectedly stopped on my powered aircraft!

So from a very early age, I wanted to be a pilot. I just wanted to fly aeroplanes, unlike this little article published many years ago and allegedly written by a young boy:

'Why I want to be a pilot'
 I want to be a pilot when I grow up because it's a fun job and easy to do. That is why there are so many pilots flying today. Pilots don't need much education, they just have to learn numbers so that they can read instruments.
 I guess they should be able to read road maps so they won't get lost. Pilots should be brave so they won't get scared if it's foggy and they can't see, or if a wing or motor falls off they should stay calm so they'll know what to do.

Pilots have to have good eyes to see through clouds and they can't be afraid of thunder and lightning because they are closer to them than we are.

The salary pilots make is another thing I like. They make more than they can spend. This is because most people think that plane flying is dangerous, except pilots don't because they know how easy it is.

There is not much I don't like except girls. Girls like pilots and all the stewardesses want to marry pilots, so the pilots have to chase them away so they don't bother them.

I hope I don't get airsick because I get carsick, and if I do I could not be a pilot and then I would have to get a job.

Out of the mouth of babes? Well, I wanted to fly and was totally ambivalent regarding money or girls.

Of course, aviation was not my only childhood interest. At an early age, as so many of my contemporaries did, I joined the Boy Scout movement. Wolf cubs led on to scouting, which in turn led to the Rovers. I enjoyed many a campfire in the open and countless nights under the stars. These valuable experiences were instrumental in the formation of my character. They toughened me up considerably, paving the way towards being better equipped to survive forthcoming Officer Training. I certainly was not a 'Mummy's Boy'!

The next time I had cause to call on the services of my angel was later in boyhood while rock climbing in the Llanberis Pass in North Wales. I was climbing a large rock overhang using pitons (large metal spikes) to secure my rope and étriers (small rope ladders used in artificial climbing). I inadvertently selected the same crack in the rock face to bury my next piton, which must have opened the crack slightly thus allowing my previous piton, which was securing me, to come out. I fell some 10 feet to the ground and broke my arm. My angel must have been on holiday that day, thus Bangor hospital got my trade.

Scouting had given me the chance to experience and later excel at mountaineering. As a very young lad, I climbed many towering peaks in the Cuillin of Skye to the French Alps. Every weekend saw me and my chums hitching lifts to Snowdonia in order to climb in the fabled Llanberis Pass, the scene which was later to witness my third 'non flight'. Many happy nights were spent in a sleeping bag living rough among the boulders under the shadow of some of the fiercest rock climbs in the UK. How times have changed! Now my hotel room must offer all the usual modern creature comforts! Incredibly, by the tender age of sixteen, I had climbed lofty peaks all over Europe. I suppose some credit must be given to my mother for allowing a mere infant to experience such adventures. In this modern age of computers, iPods, and mobile phones, some youngsters do not even venture as far as the next country, let alone taste the thrills of the frozen 'Roof of the World'.

Though flying was the ultimate goal, climbing did take up most of my time during my schooldays. Climbing in the UK had provided many thrills and spills, but two chums and I wanted to venture further afield to broaden our horizons and create new challenges. So, despite the fact that we were in reality 'babes in arms', total novices, and rather naïve, we decided to conquer Mont Blanc in the Alps, all 15,781 feet of it. The fact that this was also one of the most dangerous mountains in the Alps did not seem to bother us, nor my parents. It has the highest fatality rate of any mountain in Europe. Some estimates put the fatality rate at an average of 100 climbers a year; others estimate that more people die each

The author in climbing gear, *c.* 1962. (*Author's collection*)

year in the Mont Blanc range than in any decade in the Alaskan mountain ranges. So it perhaps bothered my guardian angel for I suspect she wanted that fortnight off. With me ascending into the stratosphere without much experience of snow climbing at all, she must have cancelled her leave and prepared herself for hard work. Just as well that she did as not for the first time, but definitely not the last either, her protection was most certainly required as never before.

Reading back now on an article in my local paper, I was quoted as stating that the ascent of Mont Blanc was no more than an 'afternoon stroll'. It was hardly that, as it took three days! Moreover, rock falls, snow blindness, and dysentery all took their toll on us three intrepid (foolish) youngsters that week and we were lucky to extricate ourselves from the mountain with our lives, but had some great memories. Were we foolhardy? Yes, of course. Were we stupid? Most certainly. Were our parents less protective of us than they should have been? Well, maybe, but do not forget just fifteen years previously, thousands of lads not much older than us were dying for their country in a vicious world war. Those heroes experienced far greater dangers than we did on that lethal mountain back in 1961. In that terrible war, many young men took risks far greater than I have ever dared to take and they paid the ultimate penalty. My uncle was just one of them when his luck ran out.

3

In the Service of Her Majesty

Before Her Majesty would let me loose in one of her shiny aeroplanes, I first had to be selected for pilot training. Not an easy task as competition was fierce. Initially, I applied to join the RAF after my sixteenth birthday, having just passed a measly five 'O' levels at my grammar school. So off I trotted to the Aircrew Selection Centre at RAF Biggin Hill, that well-known Battle of Britain fighter base. Here I was subjected to numerous hand–eye co-ordination exercises, leadership tests, and the all-essential comprehensive medical examination. In those days, we did not have the benefit of computer games, so their fiendish devices, designed to test my co-ordination, were very new to me. Nowadays, such co-ordination exercises are hardly a problem for modern kids. However, at least I think I was fitter than most youngsters of today, but, unfortunately, after a few days of torture, I failed to impress. I suspect the team there were rather polite, but sadly turned down that rather spotty immature youth with the question 'What will you do if you are unsuccessful?' My reply was to return to school and sit my A-levels. Their reply was 'Good idea', so that was exactly what I did, only to apply a couple of years later armed with another batch of mediocre examination results.

That said, this time I was more successful, although initially I thought I had failed once again. Maybe Her Majesty was desperate for pilots. Many tasks were thrown at me and I think I did quite well apart from the leadership exercise, which proved to be impossible. The team that I led unfortunately failed to cross the imaginary river, using just a couple of oil drums and some planks of wood. I thought my chances were slipping away. However, to my surprise and incredible relief, I was accepted for officer training and ultimately pilot training. When I asked why, as I had failed miserably in the leadership exercise, I was told that I had actually scored very highly. Apparently, my particular leadership exercise had no solution; all they were interested in was how I would control my team when presented with a totally impossible task.

Early in October of that year, I received a confirmation letter from the Air Ministry commanding me to report to RAF South Cerney on the evening of 7 December 1964 to begin my career as an RAF pilot. Hopefully, I would make the grade. Time would tell.

So it was on a cold dreary December morning in 1964 that my mother drove me in her venerable Morris Minor down to RAF South Cerney, Gloucestershire, to begin my officer training and a lifetime of service before the Colours. It obviously was not the enticement of the money that attracted me as I was paid the princely sum of £7 10s per week. If I had signed on for a short service commission, rather than one to the age of thirty-eight, I would have only been paid a miserly £5 per week, and so I commenced some thirty-nine years with the RAF. Little was I to know that years later I would return to the Cotswolds to be trained as a flying instructor, nor in fact that very much later I would actually retire there.

Unfortunately, South Cerney was a grass airfield without aeroplanes. Later it would act as a relief landing ground for the Central Flying School at RAF Little Rissington, just a stone's throw up the Fosse Way. Unknown to me at that time, many years later, I would end my flying career in the skies above this little aerodrome. However, way back in the '60s, not for us officer cadets was the pleasure of being able to watch aeroplanes perform, so at times we all needed some encouragement. Yet I was confined there for some four months, learning how to become an officer and a gentleman. Though I had passed the minimum standards for entry into the officer corps, judging by my final assessments, more than one of my tutors had doubts that they could turn this rough-spoken boy into anything half decent—but they tried!

Four months. Not long to change me from an uncouth lout into one of Her Majesty's finest. For four months we endured square bashing, academics, Air Force Law, Officers' Mess etiquette, flying subjects, and even how to eat peas from the correct side of a fork. I never really passed that bit, and even today, my peas are consumed using the fork as a form of spoon. Moreover, we certainly did not live the life of luxury. Twenty-two or more officer cadets were billeted in a single room—no carpets, no en-suite facilities, no wardrobes. Reveille was at 6 a.m., and breakfast was preceded by exercise. A parade was held outside after that, come rain or shine. It toughened us up. We were not even allowed off camp during the first month of training, apart from the one officer cadet who ran home to mummy on the second day of the course just because he became heartbroken that his golden locks were all shaved off. A lot worse was to come.

The other events that took place were leadership, hardship, and comradeship. We became as fit as Olympic athletes, we climbed mountains (something that came naturally to me), and we forded streams with minimal equipment. Given that my course started in December 1964, which was one of the coldest winters on record, our camping expeditions to the Brecon Beacons certainly changed us from boys to men. Though I personally had many rough edges, I think I shone at this stage, given my previous Boy Scout and climbing achievements.

However, that was not before a number of events that I still recall to this day. I vividly remember that out of some thirty or so officer cadets, only a handful were the proud owners of motorcars. Naturally, in those days, pre-MOT (an annual vehicle safety check), they were unsafe wrecks. I do recollect some six or so of us young bloods popping over to Cheltenham Ladies College in a cadet's ancient motor. Returning up Birdlip Hill, I remember being asked, along with others, to get out and walk while the owner drove up in reverse, such was the limited power of his motor. I myself still did not own a motorcar, nor would I for some time.

I also recall having to 'bull' up our accommodation prior to inspection by the Commanding Officer. One such event ended in chaos when a wretched fellow accidentally knocked over a foam fire extinguisher immediately prior to inspection, covering the corridor with copious gallons of foam. That wretched boy was me. My chums were not amused. For my sins, I was made to run around the airfield perimeter track carrying a very heavy gym bench. That helped to toughen me up even more, though I have to admit that as it was rather a foggy day in January, I did allow myself a five-minute break in the fog using the bench as a makeshift bed.

All too soon, or should I say 'after a lifetime', the four months at No. 1 Initial Training School came to an end and I passed out as Acting Pilot Officer Sharp. On 1 April 1965, I became an officer. April Fools' Day—was that an omen?

4
Basic Flying Training

I progressed to the next stage of my extensive training and made my way to RAF Leeming in darkest Yorkshire to begin my pilot course. However, before that could commence, I was informed of a backlog in training and that I would be temporarily attached to the 'Student Pilot Holding Flight' at RAF Dishforth, just a few miles down the road from Leeming. After a few months of kicking my heels and flying in all sorts of now obsolete aeroplanes, such as the huge Blackburn Beverley, I eventually arrived at No. 3 FTS.

Here I started my acquaintance with the other love of my life: motorcars. Having recently passed my driving test, I needed personal transportation, as the majority of RAF airfields were situated in the wilds and I needed mobility. Cheap cars in the '60s were plentiful as the MOT was some years hence. Thus I purchased an old 'sit up and beg' Ford Popular for the princely sum of £7.50. It had a plethora of features, including air conditioning—I could see the road through the floor! It also possessed other quaint features, for example on acceleration, the vacuum-driven windscreen wipers actually went slower, just when one needed them to speed up. Years later, when I began to collect models of all the cars I had owned, I purchased a 1:43 scale model Ford just like my first car. Sadly, it cost me more than twice what I had originally paid for the full-scale vehicle. I later moved on to something far sportier, a 1946 MG TC, which proved to be even less reliable than the Ford. The doors were termed 'suicide doors' as they opened backwards and had a habit of opening at speed. Moreover, whenever I filled up with petrol (only half a tank as my car had a hole in the fuel tank halfway up), I had to top the radiator up with water as well. The MG was eventually sold for a paltry £14; pity that I did not keep it in a barn for forty years as they are now worth more than a thousand times that. Whatever, that lovely old sports car was the start of my love affair with fast cars. I would have become very wealthy if I had stuck with economic family saloons, but not so contented.

Now they do say that pilots are born not trained. In fact, one of my early heroes was Robin Olds, a crack American pilot. He once wrote: 'There are pilots and there are pilots; with the good ones, it is inborn. You can't teach it. If you are a fighter pilot, you have to be willing to take risks'. Well that may indeed be partly true; certainly, the saying 'He has a good pair of hands' has validity and hand–eye co-ordination is a prerequisite. Nevertheless, the alternative saying that 'There are old pilots; there are bold pilots, but there are no old, bold pilots' also rings true. So it remained to be seen which sort of pilot I would become.

For the record, I was one of the first to start my flying training on pure jet aircraft, but it was in Yorkshire that I learnt the basic elements of my trade that would stand me in good stead for the next fifty or so years. Take-off and landing was an essential skill, but we were also taught navigation, stalling and spinning, instrument flying, aerobatics, formation flying, low flying, and flying at night to name but just a few disciplines. All would be useful in later life.

However, I get ahead of myself. The basic flying course lasted a whole year. Following that would be advanced training on much faster jet aircraft (if I was considered good enough to be a fighter or bomber pilot), transport aircraft, or helicopters—the latter if I had sufficient hand–eye co-ordination. Yet of course, those options would only be available if I passed the course. No mean feat, as the failure rate was at least 25 per cent.

Nevertheless, before we even got airborne, we had to pass out of Ground School. In those days, when the pursuit of excellence was paramount and long before accountants ruled, we had to endure many weeks in the classroom learning the ways of the air and we needed to know exactly how everything worked. At times, it seemed that we were required to even know how to manufacture an aeroplane. Airmanship (common sense of the air), navigation, air law, meteorology, aerodynamics, technical subjects, etc. were just a few of what we were subjected to. Interspersed with all that would be yet more officer training, survival after baling out, parachute training, and sport. Drinking was not optional. However, I recall that I passed out of Ground School with a reasonable mark, though not flying colours. Now the fun would begin.

Following on from academics, we were introduced to the Jet Provost Mk 3, a variable noise, constant speed machine. It was underpowered and hardly a rocket ship, but it was more than adequate for training. Though at the time it seemed pretty hot to me, especially after my air experience in Chipmunks, it must have bored some of the instructors rigid, especially those who had only recently left supersonic jet fighters. My own QFI (Qualified Flying Instructor) was a chap called Peter Gover, later to become an air commodore. I would love to know what he really thought of this brash and cack-handed youth, but he had a job to do and he did it amazingly well. Though possessing a modicum of natural skill, it is correct to say that I was a slow learner.

Firstly we had to learn a plethora of checks before even being allowed in an aeroplane. In those days, we did not have the benefit of a real simulator, merely a static inert cockpit trainer to help us memorise the checklists. Later, we also were introduced to the venerable 'Link Trainer', which was a rather rudimentary cross between the inert cockpit trainer and a modern simulator. Finally, and despite the affliction of being a slow learner, on 15 July 1965 in Jet Provost Mk 3 serial number XN465, I was the very first of my course to go solo. Though sluggish to pick up new skills, it was therefore perhaps surprising that I went solo in just about record-breaking time. Conceivably, my initial meteoric progress may have been due to a combination of facts. Firstly, I had an excellent and rather pushy young flying instructor. Secondly, I must have had some talent and a little experience carried over from my earlier air cadet Chipmunk flying and the plethora of gliding done with the Cadet Force. Or was there some other reason? Was this in my genes, or did I get some ethereal assistance?

Though it is said that the majority of pilots never forget that flight, I sadly do not really recall my first solo at all. My later instructor's handbook begins the relevant chapter with the

The author in a Jet Provost Mk 4, 3 FTS 1966. (*Author's collection*)

sentence 'A successful first solo flight, free from incident, gives the student added confidence which is often apparent as an improvement in his flying ability'. Unfortunately, that flight was perhaps the pinnacle of my basic flying course and I seemed to have struggled for the remainder of my time at RAF Leeming. I am not sure why I failed to retain my momentum after that auspicious occasion, but it seems that my subsequent progress was rather slow and gave my instructors some cause for worry. Was it a fluke that I reached the required standard early, did my man push me too hard for his own ends, or did I afterwards become complacent? Possibly it was a mixture of all three. Sadly, that first flight has been eroded completely from my memory.

Either way, being the first to go solo did me little good as from then on much was expected of me. Regrettably, as I have previously stated, I failed to live up to early expectations and passed out of my course well down the pecking order. Was that the same with my Uncle Derek? Did he too want to become a fighter pilot, but was deemed more suitable for heavies? Something has always drawn me to those halcyon days of the Battle of Britain and I read any novel or non-fiction book about those turbulent, but incredibly exciting times. Nevertheless, how I survived my early blunders (and they were numerous) has never been fully explained. Other student pilots were even less fortunate and the mortality rate was quite significant in those early days. This was something that later put my elder son right off a flying career as he noticed me often going to work in my best uniform, sporting a black arm band.

I now have very little recollection of that demanding course, though I must have done reasonably well to graduate at all. Others did not and suffered what we called at the time 'the Chop'. The best that I achieved was a 'below average' assessment, one grade above

The author's Wing's Day, RAF Leeming, 1966. (*Author's collection*)

failure. Nevertheless, I suppose that being slightly less able than my exalted peers (who were obviously superstars) was not too bad. Being last in a Formula One race still puts you in the top 1 per cent of drivers. Few schoolboys wishing to become pilots got as far as I had done by that stage. On 13 May 1965, I passed out of No. 3 FTS RAF Leeming, clutching my flying logbook inscribed with the words 'Low Average', Remarks 'Nil'. Hardly an auspicious start to my flying career!

Interestingly, and despite my deep inner wish to fly jet fighters, my family background perhaps led me to request a tour on the Avro Shackleton four-engined maritime reconnaissance aircraft, a successor to the Lancaster bomber in which my uncle had died. Perversely, my superiors were so disenchanted with my ability I was posted to advance jet training. Woefully, not because I was any good. Perhaps they thought I would either fail the course, die, or significantly improve. From now on, I would be trained to fly solo operationally; apparently, if I was going to kill myself, it would be wise not to take anyone with me. My subconscious wish to become a fighter pilot was about to come true. Or was it?

Thus I said goodbye to the foggy Vale of York and RAF Leeming. I had flown a total of 155 hours in the Jet Provost and would return many years later to fly it again, at that very same airfield.

5
Advanced Flying Training: The Pocket Rocket

In early 1966, I was posted to RAF Valley on the Isle of Anglesey in the shadow of Mount Snowdon, a part of the county I knew very well from my previous climbing days. Here I was to meet a formidable training aeroplane, the lovely Folland Gnat T.1, designed by the former Westland Aircraft chief designer Mr W. E. W. Petter.

So a miniscule, but most capable little fast jet trainer, which saw service with the Indian Air Force as a pure interceptor, thus followed the Jet Provost. In fact, during the Indo-Pakistan wars, the Gnat proved to be a frustrating opponent for the technically superior opposition and had lived up to its Indian Air Force nickname of 'Sabre Slayer'.

Its rate of roll (up to 480 degrees per second) also made it perfectly suitable as a display aircraft. The Gnat found fame with its participation in formation aerobatics—first with the Yellow Jacks team who displayed during the 1964 season, and later with the Red Arrows, making their first public appearances in 1965, the year prior to me arriving at RAF Valley. Ten aircraft were permanently assigned to the Reds—seven to fly with three spares (later to be increased to eight, then nine flyers with just the one spare). While initially based at RAF Little Rissington (where I later would be posted), they would soon move to RAF Fairford and then, in 1966, to RAF Kemble, which would be their home for the next thirteen years or so. Interestingly, many years later, I would keep my own aeroplane in the very same hangar that they used all those years previously. The Gnat was considered to be an excellent aerobatic type by the Reds and soon became the RAF's premier display team and a firm favourite with the public.

However, like many thoroughbreds, it could bite, and bite it did. Unfortunately, several friends were lost while I was undergoing advanced training, mainly by impacting Mother Earth. The trouble was that when the hydraulics failed, and they often did, the all-moving tailplane failed too. That meant that all pitch control was lost and if the pilot did not take immediate action such as abandoning the aircraft, both plane and pilot would end up in a smoking heap in the ground. Luckily, Mr Petter had thought of this and incorporated a little handle in the cockpit which, when pulled, released a small secondary pitch control. Unfortunately, it was imperative that this was done at a certain speed otherwise the pilot would lose all control while landing and end up usually in the lake just short of our airfield. In later years, the Hawk, an altogether much easier aircraft to fly, and thankfully significantly more forgiving, would replace the Gnat.

Things did not go quite to plan on Anglesey, but on 11 July 1966, I did go solo in XP532. During advanced training, I probably used up quite a few of my nine lives. One such mission was a 'High, Low, High' navigation exercise to Scotland, across the Irish Sea to coast in around the Mull of Kintyre. On 11 October 1966, I was authorised to fly the navigation sortie solo in XR953. As this was towards the end of my course, and immediately prior to my final navigation test, I was allowed down to 200 feet above ground level. The weather was not particularly good, though was forecast to improve over the land. I took off late morning and climbed up into the ominous black clouds. I had my instrument rating and the end of the course was in sight. What could possibly go wrong?

I had planned to let down abeam Blackpool so as to be at low level prior to coasting in close to the Mull of Galloway. After an allotted time in cloud, I began my let down over the sea. Hopefully I had planned my mission correctly and taken into account a stiff breeze blowing from the west. As this was years before the advent of GPS, my only electronic navigation aid was TACAN (Tactical Air Navigation System) that was often quite useless as it relied on ground beacons that were not always within range, especially if the aeroplane was at low level.

It was considered safe to descent in cloud to 1,500 feet above ground, and as I was over the sea, I descended to that height on the altimeter. Unfortunately, at that height, I was still in cloud, so assuming that I was still over the sea, and assuming no large ships in the vicinity, I broke one of the cardinal rules of aviation and continued my descent. With my minimal experience and considerable bravado, I assumed it would be quite fine continuing down to 500 feet.

At that height, I levelled and was pleased to note flashes of water beneath me. I was obviously on course. So I let down further to establish full contact with the sea. After all, I had been cleared to 200 feet. Suddenly a beach appeared in front of me, then, almost immediately as I was flying at some 6 miles a minute, Blackpool Tower flashed by on my port wingtip. It was higher than me, for it stands some 518 feet above ground. I had come so close I nearly hit it!

I pulled hard on the stick and zoomed back up into cloud. What had gone wrong? I must have been many miles off track. I could have been killed. I would have gone down in infamy as the pilot who crashed into Blackpool Tower, probably killing hundreds. I checked my instruments, and my gyro magnetic compass. I also managed to get a navigation fix off the beacon at Wallasey. My compass was some 30 degrees in error. Had I set it properly before take-off or had it failed? Who knows, but I managed to home back to RAF Valley terribly shaken. On the ground, I was asked how the trip went. Fine, I replied. Piece of cake. If only they knew. Even today, I have absolutely no idea what went wrong. Bad planning? Duff compass? It matters not. It was fifty years ago, but my RAF career might have ended there, with my life.

Several other escapades befell me while on Anglesey. As the course was some six months long, Les Hatcher (a friend from the very beginning of my RAF career) and I decided to go on a short holiday to the West Country. Les picked me up at my parent's house in High Wycombe and we set off west in his rather elderly 'Auntie Rover'. The journey passed fairly uneventfully and soon we were making good progress westwards down the A361. Upon departing the small town of Devizes, we trundled down Caen Hill; in those days, a mere

The author in a Folland Gnat, 4 FTS, 1966. (*Author's collection*)

normal 'A' road, but today is a fast-flowing dual carriageway. Towards the bottom of the hill, we passed J. Jones's motor salvage—in short, a scrapyard. It is still there today.

As we passed by, I noticed a turntable fire escape sticking up above the scrapyard. Later, we discovered it to be attached to a 1942 Merryweather fire engine. Merryweather & Sons Ltd of Greenwich, London—a company established in 1690 and a specialist in fire-fighting pumps and equipment—built the body. We had to buy it. That much was obvious, as it would indeed serve as a truly superb run-about for the boys at Valley. Trouble is, how would we get it there? Firstly, it weighed 9.5 tons, had a top speed of 55 mph, and a petrol consumption of 6 mpg. We paid a deposit and informed the proprietor that we would be back in a few days to collect. That we did.

Les drove it slowly to RAF Valley while I followed in his Auntie Rover. We soon discovered that it needed rather a lot of TLC, but that turned out to be an insignificant problem as the airfield fire section readily befriended our red monster given that most of their time was spent playing cards and thus they had plenty of time to refurbish the appliance. Moreover, no one asked where their materials came from. No one did in those heady days before accountants ruled the earth.

Once the refurbishment was complete, we spent many a happy hour driving from pub to pub, often with twenty mad student pilots clinging on like grim death. No doubt we lost a few drunks on the way! The last I heard of that red monster was that it was sold to Pinewood Studies to be used in a film. Les passed out from RAF Valley with flying colours and proceeded to fly the mighty English Electric Lightning. I too would pass out and proceed to another English Electric aeroplane, but not with flying colours, nor to an interceptor.

By this stage, my embryonic flying career was going downhill fast. Despite my early advantage at Basic FTS, sadly I did not excel in Flying Training. Furthermore, my instructor at Valley indicated that I would never become a good flying instructor. Years later, it was my pleasure to convert him onto a new aeroplane at a unit where I was the senior flying instructor. I reminded him of his prophecy and asked him for his comments. He replied, 'Well, they do say that practice makes perfect'. I discovered quite early on that by dint of sheer hard work and considerable enthusiasm for aviation, I would achieve more than most of my peers. Indeed, when later converting on the Vickers VC10, my instructor prophesied that despite my cocky assertion that it was my ambition to reach the top grade, I would never achieve the exalted pilot grade of 'Exceptional', the highest assessment of all. Nevertheless, I finally reached that pinnacle after some sixteen years of flying the Vickers VC10 and thus proved him (and others) wrong. I learnt very early on to 'never say never' and 'practice does indeed make perfect'.

It became my turn to graduate from No. 4 FTS and pass out with wings proudly (and permanently) attached to my chest. Sadly, as I previously mentioned, not for me the life of a glamorous fighter pilot such as Les and others had achieved. I was destined to join my late departed uncle and become a member of Bomber Command. I had drawn the short straw of a posting to Canberra medium bombers, but it was not to turn out too disastrously.

There was also another short straw. It appeared that there was an enormous backlog of students waiting to get onto Canberra courses, so I was detached to RAF White Waltham in Berkshire to fly air cadets in the trusty de Havilland Chipmunk for a few months. This was to have a profound effect on my future life, if for no other reason than I met a super chap who became my best man at all my weddings (yes, really), and even today, over fifty years later, he is still a very close friend. We were later both posted overseas, occupy adjacent rooms in the Officers' Mess, and to get up to the most abominable immature escapades together—but more of that later. Suffice to say that at this stage of my career, I thought I was immortal!

6

500 Hours:
A Dangerous Time

Later, very much later in my career, I did achieve everything I set out to do, but I was not always 'Exceptional'. In fact, I was initially graded 'Below Average'. That actually is just a millimetre short of the sack! Additionally, it is well known in aviation circles that when a baby pilot reaches the important milestone of 500 hours aloft, he can become a danger to himself, his crew, and any poor mortal who is unfortunate enough to stand underneath his aircraft. Whether at that stage in my life I was complacent, careless, or just plain unlucky, I will never know. Possibly it was a mixture of all three. However, I suspect that my superiors were in no doubt as to my ability! I have the unflattering comments in my flying logbook to prove it, but I will not share them with you.

Conceivably because of poor tuition, or more likely because of limited ability and over confidence, I began my illustrious career with a serious of near disasters. While they now bring a wry smile to my face, at the time, such incidents could have been terminal. Moreover, they did little to enhance my reputation as a 'steely ace'. One such aircraft that sucked me into an air of complacency was the trusty de Havilland Chipmunk. Designed as a simple basic trainer, this little aeroplane rightly earned the nickname 'Wolf in sheep's clothing'. In the summer of 1966, many a 'wet behind the ears' cocky young pilot, fresh from advanced training on the supersonic Folland Gnat, would spend a few summer months flying young air cadets while waiting for a conversion to even faster jet fighters. The little piston-engined Chipmunk could only manage a shade over 100 knots, thus our intrepid jet jockey stupidly regarded this aircraft as a pussycat. After all, we were mega steely aces. How wrong we were.

One of the many problems the Chipmunk suffered from was a distinct lack of forward visibility while on the ground. This was entirely due to the fact that unlike some modern aircraft it does not possess a nose wheel, thus sits quietly on its tail wheel with its nose in the air, totally obscuring the way forward. Pilots were told to weave the nose from side to side while taxiing out to the runway in order to clear the way ahead. Those who failed to observe this simple procedure did so at their peril. In fact, years later as a flight commander at a FTS, when gazing out of my office, I watched a fellow pilot start up and taxi straight into another Chippy, which had just taxied into the parking slot in front of him while he was diligently performing his pre-start checks. I rushed over to check he was all right to be told personally that he 'assumed, but did not check'. In short, he was guilty as charged.

Stupidly, at that stage, I assumed that as an important witness to this accident, I would not be asked to be part of the Board of Inquiry. Sadly, I was wrong, but I did suppose that having borne witness to the accident and indeed received the full and frank confession, I might have been just a little prejudiced.

Nevertheless, I probably was just a little sympathetic, as I too had screwed up in a similar fashion many years previously. One particular day, while holding at an Air Experience Flight, immediately prior to my operational training, I was tasked to fly young cadets in my Chipmunk. These thirty-minute flights were what originally had inspired me to become a pilot just a few years previous. Now I was returning the favour. The whole system was a little like a cab rank. One landed with the previous cadet, taxied up to the holding point, deposited the young lad (with perhaps his sick bag), and waited while the new cadet passenger climbed aboard and was strapped in. On this particular sunny day in May, I collected another victim and started my taxi towards the runway. While on the move, I briefed the passenger on the safety procedures and asked the small boy in the rear seat how long had he been a member of the ATC. When he replied thirty years, I turned round in surprise. The 'small boy' turned out to be a veteran ATC officer. Sadly, however, in turning round, my concentration wilted and in doing so I allowed the aircraft to proceed direct to the scene of the accident. In short, I impacted my wing tip on the corner of a radar building situated in the middle of the grass airfield. Unfortunately, this was not the only time my carelessness cost me my pride. It also cost me a major earache later in the year when I received a grade one reprimand! Not the last one I would be privileged to receive either.

However, as I previously stated, I was lucky enough to survive the dangerous 500-hour mark and, as they say, experience is a wonderful thing: you cannot buy it. They say that 'there are old pilots and there are bold pilots', but no old bold pilots. Now I am just old.

7

Another Petter Masterpiece

I left No. 4 FTS at RAF Valley with only a 'Proficient' assessment, a damning indictment of my limited ability. Well at least that was one better than my assessment of 'Low Average' from basic FTS. So I had a very long way to go to reach my final assessment of 'Exceptional'. In fact, another thirty-five years would pass before that auspicious milestone would be reached. Not for me the pinnacle of being able to call myself a 'fighter pilot', but that would come to pass eventually. In the meantime, rather than achieve my hoped for posting to Hawker Hunter DFGA (Day Fighter Ground Attack), I settled for the slightly less glamorous role of English Electric Canberra light bomber. This actually would not be quite as boring as it appeared. Though early on in its career, the Canberra (another masterpiece from Mr W. E. W. Petter) had been designed as a high-level jet-engined medium bomber, later in its life it achieved incredible success as a ground attack and night interdictor machine. So much so that is was one of the very first aircraft to be purchased from the UK by the USA and achieved considerable success in the Vietnam War.

This was going to be a significant step forward for me. For a start, from the diminutive size of the Folland Gnat, I would now be destined to pilot a machine almost as large as the Avro Lancaster in which my Uncle Derek went to his maker in 1943. However, the Canberra possessed almost infinitively more capability. It could fly as high as 60,000 feet, carry as much as an early Lancaster bomber, and think nothing of flying over 1,000 nautical miles at sea level, something modern strike aircraft struggle to achieve today, and all this from a machine initially designed in the twilight of the Second World War.

So it was, on 12 December 1966, I found myself at the gates of RAF Bassingbourn, the home of No. 231 Operational Conversion Unit, the training establishment for this remarkable flying machine. It was a posting that I would not regret. It was also the same RAF Station that my father had been a member of some thirty years previously.

From the initial disappointment of being relegated to 'medium bombers', my spirits rose when I discovered that Canberra squadrons were based in the far-flung outposts of Empire. Moreover, my fate was sealed on the very first night of the course when I was informed that should I be so lucky as to pass the course, I would be posted to the Near East Air Force. I had no idea where that was, but it did seem quite exciting for someone who had never ventured further than central France.

8

Operational at Last

So I came to Cyprus, that island that is today, as I write this book, still torn asunder by political unrest. Even on that fateful day in May 1967, which saw the arrival of myself and my crew on the Sovereign Base area of RAF Akrotiri, it was a land of conflict. It is also a beautiful island, steeped in history. Invaders with such iconic names as Richard Cœur de Lion, Alexander the Great, and Harun al-Rashid have all visited Cyprus. History is plentiful, but for many years I had little interest in such esoteric subjects.

Politics too abound, but I was to find out much later how this would affect me personally. On that beautiful May day when I first flew out to Cyprus, I was completely unaware of anything to do with politics and just took in the moment of arrival. Years later, when piloting RAF transport aeroplanes, I became quite used to the overwhelming experience of the heat of a tropical day, but as I disembarked from the Bristol Britannia at midday, it was like walking into a solid wall of heat. We had truly arrived and I remember it as if it was yesterday.

Of course, in 1967, I was the proverbial 'Innocent Abroad' and completely gullible. Having disembarked from the Britannia, I was met by two young pilots from my new squadron who handed me a note from the squadron commander. The note explained that promotion exams were being held that very day in the base education centre and that, as I was likely to be away on detachment when the subsequent exams were next held, my young navigator and I should sit those exams that very day. We fell for the jape—hook, line, and sinker. However, as I had absolutely no idea of even the syllabus, let along had done any study, I politely declined what I thought was the first order from my boss. Yet the jape continued.

After dropping our bags off at the squadron domestic accommodation (all the operational squadrons, of which there were many, lived in purpose-built brick accommodation blocks), we were driven down to our new squadron to meet the key personnel. First to greet us was the squadron 'Roman Catholic padre', who ushered us into the squadron 'chapel' and proceeded to insist that we signed for our own personal bibles. We started to smell a rat when we noticed a number of handmade posters on the wall stating certain quotation such as 'Cursed are those who land wheels up' and 'Navigators, know thee the way of the Lord'.

Following that, we were then taken to the squadron crew room where we came across aircrew playing board games, dressed in winter greatcoats, surrounded by paraffin heaters that had raised the temperature to well in excess of the outside, which already was touching 40 degrees. By then, both my navigator and I smelt more than a rat.

That evening, we attended a dinner in our honour and I was surprised to spot the 'RC Padre' smooching with a lady. The penny then finally dropped, and so began my relationship with Aphrodite's Isle, the island of Lawrence Durrell's *Bitter Lemons*, and my RAF flying career proper with No. 73 Squadron. This historic island is still today the key to British foreign policy in the Middle East, and I was later to revisit it on many occasions during the two Gulf Wars.

A military pilot always remembers his first squadron. I am no exception. No. 73 Squadron was formed on 1 July 1917 at Upavon as a fighter unit. Equipped with Sopwith Camels, it moved to France in January 1918 to fly fighter patrols and bomber escort missions over the Western Front. During the Second World War, it bred the very first 'Ace', Cobber Kane. Years later, in 1957, No. 73 converted to Canberras in Cyprus until it was disbanded on 17 March 1969. The motto was '*Tutor et ultor*', which translates to 'Protector and Avenger'.

The squadron badge was a demi-Talbot rampant, charged on the shoulder with a maple leaf. Of course, I wore it with pride and indeed still to this day it is adorning one of my tattered old flying suits.

I settled into squadron life, but it was not long before my inexperience showed. Blunders were commonplace in those early days of my flying career, and I suspect the reason why their airships did invite me to leave was that I was not alone in screwing up. Far from it, as blunders, crashes, and fatalities were unfortunately commonplace.

Carelessness. Was I careless that beautifully hot Cypriot summer morn early on 5 July 1967 or was I merely an accident waiting to happen? However, blowing off the canopy of Canberra T4 WJ566 by stupidly selecting the wrong switch was not exactly smart. Whatever, I later learnt that I was the twenty-fifth person to make that same mistake (and not the last by any means). Nevertheless, good old Auntie Air Force had to have its pint of blood, and I got a good rap on the knuckle from the Officer Commanding Akrotiri Strike Wing.

Here is what happened: this was my very first tactical formation sortie on the squadron. In fact, it was my very first large formation, as about twenty aircraft were to take part in a simulated attack. I was to fly dual (thus supervised) with the Squadron Qualified Weapons Instructor (QWI). Consequently, I was very much on a steep learning curve. To say 'lamb to the slaughter' would not be an exaggeration. I was most certainly over-awed by the situation having never experience anything similar before. What you, dear reader, must know is that, up until this time, the complicated pre-flight checks had been performed while the aircraft was stationary. It was not deemed sensible for an inexperienced pilot to taxi his large aircraft and carry out complex checks at the same time. A wise policy, as it turned out.

In my vintage attack aircraft, I could escape if all went wrong by pulling that veritable yellow and black handle, thus automatically being ejected from the aircraft still strapped to my seat. Subsequently, I would be gently lowered to earth courtesy of Mr Irving's remarkably fine parachute. Before this could occur, I had to jettison the cockpit canopy, though this was all part of the automatics.

However, to avoid nasty little boys like me from operating it by mistake, the canopy jettison system comprised of two switches. One to arm the system, the other to complete the circuit and fire off the canopy should that be required.

An additional problem could occur if an engine failed on take-off. Unlike safe modern airliners, the venerable Canberra, when loaded with bombs and ammunition, would not fly if an engine failed on departure. Consequently, I was provided with a neat little switch that, when selected on, conveniently jettisoned all the bombs and external fuel tanks from the aircraft.

Anyway, on this very hot sunny day in July, some twenty light attack bombers, including mine, set off on their mission. Bringing up the rear was yours truly, struggling to keep up with the mad rush and at the same time performing a plethora of complicated cockpit checks. When my navigator called for the Master Armament Safety Switch (MASS) to be selected on, I inadvertently selected the Canopy Jettison Switch instead. Well, in my defence, I had little time to identify the wretched thing. Of course, nothing happened because the MASS was still in the off position.

The sortie passed without incident and I subsequently returned to base drenched in sweat and glad to be still alive. On vacating the runway, my trusty navigator called for the MASS to be deselected. Well, you can imagine my surprise when, on selecting the MASS to the opposite position to where it currently was, there was a tremendous bang, the cockpit filled with smoke, and the canopy departed the aircraft. By selecting the MASS to the opposite position (with the jettison switch already in the 'on' position), I thus completed the circuit and deposited my canopy on the taxiway. That got me into big trouble.

However, not as much as a colleague of mine a few years later. A similar switch pig on 25 May 1982 resulted in a Jaguar from RAF Brüggen being shot down by a fellow RAF pilot flying a Phantom from RAF Wildenrath, the very airfield I would be posted to after my tour in Cyprus. It was just a routine practice interception, but the Phantom carried live missiles. During the intercept, the trigger had to be pulled to enable the gun camera to record the event. Unfortunately, the pilot of the Phantom selected everything live and fired the missile, with devastating consequences. Jaguar GR1 XX963 was no more. Luckily, my chum literally did not know what had hit him, but survived with minor cuts and bruises; the miscreant had his bottom smacked and his tealeaves read.

No. 73 Squadron Canberra formation over the Mediterranean, 1967. (*Author's collection*)

The Phantom pilot joined the illustrious band of pilots who had selected the wrong switch, just like me. Silly boy! At least I did not get tried by court-martial, unlike that chap. I got away with a mere dressing down from my wing commander.

Incidentally, looking again at my logbook, I note that the QWI in my dual control Canberra had put me down as 'captain', possibly after the event. Consequently, I got the reprimand and not the instructor.

My 'bad luck' did not end there. My introduction to operational flying had a vertical learning curve and I could hardly keep up. Moreover, those were the days long before the advent of behavioural scientists able to analyse why pilots screwed up. My next disaster was typical of that.

One of the great attributes of the Canberra was its amazing versatility. Designed by W. E. W. Petter as a high-level jet bomber immediately after the Second World War, it was much developed into a ground-attack aircraft. Few aircraft today can fly as far unrefuelled and carry as much armament as the B.15 version I flew in the Middle East in the late '60s.

Armed with guns, bombs, flares, missiles, and rockets, it was a formidable fighting machine. Perhaps it was the last attack aircraft that required the pilot to use all his skill to hit the target. Not for him the luxury of laser-guided bombs, but that only added to the fun. It was while undergoing my rocket training that I learnt not only about aiming, but also about passing the buck!

This second more serious blunder nearly caused serious loss of life. This time, I am convinced that the incident was definitely not my fault, but a mixture of bad luck and poor supervision. It all began on a glorious day in late 1967 on an idyllic island not far from Lebanon. I was briefed to fly my Canberra light-attack aircraft to a nearby weapon's range, locate a 3-ton truck, and blow it to smithereens using two-inch rockets. For those readers who are not familiar with two-inch rockets, I must hasten to add that they are not 2 inches long. Moreover, seventy-four, when fired simultaneously, can inflict significant damage on light vehicles and personnel!

Sadly, and unknown to me, a group of local peasants had decided that collecting brass cannon shell cases, expended from aircraft using this weapon range, was a most profitable business. Thus they tended to lurk on the range, out of sight of the Range Safety Officer (RSO) to illegally collect their ill-gotten booty. On this particular summer day, three locals had driven onto the range in their battered (and stolen) 3-ton truck to see what they could find. Sadly, too, as they positioned their vehicle behind a sand dune and completely out of sight of the RSO, I tipped into my attack dive, ready to obliterate my designated 3-ton truck. Given that this was fairly early in the morning, the sun was low on the horizon and immediately behind the target area. However, my steely young eyes soon identified the target and I was given clearance to fire by the RSO. I let loose a salvo of seventy-four deadly rockets, most of which scored dead hits on the 3-ton truck. The wrong 3-ton truck.

Shortly afterwards, the RSO realised what had happened and sent me home in disgrace. I am not sure if the local peasants were so lucky! During the subsequent investigation, my gun-camera film, which recorded the event, showed that the vehicle concerned was identical to the official target and was parked well within the danger area. I doubt if those poor locals continued to earn a living that way ever again.

Mind you, it was not just me doing the shooting. The Base had a number of low-level navigation routes around the island. At that time, it was not divided politically, though the north was predominately Turkish and the south Greek. I used to love flying the longest of the three routes round the island—the one that took me along the foothills of the Kyrenia mountains, past crusader castles and signs of Turkish deviance at the predominately Greek Administration. Maybe they thought I was a Greek pilot, because I often returned to base with bullet holes in my fin. Lucky for me that the protagonists on the ground did not allow for the speed on my aircraft when opening fire, as they would surely have hit the cockpit. This book would then not have been written. Maybe that was one of many of my escapes.

Actually, bombs and weapons going astray were par for the course in those days. Firing my rockets at the wrong 3-ton truck was not the only time my weapons were released at the wrong target. Nor was I alone in doing so.

Several times in the future, as you will later find out, weapons have been released in the strangest of places. Besides guns, rockets, and ordinary iron bombs, one of the more deadly weapons we were issued with in Cyprus was a mighty big nuclear bomb—all 1,750 lb of it (goodness knows why it was called the 2000 MC). We had forty-eight in total, enough to wipe out most of the world. Code named 'Red Beard', the yield of 'our bomb' was equivalent to 25 kilotons of TNT. I suppose it was just as well that at least one member of my crew was older than twenty-one with that amount of responsibility. Quite a bang! Consequently, we aircrew did not want to be anywhere near this nasty thing when it exploded. So a method of delivery to drop the bomb was devised so that we threw (tossed) the 'bucket of sunshine' (as we called it) forward some 6 miles, which enabled us to escape before the bomb vaporised everyone and everything into a sea of red mist.

Unfortunately, this delivery method had its drawbacks. One obviously had to release the bomb in the right place, though I suppose a quarter of a mile or so would make little difference. For safety, our weapons were always discharged on an approved air weapons range. Such a designated area was called CY2, an area of sea just off the cliffs of RAF Episkopi. If the bomb was slightly inaccurate, no harm would be done. We would rush into the target area at some 400 mph, then at a predetermined spot (a small raft in the sea), pull up into a loop and the simulated bucket of sunshine would release itself at about 60 degrees of pitch and be thrown forward onto the target. Trouble is, though our attack aircraft had fairly accurate instruments to ensure all this, the pilot still had to identify the little raft, which was not that easy to do if the sea-state was more than moderate. The raft represented an initial point (IP) and the entire sequence commenced overhead that point. If the pilot missed the IP, he could still proceed to the target, which I hasten to add that in real life was probably very heavily defended, hence one of the advantages of pulling up into the loop some 6 miles short of the target. If the pilot decided to go for this 'Alternate attack procedure' he had to move a switch from the 'Normal' position to 'Alternate'. This would ensure the bomb was released at about 110 degrees and fall back onto the unlucky target. Failure to select the alternate delivery profile ensured the bomb would still be tossed some 6 miles forward and thus miss the target by some 6 miles!

Yes, you have guessed it. During our practice runs, having missed the IP, we sometimes forgot to select Alternate and thus our bomb was indeed thrown forward 6 miles, right into an orange plantation, much to the considerable annoyance of the local plantation workers. Just as well then that we only used 25-lb practice bombs and not live nuclear weapons! Still, I suspect that even 25 lb of iron falling on one's head at 400 mph might cause a few headaches. Such mistakes inevitably cause headaches for the crew who screwed up and an invitation to the Boss's office with the proverbial telephone directory down one's trousers.

Fasouri plantation was not the only place to receive a hunk of metal from out of the sky. The NAAFI shop at RAF Akrotiri was also singled out for treatment. A good friend of mine ran into the target on the air weapons range, released his weapon, and was told by the RSO that nothing was seen. Young Terence assumed that the bomb was a dud (they were designed to emit a flash and smoke so that the RSO could spot the fall of shot) so completed his detail. Anyway, our brave pilot flew back to Akrotiri and whizzed over the NAAFI shop pulling fairly hard as he did so. Sadly, the bomb was still precariously attached to the aeroplane and promptly fell off onto the pavement right outside the NAAFI. Luckily, no one was hurt. At least that particular day, I was not in trouble.

I had many escapes and, of course, I was not the only careless daredevil at RAF Akrotiri. Back in the Mother Country, we fledgling aircrew had little money and alcohol was relatively expensive. Moreover, our motorcars tended to be old bangers capable (on a good day with a following wind) of no more than 80 mph. I vividly remember my first car purchased for just £7. It went over the cliffs at Robin Hood's Bay and thus ended its days on the beach, but that is another story. Its rusty remains were still there many years later.

Though I was perhaps the apple of my mother's eye, none of us were angels. However, transport this happy band of irresponsible tearaways to the sunny Levant, pay them more money than they could possibly spend, allow them to purchase relatively high-powered sports cars, and sell copious quantities of alcohol to them for next to nothing was a certain recipe for disaster. Given also that the advent of MOTs and breathalyser were still far over the horizon, it was no surprise to find that few survived their Cyprus tour intact.

Strangely enough, despite being no different from my colleagues when it came to enjoying my time off, I was one of the very few who never pranged their sports car. This was also quite surprising given that in the sultry evenings we often drove to the local tavern, consumed vast quantities of cheap local wine, then raced our mates back to Base on pothole-ridden unpaved backroads in the dark and without the aid of lights. Well, switching on our lights would make the journey less exciting. Exciting it normally was too, though several of my colleagues failed to arrive for briefing the following day. You can guess why! That I survived at all was perhaps an early example of someone watching out for me. Someone needed to!

Of course, we would today quite rightly condemn such irresponsible behaviour; however, dear reader, please do not judge us too harshly. I suppose today we all would have been given anti-social behaviour orders (ASBOs). Then, it was just 'high spirits'. Yes we played hard, but also worked hard. Moreover, we stared the Grim Reaper in the face every time we got airborne. If we dwelled on our own mortality, we would certainly not have flown at all. Col. John Cunnick, USAF (ret'd), once wrote: 'A fighter pilot is all balls and no brain. If he thinks at all he thinks he is immortal. A fighter pilot who thinks he is going to die usually does'. The term 'Flight Safety' had hardly been invented and the mortality rate was high, and not just on the Cyprus roads. That mortality rate was to significantly increase in later years.

Of course, not everyone suffered—some gained. One chap's bad luck was another's good fortune. I distinctly remember visiting one of my colleagues in hospital after he had rolled his Triumph Spitfire, an almost identical car to mine. Through his wired up jaw, he mumbled that his beloved sports car was a write-off. My charitable reply was 'Well you won't be needing the hardtop stored in your room, will you'. Consequently, from that afternoon onwards, my white Triumph sported an almost new red hardtop.

9

Mercy Mission

Apart from visiting local taverns, obviously the Officers' Mess received our custom on a regular basis, often after a night down town. One of the many party tricks individuals played was to crawl across the beams that criss-crossed the ceiling, while fellow mess members hurled bottles and beer cans at the stupid fellow aloft. This was always good sport, especially as immediately above the beams were numerous electric fans whirling at high speed. Any upward movement of a victim's head to avoid a well-judged beer can would almost certainly result in decapitation, or at least a fall from the ceiling. Needless to say, I too suffered that fate and in doing so fell through a plate glass table top, thus severing an artery in my leg. At the bar later, I failed to notice this until a nurse pointed out that my shoe was filling up with a red liquid, which almost certainly was not red wine. Another lucky escape.

I also remember one particular alcohol-fuelled Saturday night in the Officers' Mess. At the stroke of midnight, and after I had consumed copious brandy sour cocktails, the duty officer arrived in the bar to ask for a volunteer crew to fly to RAF El Adam in Libya to pick up a dangerously ill soldier. If the poor fellow did not get to the RAF hospital on Cyprus within twelve hours, he would die. We had to collect him now.

Of course, I and my equally inebriated navigator instantly and very bravely volunteered for the mission. So, after being authorised by an equally sozzled flight commander, we set off to fire up our aircraft. On arrival at the flight line, we found our Canberra jet bomber prepared for the mission. Strangely though, the engine refused to start. Despite being totally plastered, I am convinced that I put all the correct switches in the correct position, but the engines still failed to start.

Next day, I complained to the ground crew and was told that they had taken one look at me and removed the fuses from the starter circuits. Maybe my angel was asleep that night, but perhaps had left instructions with my ground crew. By now, I think I owed that angel quite a few beers. The debt I owed would grow into a case of vintage champagne.

That was not the last time I would be involved with casualty evacuation missions; much later in my career, I took up that job professionally. I did lose a few customers in later life, but none, I am happy to say, due to my incompetence.

If you, dear reader, have come to the conclusion that my life then was entirely made up of flying, drinking, and driving sports cars faster than was good for me, then you are absolutely right, but we young officers were not like the youngsters of today. We did not do drugs; in fact, I never saw any and never knew of anyone who took illegal substances. That was perhaps rather surprising given that this was the Swinging Sixties with Flower Power and all that entailed. Possibly drugs were solely the domain of the rich and famous. I saw none and was quite content with the local beer.

Yet we were very immature and, as you have seen, prone to 'jolly japes' that sometimes backfired. The officers at RAF Akrotiri were housed in blocks of some twenty bedrooms, which enjoyed the luxury of only four bathrooms. By modern standards, this accommodation was rather austere. Though the temperatures were rather extreme ranging from very close to zero to sometimes as high as 45 degrees, none of the rooms enjoyed heating or air conditioning. Additionally, each bedroom was provided with only one wall socket. Just as well that in those days we youngsters owned only a record player or tape recorder, if anything at all. But we knew no better. Anyway, I digress, so getting back to japes. In the summer, it was quite the norm for officers to work in the morning, starting about 7 a.m., then knock off at 1 p.m., repair to the bar for an hour or so, then sleep until about 5 p.m., only arising for the evening festivities. One particular day, a colleague of ours had turned in for his usual siesta, not knowing what we had in store for him. We had acquired a few 'thunderflashes' from our Army friends. These were rather enormous fireworks designed to simulate an exploding bomb. We also purchased an enormous blood-red watermelon, inserted a few thunderflashes in it, crept into his room, placed it on the bed beside the sleeping officer, lit the thunderflashes, and retired to a safe distance outside his room. After a short time, there was the most colossally loud explosion from inside the room followed by hysterical screaming. We burst in to find our terrified 'friend' yelling that he had been assassinated, for the whole room was covered in red flesh. We had to explain to him that actually it was not his flesh, merely that of a watermelon. He never forgave us.

Interestingly, at the age of twenty-one, I was still a virgin. A red-blooded pilot still a virgin—shock horror. However, I had plenty of other things to occupy my mind. Least of which was perhaps digging myself out of holes I had dug myself into, but women featured not too highly on my agenda. I had a couple of liaisons with members of the opposite sex, but nothing serious. Cars and flying were sufficient for my needs, but one swelteringly hot day, when I was washing my trusty sports car outside my accommodation block, a pretty young lady wandered past and chatted me up. Well are they not all pretty at age seventeen? The rest was history. We married in 1970 and it lasted some twenty-nine years, producing two excellent sons. Sadly that union ended at the turn of the century, when she decided to seek pastures new, but most clouds have a silver lining, as I was later to very pleasantly find out.

10

I Learnt About Navigators
from That

It would seem that I had a charmed life, though it is true that at the time, I was totally oblivious to that or even what life was really all about. It is possibly safe to say that I was a typical product of my age and, like many of my ilk, thought I would live forever. The following incident was the subject of an article that I first wrote for an aviation magazine, but after the editor took advice from the Foreign Office, he called me to say that he could not print it. I wonder why? Anyway, here it is now, sanitised slightly. Well, perhaps sanitised considerably.

Once upon a time, a very long time ago, in a far off remote land a light bomber crew took alcoholic refreshment in a native taverna. The very next day, this intrepid crew went for a jolly in their front line attack aircraft. This jaunt was to include a three hour low level sortie over deserts and inhospitable terrain very close to the border of a distinctly unfriendly neighbourhood country whose aeroplanes had pretty red stars painted on their fins. Our brave pilot took no interest in the navigation planning; partly as he had a headache and partly because his crew contained not one but two navigators. One was responsible for map reading and low-level navigation (the Observer), the other (the Plotter) for updating the wonderful modern suite of electronic navigation aids. After every turning point, the Observer would provide the Plotter with co-ordinates to enable him to perform the update. In return, the Plotter would supply the next heading from his log. Regrettably, the Observer thought that the exercise to be flown was Route 2, but the Plotter expected to fly Route 5!

Start up, taxi and take-off went without major incident and our intrepid crew set off across Dasht-e-Kavir towards the Elburz Mountains. After an hour or so, our highly competent and most professional Observer began to have serious doubts. The headings supplied to him by his colleague did not seem to make sense. Moreover, the terrain did not quite fit the pretty symbols on his chart. No matter, he thought, the map was produced in 1945 and in any case the phrase 'Incomplete information' printed on the chart reassured him somewhat. No cause to tell the pilot, something would come up eventually, just keep on supplying the Plotter with the appropriate co-ordinates at every turn. After another hour, and having missed a number of unique features, our worried Observer asked our slumbering Plotter for an electronic position. Of course the electronics conformed to the cardinal computer rule 'Rubbish in, rubbish out' and consequently suggested that our steely crew was spot on track. There then ensued a momentous argument between directional consultants as to where on earth they were. At this point, and for the first time in the sortie, the pilot began to take some interest in the subject of navigation. How could his principle of 'We cannot get lost, we have a Navigator' equate with the fact that one navigator did not agree with the other and quite violently by the sound of it. Perhaps, for the first time in his illustrious career, he should exercise some captaincy and take charge of this rapidly worsening catastrophe. For now, he began to realise that they could be 900 miles from any airfield and all he could see was sand and sky! Furthermore, he only had fuel for about 450 miles. Oh dear, he thought, 'How am I going to get out of this.' How about a training fix; that worked when he got lost in his JP a couple of years ago. Hardly, he decided, as there was not a radar unit within two thousand miles. The same applied to radio aids, unless one used a single NDB, but then he remembered being told of that nasty habit of the unscrupulous neighbouring country of meaconing poor unsuspecting aircrew over the border and then putting them in horrible damp prisons. For those unenlightened readers, meaconing is the interception and rebroadcast of navigation signals. These signals are rebroadcast on the received frequency, typically, with power higher than the original signal, to confuse enemy navigation. Consequently, aircraft or ground stations are given inaccurate bearings

'I say,' he said to the squabbling navigators, 'Let's carry out Lost Procedure.' 'Don't be silly,' said the Plotter. 'What's that?' asked the Observer. I suggested that we fly north to the coast, turn right and look for a big river, fix our inaccurate electronic kit and go home. Of course this cunning plan depended on a number of things least of which was having enough fuel; however, what else could our very worried crew do? So off they set and after many a mile and at least one mountain range later the blue waters of our foreign sea hoved into view. 'Hoorah,' exclaimed the pilot! 'Thank God,' replied the Observer. All that was heard from the Plotter was the occasional snore. Still in the weeds, and at the speed of heat, our front-line warplane sped eastwards along the coast in search of a river. After a while, our deeply anxious boy pilot noticed that his compass appeared to have failed. It now read north instead of east. Upon waking the Plotter, the crew learnt that all the compasses seemed unserviceable as they all now read north, even the basic magnetic E2b compass. But wait, of course, perhaps the aircraft was actually flying north and this river appearing on the nose obviously belonged to the horrid enemy country which our steely aircrew were now flying over. Flying over! Shit. And those happy people down there are waving at our deeply unhappy crew. Perhaps they are thinking 'Bloody Air Force, I am going to telephone the IL-28 Beagle base at Krasnovdsk [present-day Türkmenbaşy] to complain about low flying aircraft'.

How our audacious youngsters returned to the safety of the Motherland remains to be told. Perhaps they are still rotting in jail or have 'gone native!'

Well, some forty years have passed since that little incident and how I did not end up in a foreign jail with Gary Powers I will never know. Someone guided me home, no thanks to my 'expert' navigators.

I sometimes wondered if my job was to please navigators. Occasionally, we got the chance to drop real bombs. For that, we needed a big target deep in the desert. No room for error back in Cyprus, and anyway, the natives were getting restless when our little practice bombs

RAF Akrotiri Strike Wing Canberras in formation, *c*. 1967. (Ray Deacon)

went astray. In the middle of the last century, the MOD built a huge weapons range just south of the RAF base at El Adem in Libya. We often flew over to El Adem, discharged our weapons on the range, and had lunch at the RAF base before flying back in the afternoon.

One particular day in early summer, four of our Canberras flew to Libya, dropped their bombs, then, just for the navigators, all four aircraft flew off deep into the desert, aptly named the Great Sand Sea, to find an old Second World War bomber aircraft that had crashed in 1943, some months before my Uncle Derek lost his life in Germany. The aeroplane was called *Lady Be Good*, an American B-24D Liberator. At the time, the plane was assumed to have crashed into the Mediterranean Sea and its nine crew members were classified as missing in action (MIA). In 1958, the nearly intact *Lady Be Good* was discovered 440 miles inland. Subsequent searches uncovered the remains of all but one of the crew. The wreckage of course was a difficult target for navigators to find, but it amused them to try.

Anyway, the four aeroplanes in formation set course to find *Lady Be Good*. Of course, that would leave them very short of fuel, so before they departed the weapon range, they updated the weather at nearby RAF EL Adem. As usual, all was fine: blue skies and unlimited visibility. So long as our intrepid aviators returned to El Adem with fuel for a couple of landings, all would be well. Well, we never found *Lady Be Good*; perhaps the desert had reclaimed it again. Worse was to come; on return to our lunch stop, we were met with a wall of sand, the ubiquitous sand storm that popped up from nowhere. It would be impossible to land.

We now had a problem. A very big problem. We had little fuel left and the nearest airfield was at Benghazi, a very long way away. Too far. Were we indeed going to end up like the crew of *Lady be Good*? There was nothing for it but to fly west towards a sand strip near Derna. That we all did without too much problem, other than having egg on our faces. Later that day, the RAF sent out a fuel tanker to refuel us and remove any unwanted rocks from the sand runway, which incidentally I do not think had been used since the Second World War. Luckily that time our intrepid leader got the flack and not young and innocent little me, but I learnt that day that experienced older pilots could still make mistakes. Big ones!

But I, or even my chums, did not always cause problems. Well, not intentionally. Towards the end of my time in Cyprus, I and three other crews were tasked to provide offensive air support for a large NATO Fire Power demonstration in the Mediterranean. The United States Navy were to tow an old Second World War destroyer out into the Med, then certain outfits would be allowed to test their ordinance on the target, while the top brass looked on from a safe distance, drinking their gin and tonics on the lawn outside the Officers' Club. Four Canberra light-attack aircraft from my squadron had the honour of attacking first. The whole exercise was planned to last two to three days, at the end of which (after of course the obligatory cocktail party for the senior offices and invited guests), the US Navy mega warships would pound the poor old ship into oblivion.

The big day arrived and No. 73 Squadron was, as previously mentioned, going to get first crack at the fun. I suppose that the 'powers that be' expected us to use our rockets and guns, obviously with little effect on a large warship. That would produce the most fun for us. Bombs possibly would be out of the question as our weapon aiming systems were of Second World War vintage and hopelessly inaccurate. Accuracy was not the keynote of our capability.

However, what the planners did not know was that No. 73 Squadron, as well as No. 32 Squadron, had been re-equipped with a brand-new toy: the AS-30 anti-ship missile. The AS-30 was a development of a smaller missile, the 1960s Nord AS-20, allowing both an increase in range and a much larger warhead, but it was almost identical to the earlier AS-20 in design. The AS-30 had a two-stage solid fuel rocket motor, a short burn time booster section which was exhausted through two large nozzles located mid-way between the rear edges of the large fins, and a longer burn time sustainer, which exhausted at a nozzle located at the back-centre of the missile body. As with the AS-20, the AS-30 used a simple guidance system with the pilot, or bomb aimer, aligning the flares located near the missile's rear with the target and controlling the missile in flight after launch, with a small joystick steering commands to the missile via a radio link. The steering commands steered the missile back to the line-of-sight by thrust vectoring by the movement of one of four metal vanes around the sustainer nozzle. The missile's internal gyro gave the missile command unit the correct position of the missile in flight, so each of the four thrust vanes could actuate at the correct time to steer the missile back to the correct flight path. Got all that? I will be testing you later.

Given that the warhead was larger than that of our normal 1,000-lb bomb and that it hit the target in excess of 1,000 mph, we had high hopes. If only the hierarchy had known what we were up to. In the event, we fired just two missiles and naturally scored direct hits.

When the smoke cleared, the ship had sunk. We were distinctly very unpopular as we had completely spoilt their three days of fun.

Finally, in 1969, it was time to move on to pastures new and my time with No. 73 Squadron was up. In fact, it was up for everyone as the Canberra was being replaced by a big white triangle, the mighty Vulcan. On reflection, at the time, I do not think many of us appreciated the delights of Aphrodite's Isle and I suppose we took much for granted. The weather was idyllic, the girls very pretty, the food exceptional, the beer unbelievably cheap, and, above all, the flying was brilliant. We played hard and we worked hard. We spent many hours on the beach, in the pub, and weekends at that wonderful harbour in the north of the island, Kyrenia. In just two years, I grew up both as a man and as a pilot. Well, I grew up as a man and grew older as a pilot. Remember, pilots never grow up. However, I should have heeded the words of that Turkish song:

> If you should come to Kyrenia
> Don't enter the walls.
> If you should enter the walls
> Don't stay too long.
> If you should stay long
> Don't get married.
> If you should get married
> Don't have children.

Well I did get married, I honeymooned in Kyrenia, and I did have children, but that is another story all together.

11

The North German Plain

After my lengthy holiday in the Levant, I was posted to RAF Wildenrath, again to fly Canberras, this time over the North German Plain. Here, life was totally different. Gone were the clear skies and barren lands of the Middle East. The Central Plain was fertile and wet. In winter, very wet. Cloud predominated, interspersed with autumnal fogs. Many a low-level sortie was flown from church spire to church spire, which rose majestically like sentinels through the flat expanse of the stratus tops. The nights too brought their own brand of bad weather, which did not preclude low flying; we merely trundled on in the inky blackness, almost at tree-top height, hoping that our antiquated navigation equipment was sufficiently accurate to prevent us flying into hillsides in the dark.

It was here that I joined No. 14 Squadron, which was equipped with Canberra B(I)8 Interdictors. Its motto is 'I spread my wings and keep my promise', an extract from the Quran suggested by the Emir of Transjordan. The squadron was formed at Shoreham in 1915 and shortly after moved to Egypt, and it was not until 1962 that it re-equipped with the Canberra in Germany. This was the 'Cold War'. Any minute, it was expected that the vast Soviet hordes would pile into West Germany or that within a split second the Western World would be annihilated by buckets of nuclear sunshine. We would, in essence, all be instantly vaporised into a sea of red mist.

My task therefore was to maintain the Western Nuclear Deterrent. Many an hour I spent with my navigator, shut up in the QRA (Quick Reaction Alert) hut, waiting for the call to scramble. History recalls that I never did. Thank goodness. The fact that I had strapped to my own aircraft was yet another bucket of sunshine bothered me not. We merely did not think about it and I am sure we would have gone to war if ordered. After all, what would there have been left to return to?

We were on duty for twenty-four hours at a time, living 'on the job', locked up in a QRA cage like zoo animals. We ate, fed, and slept there. Due to the very nature of the task, we had to fend for ourselves as no mess cooks or stewards were allowed near the 'Bomb'. All that kept us company were a few engineers and a number of highly armed policemen. They were not just there to keep out terrorists, but also to prevent any mad pilot or navigator sabotaging the precious cargo. I recall once, during a long period of bad weather, rain ice became a huge problem and we were ordered to move a nuclear-armed bomber a few yards to avoid it becoming stuck to the ground. I as captain climbed aboard to monitor the

No. 14 Squadron Wildenrath Canberra B(I)8. (*John Galyer*)

brakes while a tug pulled the aeroplane forward. Standing next to me in the roomy cockpit was a large American policeman who held his revolver to my head in case I did something silly. He was sweating profusely and his eyes kept rolling. I think he was more scared than I. Consequently, there was absolutely no chance of the nuclear deterrent being either used or compromised. Due to the very nature of the mission and the complexity of the security measures, it would have been completely impossible for anyone to launch with the weapon. Even then, it would have been totally inert, as it required specific instructions from much higher authority to make the bomb live. Such instructions would not have been issued until just before launch.

The B(I)8 was quite different from the B.15/16. For a start, it had a fighter-type canopy and the whole crew compartment was radically revised. Sadly, the ejector seat for the navigator was omitted, in most people's eyes a big mistake, especially as the role was predominantly at low-level. I think in all its history, only one navigator was able to egress a B(I)8. The aircraft also was equipped with four Hispano 20-mm cannon, carrying 520 rounds per gun. It could also carry a single Mk 7 'Thor' weapon, a tactical nuclear bomb of American design. This was a potent weapon with a yield up to 61 kilotons (three times that of the Hiroshima weapon). Very much a 'bucket of sunshine'.

Strangely enough, though, despite the *Dr. Strangelove* nature of our mission, none of us really thought much about the morals, ethics, or politics of the situation. Perhaps we should have done. I think in reality that none of us ever thought we would ever go to war. Little did we know that future conflicts would not be fought globally or even on the North German plain, but they would be local skirmishes in far off lands. However, an amusing incident did occur to me one day back home on leave in my hometown. I was walking past the parish church when a dear old lady approached me to request that I sign a petition to 'Ban the

No. 14 Squadron B(I)8, QRA Wildenrath, 1969. (*Author's collection*)

Bomb'. My immature reply was 'Ban the Bomb? I drop them!' You can imagine the look of horror on that dear old lady's face. She must have thought I was the Devil incarnate.

But that was just a little of my job description. Our main task was interdiction. That is, the destruction of enemy lines of communication—railways, roads, and bridges. We had a plethora of 'toys' to play with. Rockets, guns, missiles, and bombs were just our tools of the trade. We flew mainly at low level, sometimes a few metres above the tops of the proverbial fog banks. We had a lot of fog on the North German Plain.

Germany was not without adventures. A fire in any means of transport is incredibly frightening, none more so than in an aeroplane in flight. After all, one cannot just stop and get out! However, there are fires and there are fires. There is always fire in the jet engine combustion chamber—that is how it works—however, an inferno elsewhere can be catastrophic, especially in the cabin or, worse still, in the hold.

Many years later in my career, when flying a large transport aircraft, the aeroplane did indeed catch fire—but more on that later. However, on one very dark night, high above the Federal Republic of Germany, my Canberra caught fire. Most of our sorties there were flown at low level, but sometimes we operated at high altitude merely to clock up hours for the statistics. One such night saw my navigator and myself circumnavigating the Federal Republic in the icy upper reaches of the atmosphere. Before long, our unheated canopy was totally frosted over, preventing any inspection of the heavens, nor indeed any external part of the aircraft. Shortly after reaching our cruising altitude, well in excess of 40,000 feet, the number two engine suffered a serious hot gas leak. The jet pipe had detached itself from the engine, allowing exhaust gases at a temperature of more than 600 degrees centigrade to play on the wing instead of being directed safely aft of the aircraft. This was to have serious consequences, though both my navigator and I remained completely oblivious throughout. My angel must have worked overtime that dark night.

Upon landing just before midnight, we parked our jet and headed for the bar. It was only the next morning that we discover the true extent of the damage to the wing when

The author standing by Canberra B(I)8 fire damage, 1969. (*Author's collection*)

an irate chief summoned me to view what I had done to his aircraft. The following Special Occurrence Report, officially submitted up the chain of command, accurately describes the event. The senior officer's comments suggested that they entered into the spirit of my opening description of the incident. How times have changed.

The following are excerpts from the genuine incident report, though I suspect a little tongue in cheek. Such was the flippant attitude of the times:

Pilot's Report

1. When I had been airborne about an hour on a night high-level navigation exercise (only eleven times this month) I noticed a rosy glow in the rear view mirror and saw that the aft end of the starboard engine was on fire. I didn't tell anyone of this since the radio had been unserviceable since take-off and with no navigation aids we did not know whom to call anyway. However, since the glow was reduced after ten minutes or so to a dimmer glare and since the flight commander had instructed the Squadron not to land early with unserviceabilities, but to do at least two and a half hours, we continued.

2. At no time did the flames cover the whole wing.

Remarks of Squadron Commander

1. I have been watching this pilot for some time; he is a typical product of the modern generation—longhaired, immoral, and, for all we know, probably on drugs. This incident

is typical of him and shows a spirit all too common amongst his type: laissezvoler. Poor motivation, no press on, no will to dice with death. I have interviewed him under Queens' Regulation 1482 (7) (Dope shops); his only comment was 'No sweat Boss, I just had to get back, sack wise'.

2. On the other hand, morale is low and I cannot afford more courts-martial. As, by his own admission, the flames did not cover the whole wing, and as he only logged 2.55 hours I am therefore recommending him for the award of a 'Relatively Good Show'.

Remarks of OC Flying and/or OC engineering Wing

1. I can only register extreme delight that this is NOT a servicing error and I will get no calls from nasty little men at Command about their bloody statistics

2. There are two valuable lessons to be learned from this incident:

a. Aircrew should seek life insurance.

b. Life insurance companies should not accept them.

Remarks of Station Commander

Faced as I am with a prodigious load of paperwork for the running of this large and busy station I am irritated by having to deal with yet another form dealing with a triviality such as an engine fire.

When I first operated Canberras in the autumn of 1924, Flt Lt Atcherley used to impress on me that the essential quality of a Squadron pilot is a 'press on spirit'. This would seem to be lacking in this case as the pilot should have completed a minimum of three hours.

I strongly recommend that Flying Officer Sharp be interviewed by the Queen for lack of moral fibre.

I did get my royal interview with Her Majesty, but not until many years later and then for a totally different reason, and that involved a lengthy stay in hospital. Again, more of that much later.

Mind you, later when serving in Germany, not for the first time did I spend a while in hospital. Like many youngsters, I suffered from impacted wisdom teeth and was confined to the RAF Hospital at Wegberg. That was when the RAF actually had hospitals. While recovering from that brutal operation, my chums from the squadron arrived to 'cheer' me up. They were each carrying a violin case, packed with beer. The ringleader calmly informed the duty sister that they were the RAF Germany band there to play for Fg Off. Sharp. Once in my room, they emptied the contents onto a hospital trolley that they had 'liberated', lifted me onto it, and proceeded to push me down the corridor to a safe place to consume copious quantities of German beer.

Sadly, though, the corridor was downhill and the team lost control. As the trolley gathered speed, they scampered after it, but were unable to prevent it from crashing into a large central heating radiator, which broke under the impact of a large trolley, a fat pilot, and many bottles of beer. Upon the loud crash being heard throughout that part of the hospital, several nursing staff arrived to see what the problem was. By now, of course, my 'friends' had totally disappeared and I was left under a pile of broken beer bottles, blankets, and an upturned trolley. Matron was not amused!

Life was good in those halcyon days. We shared an officers' mess with many expat school teachers (all female), motor cars were tax free, alcohol was so cheap that we put vodka in our vehicle windscreen washer bottles, and subsidised petrol was a mere 5p a litre. We worked hard and played hard. We had a most wonderful time. The best.

But it was not all play. One thing I was introduced to in Germany was TACEVAL (Tactical Evaluation). At least once a month, we poor servicemen were subjected to an alert exercise. It would start about 6 a.m. and the hooter (alert siren) would blow in the corridor immediately outside my officers' mess bedroom. We bachelors had exactly four minutes to get down to the squadron and into our fallout shelter. What fun it was to see a few dozen pilots and navigators, sleep still in their eyes, driving at breakneck speed down to the squadron on what were sometimes ice-covered roads. What fun indeed! I remember well the pile-up on the crossroads at the bottom of the mess road when not one car could stop.

When we arrived at the bunker, we were briefed, but then had to hang around for hours while the engineers and armourers prepared our war chariots. In order to pass the inspection, their task was to generate half of our aircraft in six hours and 70 per cent in twelve. Sometimes we had to dress in NBC kit (nuclear, biological, and chemical clothing). Not very comfortable and very difficult to work in, let alone fly. Often though we did not fly, but sat around until we were stood down for the day. Sometimes we slept in the squadron in armchairs, lucky those in QRA, who were tasked with the real stuff, had proper beds and a kitchen. As they were the official guardians of our NATO nuclear deterrent, they were excused participation in the exercise.

The exercise meant heaps of work for the ground crew, but was often very boring for us aircrew. Sometimes, though, we were tasked with operational sorties. Most times it went well, but sometimes not. Invariably, the event ended with a simulated nuclear attack on our base and we then had to spend hours in our fallout shelter, dressed in NBC suits, tin helmets, and gas masks while the specialist teams decontaminated the airfield and checked for radiation levels. In reality, we would have been there for months, if not years, until the food, water, or electricity ran out. Not much fun!

Life continued with many incidents, after all, we young things were entrusted with live ordinance. I recall one night when detailed to drop bombs on the nearby air weapon range, things went horribly wrong. Naturally, we could not see in the dark, especially as this was years before night vision goggles had even been invented, let alone supplied. More importantly, our vintage attack aircraft were naturally not equipped with any sophisticated navigation aids. The best we could muster was Decca. As this equipment was designed for use in North Sea trawlers, sailing at best at some 20 knots, it was not surprising that it hardly coped with our attack speeds of up to 360 knots. However, despite the vagaries of our equipment, at the end of a three-hour low-level exercise around Germany, we were to drop practice bombs on Nordhorn Range, in the dark and hopefully spot on target.

As we commenced our run into the range area, but with still some 30 nautical miles north of our intended target, my navigator announced 'Bomb gone', followed by the phrase 'Oh fuck'. He had misjudged the Decca readings (easy to do) and released the bomb into friendly territory. How close that was to human habitation I will never know, but we never heard of it again. Maybe that was because the unintended victim was unable to complain.

12

Survival Courses and Canberra Twilight

One thing that is always present in the Armed Forces and particularly aviation is training. There is a saying among pilots that the day one stops learning is the day to give up. We trained and trained. We also trained for the unexpected; for example, wings falling off and having to take to our parachutes. That was when the fun started! If that happened in the UK next to a pub, all well and good. Trouble is, the RAF had a global commitment in the twentieth century and one could find oneself under the silk and landing in a cruel sea, on an arid desert, a snow-capped mountain, or in a snake-infested jungle. One had to be prepared for all eventualities, including being attacked by the 'fuzzy-wuzzies' who were armed with fiendish knives ready to dismember parts of your anatomy. For that, we carried the famous 'Goolie chit', which promised the inhabitants of that country that Her Majesty would reward them well if they handed the survivor over to the British Embassy.

So enter stage left the Survival Course. Throughout my career, I have regularly had to undergo survival training. Whether it was just about egress from a passenger aeroplane or possibly having to survive a few nights in arctic conditions where temperatures dropped to minus 50 degrees Celsius, training was a necessary evil; sometimes fun, other times pretty awful.

The first one I was subjected to was sea survival. Well, initially my training took place in the UK, given that we do not have any many Alps, few tigers (unless one landed in a wildlife park, but more of that later), and not much sand (apart from Brighton beach). So after many hours in the classroom, where we learnt all about protection, location, water, and food, it was off to the municipal swimming pool and single-seat life raft drills. That was a piece of cake. We merely jumped into a warm swimming pool (in our flying suits), swam a couple of lengths (no mean feat when one's flying suit acts as a sea anchor), then inflated one's life raft and got into it. No problems. One would have to carry out this practice drill every year that one was engaged in flying duties.

The next test was something very similar, apart from the fact that it took place miles out to sea, often on a stormy day. No climbing out of the pool for a hot shower for us. This was getting pretty close to real survival, as waves were often 10 feet or so, making it difficult for the safety launch to keep track of ten young pilots as they drifted out to the centre of the ocean and further and further apart. Here we were made to survive a few hours in the dinghy before the air-sea rescue helicopter found us. However, despite being tossed around like a cork in the rapids, it was not too bad. What made it much worse in later years was when I was forced to share a twenty-eight-man life raft with some twenty or so other crewmembers,

The author at a winter survival course at Troodos mountains, Cyprus, 1968. (*Author's collection*)

most of whom were non-pilots and thus perhaps not possessing strong stomachs. This invariably resulted in most being sick, which led those with even a cast-iron constitution to feel very queasy. But sea survival was a doddle compared with winter survival!

I attended just three winter survival courses, compared with countless sea survival courses. Perhaps the reason was that winter courses were expensive to organise and fund. For a start, they were always situated when cold temperatures could be guaranteed. Hence the popular venues were either Bad Kohlgrub in the Bavarian Alps or Lillehammer in Norway. The latter was incredibly expensive due to the cost of the hotel.

Actually, my first 'winter survival' course was in Cyprus. Yes, really! Most people's impression of this Mediterranean isle is that it enjoys warm weather all the year round. After all, it is not far from Egypt. However, Mount Troodos is almost 6,500 feet above sea level, and when it is subjected to cold winds from the north in winter, the temperatures can fall well below zero. Snowfall is abundant at times, thus it is ideal for skiing and other winter sports. In fact, I have snow skied and water-skied on the same day. Nevertheless, though Troodos enjoyed a winter climate for some months of the year, the course organised by the RAF was fairly laid back and very soft. No one got frostbite, but many suffered hangovers.

The first 'proper' winter course I attended was at Bad Kohlgrub while serving with No. 14 Squadron at RAF Wildenrath. I had no choice as I was 'voluntecred'. Still, it proved to be great fun. The classroom instruction was naturally of a high standard and we were told how to build shelters from forest materials and parachutes, catch game, fish, and generally survive until help came. We also were taught to ski. The course contained many practical exercises in the snow-covered woods and on the mountainside. The après ski too was brilliant, as this was primarily a ski resort.

However, it was not all play, and the course terminated in a three-night exercise where we were teamed up with our navigators, issued with survival equipment, which included parachutes and aircraft dinghies. We were also ordered to make our way across alpine countryside to a rendezvous, which had to be reached within three days and nights. Unfortunately, there was a catch: a large team of German crack paratroops trained in alpine warfare and, unlike us victims, incredibly well equipped for night operations. Their task was to seek and capture us. When that happened, we would be handed over to some rather nasty interrogators who would not totally stick to the Geneva Convention. Bruises would be obligatory and thus we certainly did not want to be on the receiving end of their brutality. Given the harshness of the terrain and the weather, the penalty for being captured was a huge incentive to stay at liberty and reach the rendezvous (RV).

Consequently, I decided to obey one of the most important rules of war: 'There are no rules!' If my navigator and I were to succeed we would have to cheat. It seemed obvious to me that a couple of portly aircrew would never be able to cross 30 kilometres of alpine countryside without being caught. Hence my cunning plan was to lie low for half a day, then use my brain. There is a saying that a cunning pilot will always use his superior brain to avoid having to use his superior skill. So, having previously struck up a friendship with a couple of local girls, we arranged for them from outside the exercise area to collect us in their VW Beetle, hide us for a couple of days, then deliver us to a spot on the other side of the area so that we could hike into the RV from an unexpected direction. In the event, all the survival we endured was one very cold night deep inside a churchyard hedge, tucked up warmly in our single-seat dinghies, surrounded

The author's winter survival certificate, Bad Kohlgrub, Bavaria, 1969. (*Author's collection*)

by 8-foot snowdrifts. We often heard the stormtroopers going by, but they never twigged we were there. Without going into detail, the plan succeeded handsomely and we marched into the RV bang on time and fit as a fiddle. Out of some fifty or so aircrew, I think we were about the only two that made the home run. Needless to say, the directing staff were amazed!

Were we cheats? I think not. The first principle of war is 'Selection and Maintenance of the Aim'. There was only one aim: get to the RV on time. We succeeded, so I think we did OK.

The next winter survival course I attended was rather more difficult to enrol in. For a start, one was accommodated in upmarket chalets in a premier ski resort in Norway. Naturally, lovely chalet girls serviced these. Moreover, there would only be one night of survival and plenty of nights of après ski. Two types of skiing were offered: downhill and cross-country. One was great fun, the other jolly hard work, but still fun. One thing this course offered, or indeed threatened, was ultra-low temperatures. On the one night that we 'camped' out, the temperature fell to minus 50 degrees C. During the day, we were taught to build snow holes, very similar to igloos, but built into the side of a huge snow bank. Inside we constructed a ledge to sleep on and were supplied with arctic candles to warm our cosy nest. Amazingly, the temperature inside our winter shelters never fell below zero, which was a testament to the insulation properties of snow. Mind you, popping outside for a call of nature literally did freeze the balls off a brass monkey.

I never did get the opportunity to attend the desert or jungle survival courses. The desert one, held at El Adem in Libya, seemed a little boring to me. Merely heat, flies, and dehydration. The jungle course was held in Borneo and appeared quite exotic, though how I would have fared with creepy-crawlies climbing up my trouser legs to bite my privates or spending half the day plucking leaches off my bare flesh remains to be seen. I am glad that I did not attend either of those courses—winter and sea were enough for me.

Little was I to know that, many years later, the Canberra would assume vintage status. Despite a rather chequered introduction into service, it has performed magnificently. In my short time with the 'All Electric Aircraft', I grew to love it, not least because we lived in the halcyon days of the Near East Air Force and the Second Tactical Air Force. Despite being in the twilight of its operational life, the Canberra was still well ahead of the pack. If I recall correctly, it could fly 1,000 miles at low level, carry 8,000 lb of bombs, two very large air-to-surface missiles, numerous rockets, four cannon with what seemed like a year's supply of ammo, flares, napalm (oops, sorry, petrol bombs), and an enormous nuclear bomb. Its cruising speed was also not too far short of its successor, the Tornado, and could fly considerably higher than both Jaguar and Tornado. I regularly flew above 50,000 feet and the PR9 (which at the time of writing this book had only just retired from service) flew even higher. It did have a difficult start in life, but we later pilots will remember it not for its minor problems, but for its graceful lines, its performance, its capability, but also perhaps its rather nasty habit of killing its crew when one engine failed shortly after take-off. I lost a lot of good friends that way.

We brave young things, serving our country in far off places, did not realise that the sun was setting on Empire and indeed the RAF as we knew it. The Far East Air Force (FEAF) and the Middle East Air Force (MEAF) has long been disbanded. Soon, too, RAF Germany would be wound up. For a time, modern jets would replace our trusty English Electric Canberras, but within a generation, they too would be confined to the scrapyard as pilotless drones proved cheaper and more efficient. However, in those halcyon days of the late '60s, the old air force still existed, duty-free petrol was sold at 2p per litre, and I purchased a new sporty car for £500. More importantly, flying was still fun, though immensely dangerous. Night low-levels, without a decent radar altimeter or accurate navigation equipment, resulted in a large number of rather interesting sorties. I still wonder where my 25-lb practice bomb went after the navigator dropped it some 20 miles short of the air weapons range. We said nothing.

So my time flying the first ever jet bomber drew to a close and I looked forward to my next posting. Would it be a continuation of operational aviation, in short more strike attack flying? Exciting new aircraft were coming into service, least of which was the TSR-2. Now that would be fantastic, but, sadly, many Canberra and Hunter squadrons were disbanding and I would be one of many pilots seeking a plum job. Given that by this stage I had not shone as a steely pilot, I was not going to be top of the pecking order when the better postings were dished out.

All too soon my time on that lovely old jet bomber came to an end. Little was I to know that many years later I would gaze up into a blue sky and marvel how beautiful it looked, but at the end of my tour with No. 14 Squadron, the Canberra B(I)8 to me was just a workhorse. Now there is only one B(I)8 left in the world, and that is in a museum in New Zealand. Interestingly, it was the very aircraft in which I notched up my thousandth hour. My very last flight was on 29 May 1970 in Canberra B(I)8 WT 339, which fittingly was a low-level around Germany lasting just one hour and thirty minutes. A comment in my logbook merely stated that I was of average ability—rather disappointing really.

13

Learning to Fly—Again

As I have said earlier, the sun was rapidly setting on Empire and, more importantly for me, the RAF. Though I did not realise it at the time, with the introduction of SNY (Shiny New Toys) like TSR-2 and Hawker P1154, I honestly thought the future was rosy. I wanted a piece of it.

Being realistic, however, and not even enjoying an 'Above Average' flying assessment, the best I could hope for after the B(I)8 Interdictor was the Blackburn Buccaneer. This was a night capable strike aircraft designed originally for carriers. Sadly, with the demise of TSR-2 and the cancellation of F111, the British strike/attack capability remained with a few ancient and very vulnerable V bombers. To me, the Buccaneer was an exciting low-level combat aircraft that did exactly what my elderly Canberra did. This was then my logical future, but it was not to be.

It can be said that we all have a degree in hindsight. Certainly now I am well aware that when a RAF squadron disbands, there are far too many pilots looking for jobs that are simply not available. The favoured few get the cream. The less favoured take potluck. Apparently, I was less than favoured.

So instead of my posting to Buccaneers, I was posted to Central Flying School to learn to be a QFI. While in theory one had to have an 'Above Average' assessment for this course, I suspect that with me it was simply 'Where on earth shall we send Sharp?' Either way, it was not to do me any harm and I was actually taught to fly properly.

Disappointingly, in spite of asking to be posted to instruct on the Folland Gnat, I made the stupid mistake of mentioning that I had flown the Chipmunk. Given the policy of 'Supply and Demand', I got the posting to a basic FTS on Chipmunks. A far cry from flying at the speed of heat across the Central German Plain armed with a veritable arsenal of lethal weapons.

Nothing much happened to me in sleepy hollow Gloucestershire, though I discovered yet again that the Chipmunk was a wolf in sheep's clothing. It could bite. One very dark night, while practising landings on the grass with an instructor, I saw the world from various angles in the short space of a few seconds. In short, I ground looped! In the days well before health and safety, we landed on grass lit purely by 'goosenecks'. These were cans of paraffin with wicks lit to provide a flare path. To save money, the RAF in its wisdom provided lighting just down one side of the grass runway. This provided a challenge for junior pilots, as it was quite difficult to judge height and aspect from a single line of lights. Moreover, the visibility from the cockpit of a Chipmunk at night was terrible. It was bad enough during the day and especially if condensation covered the inside of the canopy. Consequently, all this led to my ground loop.

Now this was not a disaster in itself, but very shortly after we ground to a standstill, my mentor in the rear started screaming at me to move. Apparently, I had come to rest immediately over one of the flaming goosenecks. In fact, I had parked my left fuel tank, full of very high-octane aviation fuel, in just the right place to ensure we rapidly became a fireball. I am not sure who opened the throttle, but we rapidly vacated our parking place and thus saved one of Her Majesty's aeroplanes from being torched. We too were not incinerated, which is just as well as this book would then never have been written.

I graduated eventually as a flying instructor, very much on probation. My next three years teaching youngsters to fly were to pass without too much further incident. After all, no one was shooting at me, though I often thought my student was trying to kill me. Nevertheless, I started my instructional career very wet behind the ears and possessing very little ability. As you will discover, I ended that time as a totally different pilot. As well as teaching youngsters to fly, maybe I spent some of the time teaching myself. They do say that one learns from watching others make mistakes and there were many of those.

I was particularly fortunate to be posted to an outfit called HSP. When I received my appointment, I queried what and where this training squadron was. 'Helicopter Specialist Pilots, up in Yorkshire,' was the reply. Oh, I muttered, how come I have been trained to instruct on a light piston fixed-wing aircraft and yet be posted to helicopters? 'They don't have helicopters,' came the indignant reply, as if I was stupid. It turned out that the tools of my trade were indeed the de Havilland Chipmunk T10 and not some silly flying machine with the propeller on the roof. Moreover, despite the fact that this was a naval squadron, it was based miles from the sea near York.

So my first assignment as a brand new and rather 'wet behind the ears' flying instructor was to the famous 'Vale of York' where foggy autumn days often ensured early stacks to the Ryther Arms pub. The famous and ever popular 'Black Flag' days.

As stated, my flying machine was the trusty Chipmunk that had been in service since the Second World War. Nevertheless, it was an ideal platform for us to teach the rudimentary aspects of aviation to these fledgling naval aviators. I recall the comment in Pilot's Notes describing the beast:

> The aircraft is pleasant to fly; the controls are well harmonised and they remain light and responsive throughout the speed range, although they tend to become heavier as the limiting speed is reached.

Yeah, all of 173 knots. Could man survive such speed? Yet in this computer age, where speeds in excess of 24,000 mph have been reached by man-made craft, this aeroplane, with a maximum speed in a steep dive of 173 knots, seems very primitive. It seemed primitive even then. However, it was quite demanding to fly well, especially in a tricky crosswind, thus it made a superb tool for initial training. It certainly sorted the men from the boys; my boys who as men would later fly Sea Harriers during the Falklands War.

One of my very first 'instructional' sorties was with a fledgling sub-lieutenant who had passed the course and had entered the aerobatic competition that traditionally took place at the end of the course. To prevent the young bucks from killing themselves, it was mandatory for the ex-student to practise his aerobatics with an instructor in the rear, and so my boss told me to fly with the young man and that I might even learn something about aerobatics. Bloody cheek! Anyway, off we went and to my amazement, his aerobatics were far better than mine. After the sequence, he brought our tiny Chipmunk back to Mother Earth while all the while I had totally switched off, wondering if I was adequate enough to teach pupils who perhaps had greater inherent skill than I possessed. Our young pilot flew immaculately down the approach path, obviously still trying to impress the new 'Sir' in the back cockpit and then rounded out. It was only then that I woke up with a start: he had rounded out dangerously high and we were about to stall 10 feet above the grass. I quickly took control and righted the situation. Yes, I quickly learnt about students from that. Welcome to instruction!

One of the 'joys' of instructional flying is the documentation, the vital 'write-up' of the student's progress. Due to the pressure of work, especially during winter when we needed to complete a course on time, but had very few flyable days in the Vale of York, we needed to catch up on the good days. I tended to jot down notes in a little book, then write up the sortie in the students' progress books (Form 5060) at home in the evening. One day, rather tired at home, I wrote up the first six sorties, but found that I had no notes of the last one. I obviously had rushed home and relied on my memory (it was good in those days) to complete the report of the final trip, but try as I might, I could not remember it, so I made it all up. Well, I did know the student well and almost certainly knew how he would have performed. Nevertheless, I gave him quite a glowing report just in case. After met brief the following day, I took him to one side and asked him about the sortie. 'Oh Sir,' he said, 'the engine would not start and thus we called it a day.' No wonder I could not recall what we did, we had done absolutely nothing. I let the report stand as it was indeed glowing and we saved the Queen the cost of the trip.

One tangible joy was the pleasure of seeing a young spotty boy, who had absolutely no idea of how to land an aeroplane, graduate into a fine qualified pilot. Some forty-five years later,

De Havilland Chipmunks, 2 FTS, RAF Church Fenton, 1970. (*Author's collection*)

while debriefing a formation sortie at the local airfield where I flew from, a middle-aged man came up to me in the café and introduced himself as 'the worst student I had ever taught to fly'. He told me that despite his very limited ability, he had graduated as a Fleet Air Arm pilot, had a wonderful career, and ended up as a Jumbo Jet captain for British Airways. That little incident made me feel good. One does tend to remember one's first flying instructor, though I must admit my memory is now rather weak and I cannot recall the hundreds of young men that I either taught to fly or indeed converted onto advanced machinery.

Just the other day, while watching the predecessor of the Chipmunk, a de Havilland Tiger Moth, land at my local airfield, it reminded me of yet another incident that occurred to me while instructing on Chipmunks. Now the pilots among you will know that the Tiger Moth has no roof, no starter, no nose wheel, no stall-warners, no flaps, not even brakes. This is why the Tiger Moth is one of the finest basic trainers ever produced. It requires considerable skill to fly it well. Consequently, it is a devil to control while on the ground, and if the wind is breezy, 'wing-walkers' will be required to guide the aeroplane to its parking slot. Now the Chipmunk is not quite so primitive, but it too has no means of steering other than using differential brakes. At least that is more than a Tiger Moth possesses. Nevertheless, in a strong wind, the little Chippy will also require wing-walkers to help it to parking. One day, I landed in a very fierce gale and at end of the runway, two strong airmen met me to 'walk' me back to dispersal. Unfortunately, as I passed between two hangars, an enormous gust of wind, enhanced by the funnel feature of the two hangars, caught my chaps unawares and the next thing I knew I was at 50 feet and at idle power. I instantly applied full power, and due to increased slipstream over the wing, caused by the propeller, I had sufficient flying speed to recover to Mother Earth. That gave me rather a fright! Luckily, both airmen had relinquished their hold on my wingtips, otherwise they would have had rather a problem.

Then there were 'deck landings'. Well, to avoid congestion, my Royal Naval Elementary Flying School deployed to a relief landing ground for 'circuits and bumps'. There our naval cadets could take to the grass without rude remarks from their RAF colleagues from the sister training squadron. Transportation to our personal aerodrome for the youngsters was by RAF coach, while we 'mature' instructors flew the aircraft the short journey to RAF Rufforth.

However, after landing their beefy Phantom jet fighters on the heaving deck of a Royal Naval aircraft carrier, during a stormy night and without the luxury of an alternative landing strip, flying little 'puddle jumpers' was rather tame for our intrepid RN pilots. Understandably!

Hence these hardened aviators devised a wizard plan to emulate their epic sea adventures and nominated the RAF coach HMS *Ark Royal*. While the bus transported the fledgling student pilots back to base at the end of the day's flying, it became customary for each instructor to 'land' on the roof of this vehicle. When told that I had to attempt a 'touch and go', I laughed, thinking it was yet another Fleet Air Arm 'wind up'. Not so, they explained. Compared with real deck landings in a force 9 gale when the touchdown area is rising and dropping some 50 feet in just a few seconds, landing on the roof of the RAF bus was quite simple, especially if it was travelling in a straight line at a mere 50 mph. Well, I achieved my 'deck landing' status and was accepted into the brotherhood of naval aviators. But how I would have coped with landing a supersonic jet fighter on a real aircraft carrier, I will never know. Incidentally, the Motor Transport Officer never found out why his coaches all had dents in their roofs!

14

Night Landings

Night flying in a single-piston aircraft is fraught with danger. How on earth do you land the thing in the dark if the engine stops? Someone once told me to wait until close to the ground before putting on the landing light. If you do not like what you see, then turn it off again. Of course, if you have a parachute and fly high enough, you minimise the risks. Even then, do you really want to be plunging earthwards on the end of a parachute in the pitch dark? You probably are quite likely to end up speared on a church spire or drowning in a lake. Moreover, guess where the fuel gauges are situated in a Chipmunk. Yes, out on the wings and difficult to see in the dark even if one possess a half decent torch. Sadly, however, while instructing at a RAF base in darkest Yorkshire in the '60s, we pilots were mandated to teach 'Night Navigation!' We must have been completely mad. For a start, it was dark. Secondly, in our primitive Chipmunks, we had absolutely no navigation aids other than Mk 1 eyeballs—fat lot of good they are in the dark. Occasionally, if lucky, we might get a radio bearing from a nearby airfield, but usually it was dead reckoning or nothing.

One incident caused me particular concern and I will come onto that in a while. Years after my tour on the mighty Chippy, while flying for British Airways, I was trained to fly what was termed 'Category 3c Autoland'—that is, landing at an airport which was completely fogged out. That procedure is totally safe if the aircraft is properly equipped with Cat 3 landing avionics, the crew are properly trained and current, and the airfield is certified for Cat 3 landings. However, my first 'Autoland' was actually in a Chipmunk, which I do not think is 'properly equipped'.

Anyway, one starry night, my student and I found ourselves plodding on across the North York moors. We navigated partly by the lights of towns (non-existent over the moors), accurate heading (difficult with an antiquated P11 compass), time, and the occasional radio bearing from the very few RAF airfields open at night.

But at least it was peaceful, the moon was up and the flying was smooth. Perhaps I should have worried for they were ideal conditions for the formation of fog.

Just before we were due to make our final turn for home, ATC called me to suggest I hurry home as fog was beginning to form over the airfield. Well in my trusty ancient flying machine all I could do was to increase speed by a few knots and thus we started our sluggish trek home.

Then the bottom fell out of my world. ATC called 'R83, hurry up, we are now down to 250 metres'. Well with at least twenty minutes' flying time to go, I made the sensible decision and decided to divert to RAF Leeming, a large airfield close by. Unfortunately, after stating my decision, I was told that too had gone out in fog. So too had the local civil airport, Leeds Bradford. Given that I had insufficient fuel to reach anywhere else, I had no choice but to continue at top speed towards base.

Amid more and more gloomy Met reports, we gradually approached Church Fenton. As I flew into the Military Air Traffic Zone, ATC piped up to tell me that the visibility had now dropped to a mere 50 metres. It was now impossible for me to land.

Was this going to be my first real parachute jump? Church Fenton was my only option and I was down to my last ten minutes of fuel. I was worried! I had a right to be. However, as I flew into the overhead, I could make out the runway, albeit bathed in a rather ghostly haze. No problem, I thought. I was wrong!

ATC cleared me to land and I started my approach. By now I was flying the aircraft from the rear seat, hardly able to trust my teenage student. Actually, I think he was wetting himself! Initially, all seemed fine, but as we approached 200 feet above ground, I entered the fog. Mega pea soup. Trouble was I had to continue, as for the last twenty minutes or so, I had been flying on full throttle and I was rapidly running out of fuel. Not that I could see how much we had anyway. Moreover, we had nowhere else to go and I probably had insufficient fuel to even climb to 2,000 feet to bale out. But at just 200 feet per minute rate of decent, I thought that the landing might not be any worse than the usual student touch down.

I was right. I felt the main wheels firmly touch Mother Earth and I closed the throttle, keeping straight by the direction indicator. I could see nothing, not even the runway lights; however, I knew that that there was nothing serious to hit. In a very short space of time, we came to a halt and I breathed a great sigh of relief. We were alive and had even stopped on the black stuff. A short transmission to the control tower told them I was down safely and they replied that the Land Rover was on its way to pick us both up. There was no way I was going to taxi back to dispersal in that pea soup.

However, having managed to perform a miracle and successfully land my aircraft in thick fog, I was less than pleased to be almost killed by the ATC Land Rover nearly mowing us down as it hurtled past us in zero visibility. Minutes later, we were on our way back to the crew room for the usual tea and medals. My pent up feelings that night were directed towards the hapless driver, but we lived to fight another day.

Night flying, however, did bring rewards. We silly young bucks enjoyed performing aerobatics at night. With hindsight that now seems totally stupid, but we were young. However, the distinctive sound of a Chipmunk revving its engine and turning upside down not surprisingly annoyed some of the locals who often complained to the officer in charge of night flying. Consequently, knowing we might be in trouble, we always used to rush off in the opposite direction following the aerobatics, then call for a radio bearing from air traffic. If we were subsequently challenged, we could always say that it could not possibly have been us as we were nowhere near the scene of the misdemeanour. If the commanding officer disbelieved us, we merely referred him to the ATC tapes. Would I be so naughty now? Well, I am far too sensible to even get airborne after dark.

15

Engine Failures

Of course, our mission was to instruct our bright young students not only to fly our primitive aerial machines, but also to react correctly to any emergency. One such problem would of course be an engine failure. Given that the Chipmunk only had one engine, any failure of an engine meant that the aeroplane would be going just one way—downwards. In short, straight to the scene of the accident. Consequently, we taught our students what to do and how to do it properly. Given that our craft would glide quite well, the pilot of the stricken machine would naturally select a field and land in it—if, indeed, there was one. The five 'Ss' became the desired mnemonic: shape, size, slope, surface, and surrounds. Normally, there was rarely a problem finding such an emergency landing ground as we invariably operated over a rural area and, moreover, at sufficient height to allow time to select the appropriate field.

However, a more serious situation existed if the engine cut immediately after take-off. Then the pilot would have little time to react and of course would have a limited numbers of fields to choose from. Often, the plane would have to land straight ahead, taking potluck. If the aeroplane ran into a wall or ditch before stopping, there was nothing a pilot could do to prevent it.

Naturally, we often practised such emergencies. The drill was that immediately after departure from the airfield, the instructor would close the throttle and state 'Practice forced landing'. Not surprisingly, we called that an 'Engine failure after take-off' drill or EFATO for short. The student would be expected to go through the drill, pick a suitable landing spot, and simulate switching off the fuel and ignition. Just above the ground, the instructor would order the student to apply power and climb.

One day, I decided to include an EFATO drill to the sortie repertoire. At a safe height of about 600 feet and from the rear seat of the aeroplane, I closed the throttle and stated the magic phrase 'Practice engine failure'. Promptly, the front seat student correctly lowered the nose of the Chipmunk to a gliding angle, but then to my amazement, he turned off the fuel cock. The engine stopped dead. To which, I yelled, 'You have turned off the fuel cock,' and quickly put it back on. Thankfully, the engine regained power. At that, my dumb student looked down, saw that the fuel cock was now on, and turned it off again, thinking that he had made an initial mistake and forgotten to turn it off.

Now, with the engine silent and the ground looping ominously close, there was nothing for it but to land in the field that my student had initially selected. Luckily, it was a big one.

Of course, not all forced-landings were 'practice'. Given the elderly nature of the Chipmunk Gypsy Major engine, which originated in a tractor design, it had a habit of letting go. The engine itself was fairly reliable, but the ignition system (twin magnetos) was less than perfect. Moreover, failures were not confined to just when instructors were at the controls. One such incident happened to a fairly experienced student on a solo flight across the Wolds. One of his magnetos started to misbehave, causing the engine to run extremely roughly. As our embryonic pilot feared the worst, he sensibly elected to land in a suitable farmer's field before the engine quit completely. Good plan.

The field satisfied all five Ss and he made a good touchdown, causing zero damage to his aeroplane. Our now rather smug pilot wandered over to the farmhouse to ask if he could use their telephone to alert RAF Church Fenton of his plight and was told by the squadron that as he had an important flying test later that day, in about an hour, an instructor in another Chipmunk would land and pick him up, leaving a mechanic to fix the aeroplane.

So, after a cup of tea and a healthy slice of cake, provided by the very pleasant and rotund farmer's wife, our bright young thing wandered out to the field. After pondering for a moment, he remembered that pilots should not land if another aircraft occupied the runway. Moreover, though the field was of adequate size for a Chipmunk to perform a landing, his aeroplane might get in the way. So he hopped in, started up the rough-running engine (first mistake), and taxied his steed through a convenient gap in a hedge into a very much smaller field to park the aeroplane well out of the way of his landing instructor.

Thirty minutes later, the relief aeroplane appeared over the horizon. The pilot looked down and spotted the field where the student had parked his craft. 'That looks a little small,' mused the pilot, but if a student could get into that field, he most certainly could also. Well, you have guessed the outcome. The instructor, who actually had not been instructing very long, attempted a landing, missed the Chipmunk parked by the hedge, but failed to stop in time before his aeroplane ran into the hedge at the other end of the very small field. Now two Chipmunks were down. I will not tell you what happened next, as you would not believe it.

Though this book is mainly about my exploits, I am very pleased to report that incident was nothing to do with me. However, I did have my fair share of engine failures. One engine decided to quit on a lovely summer's day in perfect weather while I was performing aerobatics immediately overhead the airfield. This would be a piece of cake because the skill levels required to save my aeroplane were negligible. However, I doubted if a medal would wing my way after the incident.

Suffice to say that, after enlightening Air Traffic Control that I had an engine failure, I accomplished a perfect engine-off landing on the main runway and rolled to a halt. Imagine my annoyance subsequently when ATC ordered me to vacate the runway immediately and stop messing around. I responded with a suitable rude comment to ask how that would be possible without an engine. ATC responded by informing me that as I had not used the magic word 'Mayday', they naturally presumed it was merely one of the many practice forced-landings that took place there every day.

Memo to self: must remember to use the correct phraseology in future. I might need the blood wagon and fire engine one day. Moreover, if someone had occupied the runway just before my landing, I would have had a major problem. 'Go around' would not have been an option without an engine. The word 'Mayday' suggests that the pilot needs just a little assistance. Lucky that day all went well. It might not have done.

Later in the summer of '73, we were re-equipped with the brand-new Scottish Aviation Bulldog. The Bulldog is a British two-seat side-by-side training aircraft designed by Beagle Aircraft as the B.125 Bulldog. The first prototype flew on 19 May 1969 at Shoreham Airport, now called Brighton Municipal Airport. The first order for the type was for seventy-eight from the Swedish Air Board. Unfortunately, before any production aircraft were built, Beagle Aircraft ceased trading and the production rights for the aircraft, along with the Swedish order, were taken over by Scottish Aviation (Bulldog) Limited. All subsequent aircraft were built at Prestwick Airport by Scottish Aviation. Later, the RAF was to order 130. This was a sea change to the venerable Chippy. It was modern, the student sat beside the instructor, and it had a nose wheel. At first, we instructors were sceptical about this new instructional tool as it was easier to fly, especially as three-pointer landings would be a thing of the past. Landing speed thus would not be quite so critical and the view forward far superior. Little was I to know then that this new diminutive aeroplane would shape my retirement.

Sorry, but I digress. Having taken delivery of a fleet of bright gleaming new aeroplanes, we learned instructors decided to fly four aircraft to RAF Machrihanish (now known as Campbeltown Airport) situated on the Mull of Kintyre. We planned to fly in formation

The author at 2 FTS with Scottish Aviation Bulldog and Bulldog. (*Author's collection*)

all the way there, aiming to collect a consignment of kippers. I elected to fly No. 4 in box with my 'co-pilot', a very experienced naval airman not long off flying F4 Phantom jets off HMS *Ark Royal*. Having coasted out over the Firth of Clyde and in sight of Ailsa Craig, an uninhabited island formed from the volcanic plug of an extinct volcano, I decided to have a little snooze, confident in the skill of my colleague flying our Bulldog from the right-hand seat. Sadly, he became just a little bored and wondered how much cross-controls he could put on and still stay perfectly in formation. Consequently, this placed enormous side loads on the aircraft and, because he had elected to supply the engine with fuel solely from the left tank, the engine stopped. That woke me up! Luckily, I had the presence of mind to selected both fuel tanks and dive the aeroplane to windmill the propeller. That did the trick and the engine started. So the only result of all that was that the Steely Fast Jet Pilot (SFJP) in the right-hand seat proved that he could not fly fully cross-controlled in formation, and if it had been dark, we would still have been able to see the instruments from the glow of his red face.

Referring to that pilot saying, 'A wise pilot uses his incredible amount of knowledge to avoid having to use his incredible amount of skill', pity he did not that day and luckily I did not have to demonstrate any skill at all. Naturally, this was not the last time I was faced with the engine quitting in my aeroplane, as you will discover much later.

16
Widow Maker

After my 'penance' tour with Flying Training Command flying light aircraft, I suppose I was not well placed to 'migrate' back into frontline operational flying. I still hankered after Buccaneers and had in fact been promised them at the end of my instructional tour. Stupid me! Fancy falling for that one. 'Work hard, young man, and we will look after you.' Well, having achieved an A2 Instructor category in record time and ending up as flight commander, I assumed I had done the business. By then, the shabby start to my flying career was forgotten and I was very well thought of, but I quickly learnt that one could not trust one's poster. For a start, the usual excuse was 'Oh, he has moved on and did not leave any details of any promise'. Trouble also was that market forces prevailed. The Buccaneer was definitely in the twilight of its years, its replacement, the MRCA Tornado, was only being staffed by current members of the frontline and, worse still, my instructional prowess was needed elsewhere.

So in early 1974, when my boss told me I was posted to a ground tour, I was annoyed. I was even more miffed to discover that this backward step would take me to the wilds of northern Scotland. Little was I to know that being posted to the Jaguar Operational Conversion Unit, as a simulator and ground instructor, was to have a profound and exciting effect on the rest of my life.

Thus I was introduced to the 'Widow Maker'. When the German Air Force purchased 600 Starfighters from the USA, the deal was that pilots would be trained in America. That made sense, as Arizona enjoyed clear blue skies most of the time. Great for training, not so great for preparation for flying in weather-bound Central Europe. The young pilots, now fully trained and brimming with self-confidence, returned to the Fatherland and commenced their aviation careers. Many lasted just a few hours before becoming yet another statistic of flight safety. Of the 600 aeroplanes purchased, some 200 crashed, invariably killing the pilot. That represented a third of the total and thus the Lockheed Starfighter truly earned the nickname 'Widow Maker'.

A decade later, Her Majesty's government ordered 200 Jaguars, but history was to prove that this exciting aeroplane was to become far more of a widow maker than its American cousin, the Starfighter. Appendix I details just some of the crashes that befell the Jaguar force, but we pilots totally ignored its failings; we loved it, warts and all. As Mr Baldrick eloquently stated in the brilliant TV series *Black Adder*, if he had the bullet with his name

A painting of a 6 Squadron Jaguar low-level in the mountains. (*Peter Van Stigt*)

on it, he was safe. We crazy pilots always thought that misfortune would befall the other man! Whatever, this fighter-bomber was *Star Wars* at the time, but unlike the computerised attack aircraft of today (2018), the pilot had to do everything himself. In short, it was an ergonomic nightmare and only the very sharpest (excuse the pun) ace would survive a tour on the 'Widow Maker'.

However, all those disasters were in the future. Despite my initial and considerable misgivings, not only by being posted to a 'ground tour', but also to a distant part of the UK far from civilisation, it all turned out for the better. Being part of an incredibly futuristic fighter aircraft project, right at its inception, filled everyone on the team with immense pride. In 1973, very few people had even seen a Jaguar and even fewer had flown one. I had only read about it in aviation magazines. Now I was part of the initial project team. I discovered that in the early 1970s, the Sepecat Jaguar was light years ahead of anything even the Americans had at that time. The best that the mighty US Air Force could muster in ground attack was the venerable and elderly A7 Corsair 2. True, the US had some rather fine interceptors, but their idea of bombing was the incredibly massive B-52 bomber. Hardly a nimble beast and definitely not suitable for low-level flying, and if one was to negate the sophisticated missile threat the Soviets could muster in Eastern Europe, one had to fly at treetop level below the radar.

A few years previously, the RAF ordered a supersonic strike aircraft to replace its ageing Canberra bombers. It was simply called TSR-2. If you read Wg Cdr Rolland Beamont's great book *Phoenix into Ashes*, you will learn what happened to that wonderful aircraft. Like the Jaguar, it was light years ahead of the opposition, but the RAF had a problem: because future aeroplanes like the TSR-2 were so advanced and so quick, it was decided that a suitably fast trainer was needed to replace the diminutive Gnat that had served as the RAF fast jet trainer for many years. Previously, in 1963, the RAF had issued Air Staff Target 362 for a trainer to replace the Gnat and Hunter. With TSR-2 just on the horizon, it was imperative to find a solution to AST 362 as soon as possible. Luckily, the French had on the drawing board: a fighter called the Breguet 121. It was decided that this could be converted into a fast jet trainer and a lead in to TSR-2 or, as it turned out, its successor.

If that had transpired, it would have been a disaster. The Jaguar was far too much of a handful for young students and we would have lost far more than we actually did. Providentially for many fledgling pilots, the TRS2 project was cancelled, and subsequently, the 200 Jaguar trainers were converted to the low-level tactical strike role. So No. 226 Operational Conversion Unit was formed at RAF Lossiemouth in 1973.

The Jaguar was a quantum leap forward for ex-Hawker Hunter pilots, the aeroplane it replaced, but it was not without initial problems. For me, this aircraft seemed way beyond my reach. I had previously flown an antiquated fighter-bomber and, more importantly, had spent the last four years flying a puddle jumper. However, the senior management of the unit I was a part of had an incredibly farsighted approach to staff development. Even if you were part of the ground instructional staff, if you were good enough to fly the aircraft, you did. What an incentive! I jumped at the offer and had no problem with ground school and simulator; after all, I was an instructor in both, and took to the unbelievable complexities of the aircraft like a duck to water.

On 7 August 1974, I soloed in Jaguar T2 XX838 for the first, but not last time. Now all I needed to do was to get transferred to where I really belonged: on a frontline fighter squadron again.

First I had to work my ticket. Ahead of me lay three years of classroom and simulator teaching. What I did not know then was that the experiences in the simulator were later to save my life. Being an impatient youth, teaching in ground school and simulator, with only the very occasional Jaguar flight, soon bored me. So when I 'flew' the incredibly realistic simulator, I encouraged my colleagues who programmed the emergencies to dream up the most terrible of disasters. It then became a challenge to recover to base despite flying an aircraft that had lost an engine, the other on fire, the navigation system shot to pieces, and my airfield suffering the worst weather storm in living memory. Skills learnt here became precious. Of prime importance was that I learnt how to prioritise, something that would really stand me in good stead some years later. It was a pity that many of my compatriots did not acquire the same skills.

Sadly for many, we underestimated the complexity of the aircraft and in particular its weapon and navigation systems. Many ex-Hunter pilots were used to flying with their heads out of the cockpit for 99 per cent of the time. Old fashioned 'Stick, search and report; map & stopwatch'. The Hunter was pretty basic with no navigation aids. It was also subsonic. In 1973, due to the sophistication and lack of ergonomic design of the Jaguar avionics, much time was needed to program the various system computers in flight. Flying at 600 mph, a mere 100 feet above *terra firma*, while head down programming the kit, was a definite recipe for disaster. It was said at the time that one could sort Jaguar pilots into two types: those who looked up at 50 feet, going down like the clappers, and those who did not. Fortunately, I was one of the former.

No wonder it became known at the British Widow Maker, for we lost not 33 per cent of our aeroplanes, but 50 per cent. I lost so many friends in the middle to late '70s that my eldest son changed his mind about becoming a fighter pilot.

But academia was soon to be behind me. At the end of my tour in Bonny Scotland, for once the higher-ups were true to their word and I was posted to a frontline squadron. However, even though I had been flying the Jaguar for three years, first I had to pass the conversion course on to the Jaguar! Well, the higher-ups thought that I had sat behind a desk or played with a simulator for the last few years. Moreover, my previous official flying tour was on light piston-engined aeroplanes. So obviously I needed to be 'refreshed' before starting my 'conversion' to a supersonic jet fighter bomber.

Hence I was detached to the School of Refresher Flying (SORF) at RAF Leeming. This would be fun, I thought. After flying the Jaguar at 8 miles a minute, I wondered what trundling along in the venerable Jet Provost would be like—300 knots flat out was not quite the same as 540 knots.

But I had a problem. How was I to get to darkest Yorkshire? I could drive, but my wife would need our trusty Saab motorcar. I could go by train, but that would take an age. No, the solution was obvious. My wing commander at the Jaguar Operational Conversion Unit had a surfeit of Jaguar strike/attack fighters. Too many to place each morning out on the flight line. 'Yes, of course, Derek, you can have one for a couple of weeks.' Well in those days, the RAF was like that—a flying club. All we did was train for war. Thankfully, we never had a war. They were yet to come. So in the Swinging Sixties, RAF pilots were encouraged to take a jet away for the weekend. As for borrowing one of Her Majesty's latest jet fighters for a few weeks on duty, no problem.

Hence I flew down to Yorkshire in a *Star Wars* machine, merely to attend a jet refresher course in an ancient and very slow jet trainer. You can imagine the raised eyebrows and some incredulity from the senior staff at the School of Refresher Flying and the pure delight from the young students there who were just starting their initial flying training.

After SOFT, my refresher training was still not complete. I now had to clear the hurdle of the Tactical Weapons Unit at RAF Brawdy in West Wales. All training is good value, but I was significantly immature to object to having to learn to drop bombs and fire guns again, even in a beautiful aeroplane such as the Hawker Hunter. It had been the mainstay of Britain's air defence back in the '50s, now it was relegated to being just a weapons trainer for young pilots going on to fast jets. Would I be the old man there, as by then I was knocking on the ripe old age of thirty-two? At least I was going to get the chance to fly a classic '50s jet fighter.

I did quite well on the course, after all I had flown the Jaguar solo, I had done two tours in the ground attack and interdiction roles, and I was a QFI. Due to my relatively advancing years, I was made course leader. However, it is said that one cannot teach an old dog new tricks and so it was thus with me. Though the disciplines of air-to-ground weaponry, instrument flying, and old-fashioned navigation were dispatched with ease, air-to-air firing was a bit of a struggle for me. Years later, when I was the commanding officer of a sister squadron at the Tactical Weapons Unit, I still failed to hit the air-to-air target, much to the delight of my instructors. Partly due to this and partly because I did not get on with my squadron commander, I was in trouble. What made matters worse was the old 'sand in the boots' Hunter pilot's philosophy 'Kick the tires, light the fires, last one airborne is a sissy'. After a few years doing things by the book, and to a certain extent having slowed down a tad, I was not too sharp. I also suspect that due to my rather cocky demeanour, some knives were out for me. Luckily, the Seventh Cavalry (in the form of my old boss

Hawker Hunter TWU. (*Chris French*)

at the Jaguar OCU) came to the rescue and the station commander at RAF Brawdy was requested to dispatch young Sharp back to Lossiemouth post-haste as a member of the present Jaguar course had fallen by the wayside. Hence, I passed out without finishing the course. Just as well. Nevertheless, I was awarded the grade 'Proficient' and the squadron commander thanked me for all my hard work as course leader. I wonder if he choked as he wrote those words.

The Jaguar course passed very quickly and, needless to say, I passed my second OCU with flying colours. Well, I really should have done so as I had just about flown every lesson a million times previously.

All too soon I found myself posted as an operational pilot to No. 6 Squadron at RAF Coltishall in sleepy Norfolk. The squadron was formed at Farnborough early in 1914 and shortly after moved to Belgium. It remained stationed outside the UK until reforming at Coningsby in 1969, being the first RAF squadron to be equipped with the mighty Phantom. While I was serving at Lossiemouth, it re-equipped with the relatively diminutive Jaguar and the following month moved to its home base at RAF Coltishall.

This assignment was definitely going to test my ability, my bravery, and my capability to survive, especially as, during the very first week of my tour, two of our pilots crashed and died. Given that we only had a handful of pilots on the unit, this event hit us all very hard. Would I last the year, let alone a whole tour of duty? It became rather a worry as I was now married with two children, so much so that I even wrote for my wife a little black notebook detailing what to do in the event of my death. The first page contained the telephone number of a local hairdresser. Well, my wife would then need to start looking

No. 6 Squadron personnel and Jaguars outside hangar 1979. (*Author's collection*)

for a replacement father for my children! If my guardian angel really did exist, she would definitely have her work cut out over the next few years.

This tour would prove to be the hardest of my entire career. They do say that most are promoted one rank above their pay grade. During my operational Jaguar tour, I think I was mainly operating one level above my ability. Luckily, they do say that 'There are no old, bold pilots'. As I was now getting old, thirty-two years old to be exact, I was no longer the fearless young upstart and did not push myself, or my craft, to the ultimate limit. Often my sixth sense for self-preservation stopped me from becoming a smoking pile of wreckage.

That in itself was a miracle given the tasks we were set. Chums asked me what it was like to fly a frontline supersonic fighter. I replied that, in itself, flying the Jaguar was easy. Operating was something else. Flying often at a mere 100 feet above the ground and occasionally much lower, sometimes at speeds in excess of a mile every five seconds, requires skill. Carrying out multiple tasks during that time became almost impossible, but necessary. I likened it to driving down a motorway at 100 miles per hour while playing chess with someone in another car alongside, and this entirely taking place in thick dense fog. I can think of easier more relaxing pastimes. Small wonder we lost a few of our colleagues.

By now, I think I had used up about ten of my twenty-nine lives. I was to use up a few more before I retired from the RAF.

One (of many) such incidents occurred not long into my tour with 6 Squadron. I was leading a pair of Jaguars on a typical simulated attack profile mission (SAP) and, after a most successful strike on an airfield in northern Scotland, returned to my base in sleepy Norfolk. The weather was bad, really bad.

The standard operating procedure was to lead your wingman back to base for a radar-monitored instrument landing system (ILS) pairs approach, to land in formation. This involved air traffic control feeding the formation onto the runway centreline so that the leader could continue the approach to a safe landing using electronic equipment both on the ground and in the aircraft.

To maintain safe accuracy, the ground equipment had to be calibrated at certain intervals by what was known as a 'flight checker', a transport aircraft equipped with calibration equipment. It would fly the ILS and later adjust the ground equipment if necessary.

On this particular day, I led my No. 2 back to base for just such an approach. Unknown to me, and indeed to the air traffic controller vectoring me on to the runway centreline, an ILS calibration aircraft was also being vectored onto the same runway centreline, but unfortunately was in contact with a totally different controller on a separate radio frequency.

Both my wingman and I were now on a collision course to certain death with a twin-engined flight checker, and none of the pilots were aware of the mortal danger they were in. If both elements flew accurately, we would soon intercept as my formation was flying the exact flight path, but at a greater speed.

The first thing I knew of the proximity of this other aircraft was the flash of a shadow of a large aircraft pass over the top of my formation in thick cloud. Obviously, my height error of just 10 feet was sufficient to save the lives of all that day. Apparently, the crew of the Andover aircraft did not see us, but later told me the noise of our engines was incredibly loud. Besides the occupants of the three aircraft, the city of Norwich that day was spared, as our incident took place immediately overhead the cathedral.

Both the captain of the flight checker and I later angrily confronted the senior air traffic control officer who explained that one side of his empire did not know what the other side was up to. Great, we thought, that would have looked good at the subsequent Board of Inquiry. I later learnt that the person responsible for this near disaster was subsequently relieved of his post and the crew of the Andover required an additional laundry allowance.

I mentioned that I had returned from a simulated attack profile mission. This was quite a typical sortie and one we performed most days, so let me describe it.

Of course, in a modern fighter many computerised safety measures are available to the pilot. Often the computer will prevent the man from killing himself. The Jaguar, though extremely exciting to operate, did not enjoy such sophistication, but was expected to be flown ultra-low, ultra-fast, and with the bombload placed bang on target while evading the worst that the enemy could throw at it. So what was that typical sortie, the proverbial SAP?

Well, they always say that the secret of a good flight is two hours' planning for every hour in the air. This holds true for a simple flip across the UK, but not so for a flight of four fast jets tasked with attacking two to three targets, an in-flight refuelling slot, an electronic warfare run through Spadeadam, and perhaps a little individual period of circuit-bashing on return to base. Of course, even after that mission, there would come the inevitable debrief and examination of gun-camera film to prove or disprove the outlandish boasts of the individual pilots. It was often said that one might win the mission, but lose the debrief. Many a hardened fighter pilot was destroyed during the post flight discussion and came away almost in tears. They certainly had their inflated ego reduced on many an occasion—I know that personally.

So what of the plan? Of course, way back in the '70s, it was just the dawn of sophisticated weaponry. Though laser-guided bombs, initial navigation systems (INS), and moving map displays were slowly being introduced, they were hardly reliable. Many a Jaguar pilot would launch only to find that his 'kit' failed on rotation. Then it was expected of this steely-eyed killer to continue the mission with old-fashioned map and stopwatch. After all, that was what he had been trained to do and indeed had achieved quite well (to more or less a degree) in his Hawker Hunter.

Of course, our embryonic and unreliable avionics thus required far more planning than we were used to previously. One had to plan for all eventualities, both manual navigation and automatic. Even using the INS required a fair bit of complex planning. Turning points (waypoints) had to be inserted into the on-board computer normally as latitude and longitude as accurately as possible. This meant using Ordnance Survey 1:50,000 maps and special parallel rulers to measure the positions. It all took time. Lots of time. Routes had to be carefully planned, not just to deconflict with the plethora of obstacles *en route* such as parachute jumping, airfields, and danger areas, but also the route into the various targets required careful planning to avoid all four jets over the target at the same time. Apart from the very real danger of collision, any release of bombs from the aircraft ahead would destroy the following aircraft if it flew over the target within forty seconds of the one ahead. The reason for this was very simple. A 1,000-lb bomb would explode into 30,000 pieces, which would rise to at least 3,000 feet above the target. Any aeroplane flying through that lot was doomed.

Timing was thus of the essence and synchronisation of watches was the least of a pilot's worries. Even then it was not quite as easy as all that seems. In a proper co-ordinated attack, aircraft could not all approach the target from the same direction. That would pre-warn the defences. Hence timing calculations proved to be very difficult. Add to that problems associated with weather and terrain avoidance, coupled with the very likely chance that some members of the flight would be desperately trying to outrun defending fighters, and, in doing so, flying much faster than planned, the chances of all four attackers ending up over the target at exactly forty-second intervals became almost impossible. Yet it had to be achieved if success was to be obtained. Failure could mean death.

Even during practice attacks, danger lurked around every corner. Concentrating on computer insertions resulted in close encounters with earth. Those who looked up just before impacting the ground survived with only messy underpants to show for it. Those who did not, ended up in a coffin. That is if they found enough to bury. A very good friend of mine, who joined the Air Force with me and who was arguably the much better pilot, met his end this way. How do we know that? Well, light bulbs shatter in a different way if illuminated. On the Jaguar NAVWAS (Navigation and Weapon Aiming System) were some rather badly designed switches required to perform a vital system update while in flight. When this update was being performed, invariably at ultra-low-level, certain lights illuminated on the control panel. My chum hit the ground at some 500 mph performing this update and the bulbs shattered while illuminated. Thus the air accident chaps knew what my friend was doing in the last seconds of his life.

These times were the twilight of the manned offensive support fighter. We flew low, very low, to avoid being shot down by surface-to-air missiles (SAMS). Our enemy had an enormous arsenal of weaponry that he could throw at us. Unfortunately, I never got to fly the Jaguar into battle, though many of my chums did in the two Gulf Wars. Here they learnt that flying low, albeit avoiding the majority of SAMs, they would encounter small arms and old-fashioned radar laid anti-aircraft guns. Our American allies sensibly preferred to stay at high level. Perhaps very wise, but in the heady days of the mid-1970s, we believed we would be fairly safe at low level. Moreover, we were trained for a European war and that invariably involved bad weather. Flying at height was not an option for a Jaguar, which was not designed for such conditions. However, the two Gulf Wars were flown mainly in good weather, so the medium-level option was more viable. However, twenty years previously we did not have that option and hence our practice missions were close to the ground, much to the annoyance of the general public and much to the delight of us Jaguar pilots!

However, there was a problem. The manned fighter interceptor would creep up behind us and ruin our day. Hence we chose to fly in what we called 'Battle Formation', pairs of aircraft flying some 2,000 yards apart with the second pair doing likewise some 2,000 yards behind. In essence, a box formation. Each pilot cleared the area behind the aircraft abeam him and the pair bringing up the rear did likewise, but at the same time looking after the pair in front. This worked well, but needed close co-ordination and planning when turns took place. This was the dangerous part and several pilots became unsighted of their wingman, resulting in mid-air collisions.

Navigation was, of course, always a problem at low level. The world rushed by incredibly quickly, so one very rapidly learnt to choose one's landmarks carefully. Elevation was important, and I have already mentioned that church spires were useful navigation features when I flew the Canberra in Germany. Now we had a sophisticated inertial navigation system and projected map displays to aid our progress, but the 'kit' was notoriously unreliable and the stated position was liable to drift. The heart of an inertial navigation system is called 'the platform'. On this platform were installed accelerometers and gyroscopes. All this was coupled to timers, compasses, and the ubiquitous computer. Actually, more than one computer. If the aeroplane moved in a certain direction for a certain period of time, the computer could calculate the new position; always assuming, of course, that the pilot had told it the correct starting point in the first place!

Consequently, if one fed in the wrong co-ordinates, the computer gave the wrong information. 'Rubbish in; rubbish out' is a well-known computer saying. Worse still was the fact that the platform was never completely level and this resulted in errors over time. However, ensuring that the platform rotated once every ninety minutes compensated for this. So the error appeared as a sine curve and the navigational errors were cancelled out over a period of time. Nevertheless, the navigational error could be as much as a mile out at times. This was unacceptable, thus the pilot had to physically update the computer every now and then. This could lead to him hitting the ground at high speed. Never much fun.

With the 'kit' working properly and updated often (without in doing so hitting the ground), all was well. However, the avionic equipment was notoriously fickle and one could get left with absolutely nothing; this was far worse than if the pilot had originally been monitoring his position by old-fashioned map, stopwatch, and compass. Still, if the worst happened, one could always hang on to one's leader or wingman to get to the target on time.

Falling from the sky and hitting the ground was rather unpleasant, but danger sometime lurked while on *terra firma*. Every pilot had to annually pass a test to prove that he was safe to fly in cloud. It was called the dreaded Instrument Rating Test (IRT). Later I was to become No. 6 Squadron's IRE (Instrument Rating Examiner). However, while I was training to fly the Jaguar, I had to do my initial IRT. For this, the unfortunate candidate (me on this occasion) sat in the back seat of a two-seater Jaguar and flew the entire sortie from take-off to just before landing with the entire windscreen and canopy obscured. The take-off would be performed totally blind, but the examiner would take over to land the aeroplane (a bit difficult if one cannot see out).

Although challenging to control the aircraft direction on take-off, one had to demonstrate one's ability to keep straight on the runway with reference merely to a compass heading. Anyway, my particular test progressed very well, and on arrival back at Lossiemouth, at about 200 feet, the IRE took over to perform the landing. I relaxed, my task complete, but immediately after touchdown, there was a loud bang as a tyre burst and we departed the runway for the grass. My examiner literally had his hands full and said nothing. Were we about to hit anything? I have to admit that I was rather concerned hurtling across the grass at 150 mph, totally blind, with any minute possibly running into something rather solid. Was my examiner unconscious? Should I eject? Luckily, I did not and we finally came to a stop close to the control tower. Trip over and clean underwear required!

It just goes to prove that no one ever collided with the sky and luckily my Jaguar career did not end there.

17

Top Gun

Occasionally, one would get selected to represent the RAF at the premier fighter/weapons competition in the United States at Las Vegas Nevada and entitled Red Flag for obvious reasons. After all, the Cold War was at its height. Nellis Air Force Base annually played host to air forces from selected nations (invariably the UK and Canada) to enter a fairly accurate simulation of war over the deserts of that part of the US. Unlike the UK, land was relatively unpopulated and vast areas were available for offensive aircraft to drop live munitions.

Another similar major exercise called 'Maple Flag' is based in Alberta, Canada. Maple Flag is an advanced aerial combat training exercise hosted at the Canadian Air Force Base Cold Lake. Established in 1978, Maple Flag is one of the largest of such exercises in the world, as it makes use of the extensive Cold Lake Air Weapons Range. Late in my tour with No. 6 Squadron, I was selected to take part in this prestigious exercise. The area selected for our 'war games' was just about the size of England and the vast swathes of tundra are ideal for practising live weapon firing. The exercise itself currently still occurs annually over a four-week period, and provides realistic training for pilots from the Royal Canadian Air Force, as well as select allied air forces from around the world. My squadron was one of the very first RAF squadrons to attend and thus in October 1979, just a couple of days after my thirty-fourth birthday, we planned to fly to Canada to be part of Maple Flag 4.

Prior to the exercise, in early October, we trained hard in Scotland, slowly lowering our operating height down to 100 feet above ground, this being termed 'Ultra Low-Level' (ULL). During this time, based at RAF Lossiemouth, we operated against foreign F5 attacker aircraft ending up in six-ship formations flying against multiple aggressor aircraft. Finally, by mid-October, we were ready.

The problem was, how on earth were we going to get our relatively short-range Jaguar fighter-bombers there? Consequently, I was introduced to the black art of air-to-air refuelling (AAR). It was not easy. In theory, one just formated on the back of the tanker aircraft and then plugged into the trailing hosepipe. Definitely not easy. For a start, one had to find that 'filling station in the sky'. Unlike the BP garage round the corner from your house, this one was moving at 400 mph. Thankfully, we had electronic gadgets that helped us in this task, but it still was not a piece of cake.

For those who have not flown at 400 mph while filling up their fuel tanks, let me explain further. I suppose it might be quite like trying to fill up the tank in your motorcar while following a tanker lorry across a particularly rough field. The lorry is bouncing up and down, your car is bouncing up and down, and both might be driving in thick fog. So I suppose it would be a little like trying to get the fuel hose into your moving motorcar having drunk ten pints of beer.

I make it sound quite simple, but unfortunately it is not as easy as that. Experts, of which I am not a member of that club, do make it look easy. It seems that all you have to do is plug your refuelling probe into a basket (the size of a waste bin) trailing from the tanker aircraft. However, as stated, that basket is also bouncing up and down. More importantly, due to the disturbance of the air between both aircraft, as your probe approaches the basket, it smartly wizzes out of the way. Hence, the trick is to manoeuvre your probe into a space that at present is empty but hopefully when your probe gets there, the refuelling basket will jump to the same position as your probe. Well it must have been black magic as someone once said 'air-to-air refuelling is like trying to push wet spaghetti up a cat's backside'.

All this can take place in thick cloud, at night, or both. Critically, failure to take on fuel might just result in one running out of fuel, which is always embarrassing halfway across the pond. Moreover, failure was not just a possibility, it was relatively likely. The Jaguar often destroyed refuelling baskets, hoses were pulled out from the tanker aircraft, and, to cap it all, the Jaguar probe was positioned immediately in front of the right-hand engine, so that engine could not be used, but had to be restricted to low power to prevent stalling and thus subsequent meltdown. In essence, the lightly powered twin-engined Jaguar then became a single-engined aeroplane. If one is cack-handed, one can miss the middle of the basket and push one's probe through the spokes that hold the rim of the basket in place. This is not surprisingly called 'spokes'. If one then panicked and closed the throttle(s) too quickly, there would be a great danger that the basket will detach from the hose and remain on one's probe. That would not only screw your wingman waiting desperately for fuel (in fact, his low fuel warning light may already be illuminated), but your right-hand engine will now flame out—i.e. stop. As you cannot any longer maintain height, you will have to divert to the nearest suitable airfield. Not too many in mid-Atlantic! Not your day, especially as that water is rather cold and, with a 50-mph wind blowing at sea level, any parachute decent will almost certainly result in one drowning.

But to get to our exercise airfield in Alberta, all this had to be risked—was refuelling our only problem? Actually, no. Fifteen hours or so in a little tight squeeze of a cockpit, no autopilot or men's facilities, would put a severe strain on not only our stamina, but literally on our poor bladders. Initially, we came up with a simple solution, namely a pee tube. One liberated one's member from the copious straps and survival clothing and deposited the contents of one's bladder into a special receptacle. Simple in theory, but almost impossible in practice. Due to the watertight design of our immersion suits, vital equipment for surviving a dunking in the middle of the ocean, combined with the fact that one had to fly the aeroplane at the same time, one could not guarantee everything being captured by the receptacle. In the end, we settled for good old-fashioned Terry Nappies.

But everyone got there safe and sound, ready to do battle with the world's finest air forces. It also proved to be incredibly interesting and very satisfying as we were flying an aeroplane that was streets ahead of the opposition. Compared with the transit there, the competition itself was rather a doddle and most enjoyable. In the years before the Gulf

Wars, this was as realistic a 'war game' as could be possible. The complex exercises of Maple and Red Flag exercises were to provide comprehensive and realistic training for allied air forces, including fighter, bomber, aerial refuelling, transport, air defence, airborne early warning aircraft, and electronic warfare crews. Participants joined forces against a hostile aggressor and each two-week phase involved a combination of air-to-ground, air-to-air, and other missions. It was great fun: rivalry was intense and we were immensely proud if we did well against the cream of NATO air forces.

Even the mighty USAF F-15s had trouble stopping us. But it was a breath-taking exercise, even down to the incredible B-52 bombers running into the target with us, having taken off from bases thousands of miles away deep inside the USA. It was marvellous in the extreme, especially as for several of us this was the first time we were able to participate in all aspects of a simulated aerial battle and operate with our fellow NATO colleagues. I flew my first mission on 25 October and my last on 7 November, both sorties in XX818. I think we acquitted ourselves very well, won a few trophies, ate a million burgers, and drank a few pints of beer. In fact, all the Brits did well, but I do not remember personally getting any prizes. However, I survived.

The fun soon came to an end and we flew back by passenger aeroplane. We left the jets there for the RAF Germany Jaguar pilots to play with for the second part of the exercise together, with a few Coltishall pilots who would fly the jets back to the UK, as German Jaguar pilots were not air-to-air qualified.

Actually, my time at RAF Coltishall was dispersed with many such exercises, from northern Norway with its vast expanse of snowy mountains, to the sunny Mediterranean. One exercise that does stick in my memory was the annual trip to Denmark where we had to endure three weeks in tents in wet and very cold conditions. Pilots, ground crew, and aircraft suffered from the inclement weather and most of us contracted flu before the exercise finished. At least we managed a trip to Copenhagen to see the Mermaid and sample other delights.

A more enjoyable detachment was to Decimomannu Air Base for our annual weapons practice camp. Deci, as it was fondly known, is an Italian Air Force base located close to Cagliari on the island of Sardinia in Italy. Besides the professional aspects of the detachment, we also had much opportunity to enjoy the coastal climate and sport available in the local area. One such delight was playing golf at the international resort of Is Molas located close to nearby Pula.

We would often check into the hotel resort on a Friday night and stay until Sunday, playing golf (I still hold the world record for the most number of golf balls lost on the ninth fairway), swimming and generally relaxing by the pool. By this pool was a piano and, after a few beers, we would often gather round and sing a few military songs. Some would be stirring German versions. Sadly, however, they would not always go down too well with the resident German hotel guests and I distantly remember one such occasion when halfway through a rousing number we were approached by a couple of our German friends who explained that they were not allowed to sing such songs in Germany and would we desist. Unfortunately, we did not, whereupon the German guests lifted the piano, complete with squadron leader pianist, and deposited the entire combo into the swimming pool. It is to our pianist's immense credit that he continued to play as the piano and he floated towards the centre of the pool. Suffice to say, we all were invited to leave.

Hijinks were not just confined to overseas detachments. Back home in sleepy hollow Coltishall, we also worked hard and played hard. We actually had an officer in charge of the 'gin mine'. His solemn responsibility was to ensure that the special oak cabinet was always full of gin and bottles of tonic. At the end of a day's flying, there also had to be sufficient ice available to make the perfect G&T. I am pleased to note that on a visit to No. 6 Squadron, more than thirty-five years later, the gin mine was still in existence. Additionally, when a new pilot became operational—i.e. was qualified to lead another Jaguar into battle—he was frog-marched to the officers' mess bar and forced to drink from the 'Op Pot'. This was a yard-long glass, full of ice cold lager. When he had finished all that, hopefully in one go, the poor young man then had to drink a ladle of warm whiskey. Standing behind him would always be a senior pilot, holding a bucket, ready to catch what would inevitably be brought up.

But it was not all hijinks. We lost a lot of pilots at about the time that motor racing also lost a lot of drivers. I suppose, not too long after the Second World War, people were prepared to take risks. Today both motor racing and flying fast jets is eminently safer and so it should be, but such safety came rather too late for some of my colleagues and I can still remember all their names.

No. 6 Squadron, RAF Coltishall Officers' Mess, 'Op pot' ceremony. (*W/C Robertson*)

18

Pastures New and Past Over

Part of the rich pageant of life within the RAF in the '70s, the advantages, and indeed disadvantages, was that one was moved on every three years—sometimes to another squadron operating the same aircraft, sometimes to a new aircraft but the same job, other times to a completely new aeroplane and new job. It made for variety, it produced pilots that were jacks of all trades, but never masters of any. Those who did manage to stay flying the same jet, doing the same job, progressed significantly in ability and were well rewarded for their efforts, either by promotion or accolades. My luck, if you were to call it that, was to move on every three years. That made it very difficult for me, a pilot of limited ability, to progress. I was always learning new tricks, learning new aircraft, getting to know new comrades, and, more importantly, learning how to deal with new superiors.

So it came to pass that after three years or so of wonderful operational flying with No. 6 Squadron, a posting mixed with excitement and fun, I received a new posting. Initially back to Lossiemouth in the wilds of Bonny Scotland, again to fly the Hawker Hunter, but this time as an instructor. I would have really liked to stay at Coltishall as I owned a lovely house nearby and I had made good progress over the three years. I also wanted to consolidate what I had achieved on that fast-jet squadron, but it was not to be. My farewell assessment from the squadron commander reads like this: 'Above Average Attack pilot and Instrument Rating Examiner. Many thanks Derek for your persistent hard work and enthusiasm'.

So progress had been made, and if I had moved to one of the sister squadrons at Coltishall, I am sure I would have done even better, but sadly it was not to be. If I had stayed flying the Jaguar, or even accepted the posting to Lossiemouth, my whole life would have completely different.

Fortunately, as it turned out, I was not posted to Scotland. I decided that would not be good for me; after all, the Hunter was elderly and not scheduled to last for long. In the event, I elected to move to sunny Devon to join a new squadron at RAF Chivenor near Barnstable flying a relatively new jet, the BAE Hawk. The unit was No. 2 Tactical Weapons Unit and I was to be one of their very first instructors. It suited me down to the ground. I was happy, but my wife was definitely not as it meant leaving our lovely home on the Norfolk Broads and moving into officer married quarters (OMQs) at the base. Such was Air Force life. Little was I to know that posting was to change my life in many more ways than one.

No. 151(F) Squadron Hawk formation over Lundy Island, 1982. (*BAE SYSTEMS*)

After a very brief conversion onto the BAe Hawk, the successor to the beautiful but miniscule Folland Gnat, I moved to Chivenor to form the advance guard for what was to become known as 2 TWU. Initially, I was posted to No. 63 Squadron as a tactical instructor (teaching fighter tactics to recently qualified new pilots) and also as a QFI. Subsequently, when No. 151 (Fighter) Squadron formed, I moved across as senior flight commander and later took over as the squadron commander. No. 151(F) Squadron was formed at Hainault Farm on 12 June 1918 as the very first night fighter squadron. Its badge depicts an owl landing on a *seax*; the owl representing the night-fighting role and the *seax* representing the county of Essex where the squadron was formed. We also retained the cross of St Andrews emblem on the aircraft to represent the last airfield where the squadron been operationally based, namely with Gloster Javelins at Leuchars in Scotland.

This was a happy time for me, plenty of interesting flying (the Hawk is possibly the easiest aircraft I have ever flown), a very good atmosphere, a beautiful place to live, and some very good mates. Even before being promoted, I accepted that we had a duty (at least I think we did) to mould our embryonic fighter pilots into models of ourselves. We played hard and we drank hard, perhaps too hard. Once flying had ceased for the day, we repaired to the mess bar for fun and games. Latterly, it got a little out of hand and the station commander decreed that the bar would close for one hour at 7 p.m. to allow staff to go home and students to go back to their rooms to change for dinner. Trouble was, young bucks had other ideas (egged on by their instructors), and as the time reached 6.55 p.m., the bar clock was put back to 6.30 p.m., and so on. Often the 'kill-joys' would attempt to stop this 'vandalism', but mostly they failed and often the clock was destroyed in the

No. 63 Squadron BAe Hawk formation, RAF Chivenor, 1980. (*BAE SYSTEMS*)

process. Several stupid games were played involving fire or jumping from a height, and it is no wonder that a few got injured. Such was life then and steam had to be let off. Some years after I departed Chivenor, there was a serious incident, which resulted in a civil case (Crown Immunity had by then ceased to exist) and two students were sent to jail. Naturally that was the end of their career and I suspect Chivenor became a little more docile subsequently.

Life was wonderful, though unknown to me, the dark clouds of divorce were gathering in my wife's head. Despite marrying into the RAF and thus knowing what was in store for her, she hated the life and an assignment, which required us to live in ex-officio married quarters, was too much for her. Unknown to me, her future without a husband was being conspired, but a catastrophic event later in the tour was to force her to postpone her plan. Luckily I knew nothing about that intended bale out.

However, the flying was fantastic, interesting, and vary varied. I loved it, for when I first joined Her Majesty's RAF, I had absolutely no ambition and only wanted to fly. As previously stated, my father suggested a short service commission so that I could concentrate on a career as a pilot and ignore promotion to senior rank. Initially that appeared excellent advice. I flew operationally long before any of my contemporaries who went to the officer

Hawk over Wales flown by the author, 1982. (*BAE SYSTEMS*)

Hawk firing rockets on Pembrey air weapons range. (*BAE SYSTEMS*)

academy at RAF Cranwell in Lincolnshire and much sooner than any of my chums who decided to go to university before joining the RAF.

Of course, a young man who had no accurate idea what he really wanted from life made that decision. More importantly, he had no crystal ball, thus the future was clouded with uncertainty. But I suppose with hindsight, if I had been my father, I would probably have given my son the same advice.

Nevertheless, as the responsibilities of parenthood became apparent and my colleagues gained promotion, I wondered if a full career in the RAF was for me also. By now, I had been persuaded to complete all my promotion exams and thus entered the bracket where I could be considered for promotion with my better-trained chums who had suffered the three-year-long course at the RAF College. Maybe they had a head start on me, but my energy, flying skill, and administrative ability gave me a chance. Of course, my natural abrasiveness counted against my finer points!

Lucky for me, I had at that time a squadron commander who respected ability and hard work, counting little for the obsequious aspects of officer life. I had never been one for brown-nosing, which was just as well. My boss and I got on. I worked hard for him and the squadron, ticked all the boxes, and flew my socks off. He liked that. Come annual confidential report time, I starred. Not only one year, but in the two subsequent years also. Despite being in a pool of brilliant fliers, all jockeying for promotion, I thought I stood a great chance. My boss especially recommended me for promotion and both my wing and station commanders endorsed this. Surely now fame would come my way? Not so. Well, not nearly. But I had a little stroke of luck. We all need that.

My new Air Officer Commanding, Air Vice-Marshal Hayr, wanted to be flown around his Command in a two-seat Hawk. I was chosen for this task. As his personal pilot, I got to know Ken well during those few days and he obviously gained a favourable impression of me as both pilot and officer.

So consequently, when my annual confidential report (ACR) fell on his desk with a special recommendation for promotion, he took more than just a cursory glance at the narrative. Realising that promotion to squadron leader was a most competitive selection process and that there were many more candidates with far better credentials than I, Ken took the unprecedented step of sending back my recommendation to my station commander with advice on how to change the narrative. That was duly done and I was promoted!

However, it nearly was my undoing, as you will see in the next chapter.

19

My Appointment with Donald Duck

Much has previously been written about the disastrous accident that befell me in February 1983. However, neither of the two crewmembers present during the entire occurrence have ever put pen to paper. So here then is my side of the story.

This incredible tale started way back in the mists of time. In fact, it was in 1916, two years before the First World War ended, when my uncle, Derek Minden Sharp, was born. Like my father and myself, he was to join the RAF. During training, my uncle had a couple of incredible close shaves, but more of that much later.

It is said that most things come in threes. My own personal ultra-close shave completed that trio. Actually, I am talking rubbish as usual. I personally have had more than three close shaves. But what happened to me on that fateful day back in February 1983? I was coming to the end of my tour as squadron commander of No. 151 Fighter Squadron with the TWU at Chivenor. I had been given notice of promotion earlier in the year, to be effective as of 1 January 1983. As is usual in this situation, I would be posted and eagerly awaited a decision on my disposal. Was it to be my first choice, the shiny new Tornado? I waited with bated breath.

Once again in my career, I was to be bitterly disappointed. Despite doing exceptionally well at the TWU, I failed to be rewarded for my efforts and yet again their 'Airships' merely filled a slot on their appointments board. In short, I was to be grounded and told to fly a desk. That proved, yet again, that loyalty only worked in one direction. However, to be fair to my poster, he no doubt was getting grief from his boss to fill a slot quickly and my name fell out of the hat. Maybe I would have done the same.

However, at the same time, my previous boss had also received a posting, also to a ground post, but at a Tornado base. This appeared to suit me more than what I had been offered as I saw it as a foot in the door. Just as I had moved from the Jaguar Simulator to flying the Jaguar operationally, here was the chance for history to repeat itself. Moreover, an added advantage was that I would be able to move back into my old house in Norfolk, which I had let when I had been posted to Devon.

So it was on that ill-fated day in February 1983 I decided to fly to RAF Marham to investigate what life would be like with the Tornado Force. In order to maximise the flight, I decided to take with me Flt Lt Les Pearce, who was retraining as a Tornado navigator. He would benefit from the low-level navigation exercise across the breadth of the United Kingdom and would be good company on that sortie.

We would be flying from Chivenor to Marham in Norfolk, 8 miles south-east of King's Lynn. It was a flight, allowing for doglegs to avoid obstacles, of some 250 miles. At a speed of 420 knots (roughly 500 mph), we would be there in half an hour. When we taxied out to the runway, it was daylight and our unfortunate day had begun.

I got airborne fairly early in the morning in BAe Hawk XX331. The outbound leg went to plan and we arrived at Marham on time with Pearce accomplishing his exercise most successfully. I completed my business and, after a traditional fry-up in the Aircrew Feeder, we again checked the weather and set off on a different low-level route back to Chivenor. The time was 11.30 a.m.

Our route took us across good low-lying fenland, but with useful navigational features and a maze of obstructions—chimneys, TV masts, towns, military air traffic zones—to avoid.

Keeping to the north of the bird sanctuary at Holme Fen, we aimed to cross the A1 main road at the roundabout at Norman Cross.

It was during this part of the low-level navigation exercise that, at 11.50 a.m. precisely, we struck a mallard duck weighing some 3 kg. I never saw it coming. Probably nor did the duck. Like many fighter pilots, I had experienced bird strikes before. This was different. Very different.

The following is a compilation of accounts of that accident, written just afterwards by a famous journalist and subsequently corrected in places by myself. Though he has sadly now passed away, he would have allowed me to print it here; in fact, he would have encouraged me to write this book. Thank you Ralph Barker.

The wild mallard drake, brightly plumaged male of the species, soared gracefully to 250 feet over its marshy Fenland haunts, the solitary occupant, as it seemed, of a murky February sky. But a Hawk two-seater jet fighter, pilot and navigator sitting in tandem, was approaching on a low-level navigational exercise, speeding west across the flat plains of East Anglia at 500 miles an hour.

The Hawk, like the drake, was flying at 250 feet. They were on a collision course.

The unfortunate bird never knew what hit it.

Bursting through the Hawk's windscreen, leaving a two-foot gap in the middle, the bird struck the pilot in the face with sledgehammer force and detonated like a bomb. It knocked his left eye out of its socket, broke bones in his neck and pulverised the bones and nerves in his face. It seemed inevitable that the RAF Hawk jet would crash, killing the two-man crew and possibly many people on the ground.

Blinded by debris, deafened by the hurricane blast of the airstream, and knocked unconscious by the impact, the pilot lost control of the aircraft as it swung to the left.

Sharp later said, 'It was as if someone had hit me around the head with a wet blanket. Some unconscious instinct must have made me pull the control column back, which is what you are trained to do in an emergency at low altitude. It takes you away from the hard ground and gives you more time to think'.

But Sharp had no time to think!

'I blacked out. God knows where the aeroplane went whilst I was out, but I must have been unconscious for quite some time because when I regained consciousness apparently I was flying out of control at 5,000 feet.'

As he regained consciousness, Sharp knew instinctively that is must have been a bird-strike and with a mounting sense of horror he realised that he was unable to see. He was completely blind!

Derek had suffered bird strikes before, though nothing had ever come through his windscreen. The noise alone was infernal, stupefying in its volume and amplitude.

Deprived by his blindness of any visual or instrument checks, Sharp was flying by the seat of his pants.

In the navigator's cockpit behind and above Sharp, Flight Lieutenant Lester Pearce was terrified, but powerless to help. Between his knees was the ejector seat handle, which if he pulled it, would eject them both.

However, abandoning the aircraft would be no Sunday picnic. The explosive rocket can break a pilot's back and, more importantly, Sharp was concerned that the abandoned jet might crash into people on the ground below. Importantly also, Sharp was bleeding profusely, such that if he had parted company with the aircraft it would have been quite some time before he would be found. By then he would be dead. The only solution would be to land or eject close to civilization.

Thus Sharp was relying on Pearce not to eject them prematurely, but neither Pearce nor anyone else other than Sharp could solve the problem of getting the aircraft down. Worst still was the fact that Sharp had absolutely no protection from the slipstream that was blasting through the broken canopy at a speed twice that of the worst hurricane ever known to man. This forced our badly injured pilot to crouch low in his ejector seat, well below the level of the windscreen.

As Sharp reached up with one hand to feel his face, his fingers made contact with a mushy poultice of skin, feathers and blood, loosely impacted under the remnants of his shattered helmet visor.

He later said, 'I thought I just had debris in my eyes. I kept trying to wipe it away, but then I felt this sticky mess on my fingers and realised that I was actually wiping away parts of my own face. I didn't feel any pain, but my left eye was missing and my right eye was full of blood and bits of what I found out later to be mashed duck. Everything was at the very best severely blurred.'

He felt more numbness than pain, but he sensed that his left eyeball had been driven back into the bone.

After excavating the debris from the socket of his right eye he was conscious of the first glimmers of returning vision, though he could see very little.

But what he did see appalled him.

Glancing at his reflection in one of his mirrors, he wished he hadn't.

The left side of his face, gored by a huge jagged splinter from the windscreen, was slashed right across and was bleeding profusely. He could see bone. How much blood could one lose and still remain conscious?

Despite his reluctance to depart his aeroplane, Sharp felt almost certainly they would have to eject at some stage. With such marginal vision he could hardly even attempt a landing, let alone affect a safe one. Landing a jet fighter is hard enough when fit; surely impossible when badly injured.

But any ejection must be properly controlled. To 'bang out' where the plane might come down on houses was unthinkable.

But there was worse to come. Sharp could just about make out the central warning panel, which was a mass of red lights. He knew then that not only had he suffered a catastrophic injury, but also the aircraft itself was in a very bad way. Maintaining his head below the cockpit coaming to avoid the horrendous blast and to try to read his instruments, he made out exactly which warning lights were winking urgently. The engine had failed! Feeling for fuel switches, he found them all in the off position, fouled presumably by a large chunk of windscreen.

He flipped them back on and some of the lights ceased to wink. All he then needed to do was to relight the engine to restore thrust. And to prevent the inevitable crash.

Having achieved that priority, Sharp then instinctively eased back the control column and reduced the throttle setting and thus the airspeed. Even then the gale was still thundering through the gaping hole in the windscreen.

Despite his incredibly limited vision, he could take stock of the situation. His altimeter was reading 2,000 feet, his speed was 220 knots. That much he could tell. The plane was still flying and they were in no immediate danger. He shouted at Les Pearce. 'It's OK, Les, I'm OK!'

Anyway for the moment.

As his oxygen mask was destroyed in the collision, Sharp switched his UHF radio to the emergency channel to enable Pearce to make the distress call on his behalf.

'Mayday. Mayday. Mayday.'

'Drayton Centre, this is Charlie One-four. Bird strike, Hawk aircraft, two people on board. Pilot severely incapacitated. Request immediate diversion to nearest suitable airfield.'

'Roger Charlie One-four. Stand by one.' Came the reply.

'Pilot incapacitated,' thought Pearce, was an understatement. The dividing screen in front of him was crimson with spattered blood, parts of the duck and parts of his pilot. He caught a glimpse in one of the reflecting mirrors of his pilot's face.

He was gazing at an apparition. Ejection would be the only hope, and he tightened his straps.

Sharp felt the same.

'I can still see—but only just,' he told Pearce, 'but I can't see to land. We'll probably eject when we get to an airfield.'

Drayton passed them on to RAF Wittering, eight miles distant, just beyond the Al. Soon Wittering began giving them courses to steer to reach the airfield.

They would be in the Wittering circuit, faced with a final decision, within minutes.

Struggling to cope with shock, blindness, concussion, and a 300-mile-an-hour gale, Sharp struggled to avoid hitting the ground. He was pretty certain he would have to bang out. But after 18 years of flying he had reached the stage when he couldn't just throw an aeroplane away willy-nilly, even if staying with it had its hazards. Ejection had to be a last resort.

He would make an approach at Wittering, and they would funnel him in by radar. But the climactic moment would come when he had to decide whether or not he could see to land.

'Pilot bleeding profusely,' called Pearce to Wittering. 'Get the medics ready and get us on the ground as soon as possible.'

Sharp didn't think this was enough. Moreover, when asked by ATC what was their endurance, Sharp replied, 'One hour fuel, ten minutes of blood! 'Tell them also that we'll almost certainly have to eject.'

Pearce did so. At Wittering, blood wagon, fire engines and a medical team were hastily assembling.

Sharp knew he would have to cut corners otherwise he really would run out of blood! But too many shortcuts would lead to inaccurate flying and a disastrous attempt at an overshoot.

He would do a standard, but shortened approach relying on instruments until he reached decision height, the ultimate moment when he must make his assessment. That would be the moment of decision as Sharp would then have to brave the elements yet again and subject his broken face to the icy hurricane.

As they got closer to the airfield, the controller asked how much fuel they had remaining. Pearce again replied calmly that it was not fuel they were worried about, but reminded them that Sharp had only about five minute of blood left. It was then that Air Traffic Control realised just how serious the situation was. Pearce called the controller.

'Be prepared for ejection on short finals.'

The measured voice of the talk-down controller, immensely reassuring, began to intone the familiar litany.

'Four miles from touchdown. Check wheels down and locked. You are on the glide path, height 1200 feet. Begin your descent now at 600 feet per minute. Do not acknowledge further instructions. '

Head down under the cockpit coaming, peering through one half-closed bloodshot eye at instruments on which he could barely focus, Sharp followed the ground controller's instructions.

'You are 80 feet above the glide path. Increase your rate of descent.'

A full load of fuel forced Sharp to keep his approach speed relatively high at 150 knots, not easily compatible with the required rate of descent. And he was having trouble maintaining direction.

'Left, left, you are right of the centre line. Come left five degrees, heading zero seven five.'

Pearce was monitoring the instruments in the rear cockpit. He thought Sharp was doing all right. Little did he know that his pilot was drifting in and out of consciousness!

'You are on the centre line, return to zero eight aero.'

And a few seconds later: 'You are on the glide path. Adjust your rate of descent.'

After a fifteen-second silence, the controller spoke an encouraging word. 'Coming along nicely now. Two miles.'

They were down to 600 feet.

Sharp repeated his warning: 'Be prepared for an ejection on short finals'.

Suddenly, loud and clear, the controller's voice burst in: 'You are approaching decision height'.

A mile from the runway, at 250 feet—and Sharp was raising his head.

'You are at decision height. Look up and take over visually.'

Even now, with the hurricane reduced to little more than 150 miles an hour, Sharp's head sustained such a buffeting that he almost gave up.

As his good eye, such as it was, streamed water, he blinked and was suddenly conscious of speed. He couldn't see much, but it might be enough.

Below him was the runway, all 9,000 feet of it. He was going to try to get the plane down after all.

Self-preservation was very such a part of it. He was saving his own skin, not to mention his navigator's. But even more important, he would be doing his job.

A final burst of engine, a moment of holding off—and Pearce shouted in amazement at the touchdown.

One day he might joke that Derek made better landings half-blind. But as the Hawk came to a halt on the runway, the hood, which covered both cockpits, was flung open by Sharp.

Fire tenders and ambulances were approaching, yet as Pearce, hurriedly, and Sharp, unsteadily, unstrapped themselves and stood up, the entire rescue party stopped in their tracks.

They were gazing in horror at the mutilated, blood-soaked monster emerging from the front cockpit, unrecognisable as an RAF pilot.

Les Pearce had to shout at them, 'For Christ's sake get a ladder up here.'

Back on the airfield, such had been the concern for Sharp, that Pearce was forgotten. After watching Sharp carted away in the blood wagon to the Station Medical Centre and then on to hospital, he switched off the engine, replaced Sharp's ejector seat safety pins, checked the remainder of the switches and made the jet safe. He then looked up to find he'd been left standing alone in the middle of the runway of that vast airfield.

Les had paid no small part in this adventure, but as is often the case, he did not get to share the subsequent limelight. After Sharp was awarded the highest peacetime honour for aviation gallantry (an Air Force Cross) and made a 'Man of the Year', Pearce's own bravery was not totally forgotten. Consolation came when he was awarded a very well deserved Green Endorsement for 'exceptional crew cooperation and cool presence of mind'. A lesser back-seater would have taken the easy way out, pulled the ejector seat handle and that would have been the end of Sharp. He would have bled to death in some farmer's field, before rescue services even found him.

Interestingly, Pearce later had a go at landing a Hawk jet to see what would have happened if Sharp had not regained consciousness. He failed!

Sadly the two never met again.

So there you have it. An amazing story. Pilots and anglers are often accused of 'line-shooting'. The fish is always a foot longer than what was actually caught and there is a pilot's saying 'mothing on the clock but the maker's name'. Quite incredibly, my story is totally true—it could not possibly happen as described, but it did.

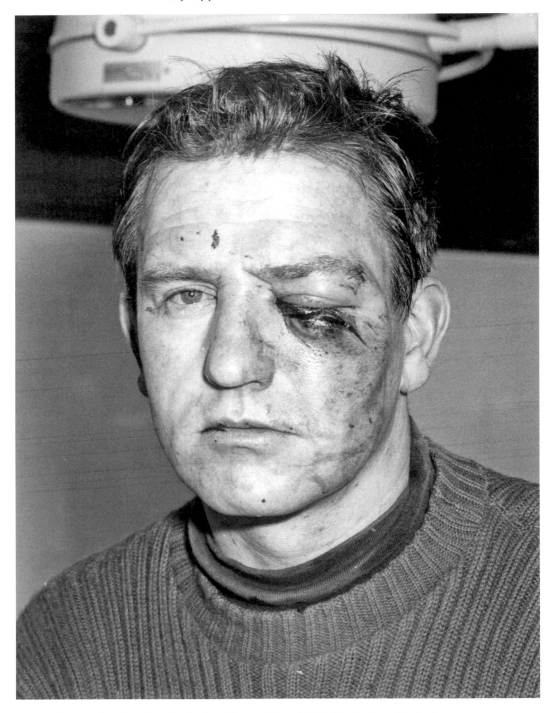

The author on the day after the duck strike accident, 1983. (*Author's collection*)

20
Aftermath

It was from RAF Wittering that I was transported to the nearby RAF Hospital at Ely for emergency treatment. Lucky for me that in those days we actually had RAF hospitals, for as you will see, I would not have been treated so well. However, one more drama was yet to unfold during that fateful trip to the hospital. The antique RAF ambulance broke down on the A1! Military transport back in 1983 was apparently not much better than today.

Eventually we made it to the hospital, though thankfully I was not asked to get out and push. They say that miracles do not happen twice in one day, and after managing to land a jet aeroplane when blind, I certainly was not expecting any more favours from the Almighty above. Amazingly, I had inadvertently chosen exactly the best place and the right day to crash land. Ely hospital that day was running one of its very rare eye clinics. Not only was my ex-flight surgeon and good friend being trained in eye surgery there, but his tutor was one of the top eye surgeons in the country, if not in the whole world.

I was wheeled into theatre almost immediately and, after a lengthy operation, they managed to save the sight of my right eye. Moreover, the ophthalmic surgeon later told me that if I had been anyone else, he would have thrown the pieces of my left eye into the slop bucket. In the event, he painstakingly put it all back together so at the very least I would not require a glass eye. Later in life, I came to value his skill and diligence as eventually I gained a little peripheral vision in that eye.

Now began a long serious of operations to put my face back together again. It was far too early to predict if I would see again with my left eye, but I personally had hopes. Ever the positive chap!

Additionally, the ENT surgeon even asked me what sort of nose I would like, as the one I had now was rather shattered. I replied that I would quite like what I had before, even though it was rather big and not particularly pretty. Was this the first time someone had turned down free cosmetic surgery?

Sadly, the sight in my left eye could not be saved, and I was grounded for a time. Today, some thirty-five years later, I still suffer from the effects of that catastrophic event. Unknown to all at the time, I had broken my neck in the incident. The effect of the duck forcing my head back into the ejector seat headrest resulted in a reverse whiplash and my head slammed forward into the instrument panel, breaking some instruments. Some five years later I could not move my head due to spondylitis. Apparently, the force of the whiplash resulted in the ligaments in my neck ripping off the bony spurs from my upper spine, but at the time no one had noticed. Well, after all, I was not complaining of pain in my neck! Years later, when a specialist asked me if I had had a car accident, I replied no, but then I remembered my duck-strike. So I am left today, blind in one eye, a displaced septum, and a knackered neck, to name just a few of the residual effects. This event changed my life, and even today, despite the residual effects, I think it changed it for the better. It made me rethink what was really important in my life and thus I suspect my character changed that day for the better. If nothing else, as I lay in my hospital bed, I remembered something a friend had said many years ago: 'Think positive'. Well, in that hospital, there were people far worse than me. OK, so at that stage I was totally blind, as both eyes were damaged and covered with bandages. Would I fly again? I was told that I had more chance of winning a Nobel Prize. Would I even be able to drive? Time would tell, but as I lay there in my bed, I reflected what my options were. They were many and, despite what the medics said, I would fly again. I would!

Later, the Ministry of Agriculture and Fisheries informed me that the weight of the duck was about 2.5 kg; it had actually calculated that from the duck's beak. Do not ask me where they found it though. Anyway, 2.5 kg at 500 mph possesses considerable energy; about the same as a sledgehammer at 150 mph. No wonder my unbreakable polycarbonate safety visor shattered under the impact. The official accident report ended with these kind words from my wing commander: 'The fact that this incident ended with a safe landing at Wittering can only be attributed to the skill, fortitude and sheer guts of the pilot'.

Thus ended my life as a fighter pilot. I was medically downgraded, told I would never fly again, and 'looked forward' to a life behind a desk. Some small consolation could be had from the final comments in my flying logbook in April 1983: 'Well Above the Average as a TWU instructor and pilot. Many thanks for your outstanding contribution to Chivenor'.

The following month, I was granted the highest peacetime aviation award for bravery in the form of an Air Force cross. That made me smile as I had always made the Royal Air Force cross! Anyway, here is what was subsequently promulgated in *The London Gazette*:

Tuesday 10th May 1983

Ministry of Defence

Air Force Department

The Queen has been graciously pleased to approve the following award: Air Force Cross
  Squadron Leader Derek John Sharp (4232596), Royal Air Force
  Squadron Leader Sharp is the Officer Commanding No 151(F) Squadron at Royal Air Force Chivenor. On 15 February 1983 he took off from Royal Air Force Marham on a low-level navigation exercise with a student navigator.

Flying at 250 feet above ground level and 400 knots about 3 nautical miles south of Peterborough, his aircraft struck a Mallard duck, which entered the cockpit. The impact shattered Squadron Leader Sharp's visor, severely damaged his left eye and fractured his nose, eye socket and sinuses.

His right eye was filled with blast debris, blood and bird remains.

Furthermore, he could not talk to his navigator.

At this stage Squadron Leader Sharp could have justifiably initiated the abandonment of the aircraft.

Instead, he climbed, reduced speed, restored partial sight to his right eye, cleared the surge in his engine and resolved a fuel pressure problem.

Having decelerated to reduce buffeting he could now communicate with his passenger, but could barely monitor his instruments.

The pressure to eject was still strong; nevertheless, he resolved to delay such action until clear of the Peterborough suburbs.

Squadron Leader Sharp informed his passenger of their predicament and that he would have to manoeuvre the aircraft in response to his passenger's directions.

He then instructed the student to broadcast a MAYDAY call.

Despite continuous pain and misgivings about his failing sight, Squadron Leader Sharp flew an immaculately judged ground controlled approach at Royal Air Force Wittering and landed safely.

Throughout this harrowing experience, Squadron Leader Sharp was in great pain, yet he showed courage and coolness of the highest order. His concern for public safety was such that he chose to fly away from a densely populated area although the circumstances fully justified his abandoning the aircraft.

Moreover, by exposing himself to considerable personal risk he saved his aircraft and crew. Squadron Leader Sharp displayed gallantry and airmanship equal to the highest traditions of the Royal Air Force, and his performance reflected the greatest credit on the Service.'

I remember quite well the day that my local postman knocked very reverently on my front door to deliver notification of the award. He also rang the front door bell; something he never did. With trembling hands he gave me an envelope without a postage stamp attached. I knew already what was inside as my Station Commander had forewarned me. However, poor Mr Postie did not have a clue, especially as the envelope was from St James's Palace and franked 'Central Chancery of Knighthood'. I never did enlighten him and I suppose he really thought that I was about to become a Knight of the Realm! I wonder how many occupants of my little village were later told that on his rounds. It must have been quite a few, as my telephone did not stop ringing for the next few days.

Later that year I was to be awarded a further accolade when the Royal Association for Disability and Rehabilitation elected me as 'Man of the Year'. This was presented to me during a ceremony at the Savoy Hotel, London and actually broadcast on British television. My mother, who had been bursting with pride, as all mothers would be following the award of the Air Force Cross to a son, very sadly never lived to see me receive that latest honour. She very unfortunately died of cancer before it was announced.

They say that everyone is famous for five minutes. Interestingly, I was famous for five months!

Following my rather unfortunate meeting with the mallard, rather calamitous for him, I was asked where I would like to be posted. I chose RAF Coltishall, partly because I could continue to receive excellent medical attention at the nearby RAF hospital, but mainly

No. 49345   6333

SECOND SUPPLEMENT TO

The London Gazette

of Monday, 9th May 1983

Published by Authority

Registered as a Newspaper

TUESDAY, 10TH MAY 1983

MINISTRY OF DEFENCE

AIR FORCE DEPARTMENT

Whitehall, London SW1A 2HB.
10th May 1983.

The QUEEN has been graciously pleased to approve the following award:

Air Force Cross

Squadron Leader Derek John SHARP, (4232596), Royal Air Force.

Squadron Leader Sharp is a senior instructor on No. 151 Squadron at Royal Air Force Chivenor. On 15th February 1983 he took off from Royal Air Force Marham on a low-level navigation exercise with a student navigator. Flying at 250 feet above ground level and 400 knots about 3 nautical miles south of Peterborough, his aircraft struck a Mallard duck which entered the cockpit. The impact shattered Squadron Leader Sharp's visor, severely damaged his left eye and fractured his nose, eye socket and sinuses. His right eye was filled with blast debris, blood and bird remains. Furthermore, he could not talk to his navigator. At this stage Squadron Leader Sharp could have justifiably initiated the abandonment of the aircraft. Instead, he climbed, reduced speed, restored partial sight to his right eye, cleared the surge in his engine and resolved a fuel pressure problem. Having decelerated to reduce buffeting he could now communicate with his passenger, but could barely monitor his instruments. The pressure to eject was still strong, nevertheless, he resolved to delay such action until clear of the Peterborough suburbs. Squadron Leader Sharp informed his passenger of their predicament and that he would have to manoeuvre the aircraft in response to his passenger's direction. He then instructed the student to broadcast a MAYDAY call. Despite continuous pain and misgivings about his failing sight, Squadron Leader Sharp flew an immaculately judged ground controlled approach at Royal Air Force Wittering and landed safely. Throughout this harrowing experience, Squadron Leader Sharp was in great pain, yet he showed courage and coolness of the highest order. His concern for public safety was such that he chose to fly away from a densely populated area although the circumstances fully justified his abandoning the aircraft. Moreover, by exposing himself to considerable personal risk he saved his aircraft and crew. Squadron Leader Sharp displayed gallantry and airmanship equal to the highest traditions of the Royal Air Force, and his performance reflected the greatest credit on the Service.

LONDON
Printed and published by HER MAJESTY'S STATIONERY OFFICE: 1983
Price 55p net

PRINTED IN ENGLAND

ISBN 0 11 659345 8
ISSN 0261-8575

Above left: The London Gazette 1983 Award of Air Force Cross to the author. (*Author's collection*)

Above right: The author poses for Buckingham Palace Investiture, 1983. (*Author's collection*)

Right: The author posing on a Hawk cockpit following duck strike 1983. (*Author's collection*)

because I still owned a house close by. So, in the summer of 1983, I was appointed to the position of SLOPS (Squadron Leader Operations) at that base. My duties were as much as I wished to take on, though they were soon to grow.

Of course it was imperative that I renewed my acquaintance with the Jaguar if I was to be responsible for the day to day running of that busy fighter airfield. Well, that was my thought anyway and the MOD humoured me. In May 1983, just three months after my catastrophic bird strike and still suffering from my injuries, I was detached to RAF Lossiemouth for a refresher course on the Widow Maker. Would I still be the man I previously was? I was not to worry. Despite being partially sighted, I completed the course with flying colours. I was delighted to read my commanding officer's end of course report on me:

> What a pleasure it was to have Sqn Ldr Sharp on the OCU. His determination was an inspiration to everyone and he has demonstrated that he has lost none of his former skills despite his loss of vision. I wish him every success in the future.

So now my ambition was to fly solo again, preferably in a supersonic fighter. I had convinced the Air Staff, now to convince the medics.

Back at my 'desk job' at Coltishall, I continued to recover from my battle scars. Part of my duties as SLOPS was to run the busy airfield should war break out. The plan was for the base commander to deploy forward into Europe with the three Jaguar squadrons, and for RAF Coltishall to receive a number of McDonnell Douglas RF4C Phantom II aircraft of the ANG (Alabama Air National Guard). I would, in effect, be their wartime base commander. It was this very desk job that was to result in an invitation to fly the mighty Vietnam War fighter-plane.

Naturally, it was imperative that I got to know the men and their machines, so I sought permission to visit the ANG in Alabama. To my surprise, my request was granted and I soon received an invitation to visit the wing headquarters in Birmingham, Alabama. Interestingly, not surprisingly, it was they who paid for my air fare and not the British Ministry of Defence.

I caught the Delta Airlines jet to Atlanta, changing for Birmingham. This was to be my first tour of duty with our American cousins. I found them to be utterly generous and incredibly hospitable. Possibly too much so, but that is definitely another story. At the time, I also found the ANG rather naïve in their approach to aerial warfare. Though most of the reservist pilots had seen combat in Vietnam, the war for which they now trained at weekends promised to be totally different. For a start, the weather on the North German Plain would be significantly different to that which they had experienced in South East Asia. I knew, having served with 2ATAF in Germany.

It seemed that navigation was to them merely flying from one tactical electronic beacon to the next. Whether these weekend warriors had forgotten the basics of low-level navigation or had never previously flown that low I will never know. However, when I pointed out that our enemies might switch off all navigation aids, my American friends looked blank. Perhaps they, like many RAF pilots, were under the impression that they were training for a war that would never happen. Moreover, perhaps this was just their way of having fun at the weekend. Better than on the golf course.

The author egressing RF4C Alabama Air National Guard, 1983. (*Author's collection*)

Whatever, I too had fun, enjoyed my stay with the Alabama Air National Guard, and returned back to RAF Coltishall in good spirits. After all, I had managed to grab a few flights in the mighty Phantom. It was worth travelling halfway across the globe for that alone.

Additionally, during my second tour at RAF Coltishall, for the first time in my life I had the chance to fly a helicopter. As SLOPs, under my command was the SAR (search and rescue) flight of three Wessex helicopters. Naturally, I needed to fly them, so I smooth-talked the flight's helicopter instructor into giving me a few lessons. I then found out why fixed-wing pilots are not encouraged to fly helicopters at the same time. For a start, the lever in your left hand seemed to do the opposite of what the lever in your left hand in a fixed-wing aeroplane does. More power in a Jaguar was forward—i.e. away from you—so when in the hover we started descending, I shoved the lever away from me (down) for more power. Unfortunately, we went down quicker, much quicker. Luckily, 'sir' took control. I just could not hover, so gave up that idea. Years later, a chum told me this: 'Hovering is for pilots who love to fly, but have no place to go'. Well, I always had places to go, so just as well I stuck with real aeroplanes.

21

The Last of the Combat Buffalos: Beirut 1983

Early into my tour as SLOPs, my appointer (the nice postings chappie) had tried to detach me (a temporary posting) to the Falkland Islands at very short notice due to the original officer breaking his leg. But I ruined his day when I suggested that he check my medical category: A4 G4 Z4. The Z4 part stated that I should not really leave the hospital grounds, let alone pop off to the South Atlantic. His only reply was 'bugger'. However, my next appointment was once again with Uncle Sam and followed shortly after my trip to Alabama. It was during the spring of the following year, while still 'convalescing', that my appointer asked if I would like to spend a few months in the Middle East. Did I have a choice? Not really was the reply. Apparently there was a war on and they needed me. You may recall that in Beirut in 1983 (actually on my birthday, but not because of it), the US barracks were bombed during the Lebanese Civil War when two truck bombs struck separate buildings housing the Multination Force (MNF) peacekeepers, specifically against the USA and many others.

Sadly, I would not be flying offensive combat operations though. My title would be 'Commander British Forces Lebanon' or COMBRITFORLEB for short. That sounded incredibly impressive. My duties would involve liaising between high-ranking commanders and the MOD. I also would be responsible for managing UK offensive air assets and would be detached to RAF Episkopi in Cyprus. However, no luxury headquarters accommodation for me; I would be based on the United States aircraft carrier USS *Guam* a mile or so off the coast of Lebanon, but would occasionally visit that war-torn country. I would also be required to report to RAF commanders in Cyprus and other units of the MNF. It all seemed very exciting and certainly exceptionally interesting. What a pity I was given just a mere twenty-four hours' notice, having been told on the Friday immediately prior to proceeding on holiday to California. Still, when their Airships said 'Jump', we minions invariably replied 'How high?'

Thus some forty-eight hours later, with my family on its way to the USA, I was landing on the USS *Guam*, a helicopter carrier and the command ship controlling the MNF. The next few months would prove to be very interesting! For a start, we were on twenty-four-hour alert for kamikaze transport planes, which were packed to the gunnels with high explosive. Great, I thought. Having survived a maniac suicidal duck, all I needed now was a suicidal fanatic crashing his aeroplane onto me.

Moreover, the environment in which I had found myself was totally strange. USS *Guam* was no cruise liner! Jokingly, I asked for an outside cabin with balcony. Typically I met with the usual lack of American humour. That came home to me very clearly when later in the operation, a fellow colleague told me he was going to the UK on leave. I suggested he 'knock up my wife when he was there'. He looked at me incredulously and asked if I was really sure. At that stage, I realised that 'knocking up' did not mean telephoning my wife to say hi. I should have known, as in a previous assignment, I soon got to learn that Americans do not really share our language.

I should have felt lucky to share a cabin with another senior officer. What I did not know was that a mere 3 inches of steel separated me from the flight deck. Moreover, the enlisted men who started work at 4 a.m. preparing the deck for the day's operations knew exactly where each officer slept. You would be astonished by the noise an aircraft chock makes when it is dropped onto the ceiling just above your head. A very rude awakening at 4 a.m. Luckily, I mixed well with all ranks and the enlisted chaps soon allowed me to sleep in.

However, despite my rapport with the seamen below, I was informed that for my own safety I should not venture below deck seven. Do not ask. That said, the worst predicament was that the ship was totally dry. Now, I do not mean that it never rained: the problem was quite simply that the nearest bottle of alcohol was 10 miles away on shore. Unfortunately, the enemy would probably shoot me if I ventured ashore on a shopping trip, so I gave that one a miss. Nevertheless, I was reliably informed that there were plenty of drugs on board, though for some strange reason that did not interest me. I just settled for the mountains of popcorn.

Nevertheless, the nonexistence of alcohol was more than compensated for by the excitement and fascinating activities. One task I had been given was to make myself known to one of our defensive/offensive ships, the gigantic battleship USS *New Jersey* (BB-62). Sadly none of this fascinating breed of warship is still in active service, but a few facts and figures are notable. She was built in the Philadelphia Naval Shipyard some five years before I was born. She weighed 58,000 tons, her armour was more than 17 inches thick in places, and she possessed, among other offensive weaponry, nine 16-inch guns capable of firing an armour-piercing shell, weighing more than a motor car, some 25 miles. She also carried cruise missiles and many other big-boys toys. She had acquitted herself very well in the Second World War, Korea, and Vietnam. I had to visit her and see her in action.

I needed, of course, a reason to visit. As I was responsible for all British forces in Lebanon, it was obvious that I was interested in what protection this magnificent leviathan could afford our small force. I signalled the ship that the RAFLO would visit the very next day. I did not want any fuss so had dropped the title of Commander British Forces Lebanon. I immediately received a reply asking who on earth was the RAFLO. I replied that it stood for 'Royal Air Force Liaison Officer'. For some reason, the USS *New Jersey* received a corruption of my message and was puzzled by the word 'Royal'. Consequently, next day, as I alighted on the immaculate teak deck of BB-62, a full honour guard and the Executive Officer, a full naval captain, met me. Perhaps this was a little overkill for a welcome for a mere squadron leader in a grubby flying suit, but I did receive the fuss that I had sought to avoid. After some difficult explanations, they did eventually see the funny side.

I only spent a day on board, but I was privileged to witness the firing of her amazing 16-inch guns in anger. A full broadside was planned and as this was obviously going to be incredibly spectacular, I asked to remain on deck when this occurred. The Executive Officer looked at me as though I was an imbecile, but then went on to explain that the

USS *New Jersey* off Lebanon, 1983. (*Author's collection*)

over-pressure caused by the firing would in fact kill me. It seemed that all personnel had to retire to safe, shockproof quarters during any mega broadside.

As I have stated, USS *New Jersey* was equipped with nine incredibly potent 16-inch guns. While I was tucked up safe below decks, the firing took place, and I was told by my shipmates on board USS *Guam*, some 5 miles distance, that it was indeed incredibly spectacular. The *New Jersey* that day fired one of the very last broadsides of nine 16-inch guns in history. Sadly, we will never ever see its like again, and I was lucky enough to be present that day.

Woefully this great vessel is now a museum ship in the United States and will never set sail again.

It was luck that I visited the mainland of Lebanon infrequently; after all, it was a highly volatile and an incredibly dangerous place. One such time I did dare to set foot on dry land, I was fired upon by a person or persons unknown. That day, I reminded myself why I did not join the Army. Anyway, to cut a long story short, while standing gossiping on the Cornice on the Beirut seafront with a fellow colleague, a most unpleasant individual opened up with an anti-aircraft gun in our vicinity. A tremendously large bang close by alerted me to the fact that I really ought not to be there and I turned to my colleague to remark just that, only to find that he most unfortunately had become the recipient of a ricochet and would take no further part in that conflict. In fact, he would take no further part in any conflict. Was my angel looking after me that day, or was it just Lady Luck?

One of my other responsibilities in Lebanon was intelligence gathering. For obvious reasons, I felt rather reluctant to wander the streets of Beirut so I devised a wizard plan to keep my masters informed of exactly what was going on in that country. A quick helicopter flight to RAF Episkopi in Cyprus to purchase a copy of the *Sunday Times* would provide all the intelligence the mighty planning machine of the MNF would need. After all, such information had indeed been gathered by foolish war correspondents based inside Lebanon

BEIRUT, LEBANON
USS GUAM (LPH-9)
6FEB84

The author aboard USS *Guam* as part of the Multi National Force. (*Author's collection*)

reporting for television and the newspapers. Not only that, it was accurate and up-to-date. Much better than some of the target photographs my American friends supplied.

One such useless photograph depicted a Russian-made anti-aircraft system. Obviously this was a considerable threat to our offensive air support and it was decided to destroy the facility. However, just before the A6 bombers were scrambled to attack the facility, I calmly pointed out to my colonel that the date of the photograph was some fourteen months previous. I also pointed out that the machines were self-propelled and thus might not necessarily still be there over a year after the photograph was taken. I am not sure why his highly skilled team of intelligence officers did not spot that obvious fact. Perhaps that was why they employed a sensible Brit!

All too soon the war ended and my Middle East holiday came to a close. I said my goodbyes and I left the Eastern Mediterranean by helicopter for Cyprus. After being debriefed by the 'high and mighty', I boarded a transport aeroplane back to Blighty. Apart from my miniscule luggage, I carried with me a plaque inscribed:

Squadron Leader Derek Sharp
Best Wishes
To the last of the Combat Buffalos
Lebanon 1984

Of course, I took home with me many very interesting memories. Why the phrase 'Combat Buffalo'? I just suppose that was American humour. I was the last RAFLO to see combat in the region.

22

Truck Driving

My time as SLOPS soon came to an end and I was faced with one of the most difficult decisions of my life: do I continue in administration and almost certain promotion, do I retire from the RAF, or do I move sideways and become a professional aviator without chance of further promotion? The first choice did contain the important carrot of increased salary and position. The second would be a step into the unknown and I never was much of a risk-taker. The last choice would provide the most fun. After much soul searching and some advice, I went where my heart lay and opted for flying. It really was a no-brainer.

However, it would not be easy. Initially, I thought the new RAF Tri-Star would be great, but the job was not. So I visited RAF Brize Norton to investigate what flying the wonderful but rather elderly Vickers VC10 would be like. Little was I to know that despite its age, I would still be flying it some seventeen years later. However, having elected to fly the venerable 'Queen of the Skies', I was told categorically by a crusty old instructor that the last fighter pilot who tried to make that transition was chopped; he got the sack because he could not fit in with a crew. For those who do not quite understand the rivalry between multi-crew pilots and single-seat fighter pilots, let me explain. Col. John Cunnick once described fighter pilots as 'All balls and no forehead. If he thinks at all, he thinks he is immortal; God's gift to women and his airplane…. When the fighter pilot returns to base, that's when the bullshit starts. Yes, they are cavalier because a fighter pilot who thought about dying usually did die'.

Many transport pilots with no fighter background would agree with Col. Cunnick and perhaps there is some truth in what he said. However, flying a jet fighter is often 90 per cent fear and excitement and 10 per cent boredom, the complete opposite of flying a heavy passenger plane. A fighter pilot usually only has himself to look after, but a multi-crew pilot, especially a captain of a large airliner, has many lives to consider. That is enough for the moment, but I will come back to this topic later.

Was I making a big mistake? Certainly, there is no room on the flight deck of a four-engined airliner for a one-man band or anyone with a cavalier approach to flying. Was I the right man for the job? Would I be setting myself up to fail for the first time in my life? Hopefully, I thought my experience flying Canberra jet bombers might prevent prejudice. I was soon to be disappointed on this score.

Moreover, there was worse to come. Having risen to the dizzy heights of squadron commander, leading up to sixteen fighters at any one time, I was now re-mustering as a co-pilot. Would I be able to swallow this? I had to if I wanted to succeed, but my egotistical fighter-pilot nature would be an obstacle to overcome.

To help me overcome my 'single-seat' nature, in May 1986, I was detached to RAF Finningley in Yorkshire to the Multi-Engine Crossover course to fly the Handley Page Jetstream T1, a small twin-engined turbo-prop airliner. The course lasted just two months and was rather a doddle, given my previous twin-engined experience with the Canberra. Remarks in my flying logbook are: 'High Average. A new role and a new aircraft. A most encouraging start in the transport world—well done'. So I must have done reasonably well. Now off to RAF Brize Norton!

The VC10 Operational Conversion Unit (OCU) was some six months long. The ground school was at least six weeks. In typical RAF fashion, we learnt how to build a VC10. I did think at the time that this went a little over the top seeing as we carried a flight engineer on the flight deck. We also invariably carried two experienced ground engineers on every flight.

Having passed ground school, we moved onto the dreaded simulator. Here we learnt to actually fly the aircraft. Well, at least to learn checks and procedures. It was not until a year or so later that we received a simulator that really resembled the VC10. However, at least we knew what to do when two engines failed or the wing fell off. The former required a carefully thought out procedure developed over many years, the latter ensured one resorted to prayer. In fact, every time I flew a VC10, I had to remind myself that both ejector seats not only were unserviceable, but also had never ever been fitted. That concentrated the mind when things went horribly wrong. No easy escape by pulling a little yellow and black handle.

So having learnt how to operate the controls, switches, and knobs in the right order, we were let loose on a real aeroplane. Nowadays, one progresses direct from airliner simulator to operational flying—modern simulators are that realistic. Ones very first flight may well have 300 passengers on board, but for me, some seventy hours of flight training lay ahead, from circuits and bumps, graduating to a global trainer, circumnavigating the globe in an empty aircraft.

Of course, by this stage of my life (I was forty-one years old with many hours in my logbook), I was considered an experienced pilot. However, in the simulator, I had only just begun to understand how to deal with a flight deck comprised of a captain, a co-pilot (me), a navigator, and a flight engineer. A modern flight deck normally comprises just two pilots as computers do most of the work. In fact, it has been said that the Boeing 737 was built to be flown by just one pilot and a dog. The pilot watches the computers and the dog is there to bite him if he touches anything!

Most of my life I had done everything myself. Now the workload was shared and that took some getting used to. For example, I had to listen to at least three conversations at once, the crew, air traffic, and weather reports. Already my hearing had deteriorated, a product of many hours listening to aero engines. Now I had some trouble understanding who said what, but that improved with time. Slightly more difficult to grasp was the fact that my flight engineer moved the throttles. Previously I had instinctively moved them if I need more or less power. Now, if power change was required, I had to think of what to say, say it, the engineer had to hear me, do it, then I had to check if the adjustment was sufficient. This all took time and thus anticipation was vital. More importantly, I could no longer be 'gung-ho', no longer for me the immortal words of that fantastic pilot Captain Eric 'Winkle' Brown: 'Kick the tires, light the fires and last one airborne is a sissy'. Shock horror, I was now had to become responsible.

Finally, after what seemed like eternity, I graduated and joined No. 10 Squadron at RAF Brize Norton, home of the VC10. No. 10 Squadron, like No. 6 Squadron, was formed at Farnborough in 1915. Interestingly, it also had been equipped with Canberra jet bombers, but now it boasted ownership of the 'Queen of the Skies'. Though I had great ambition for the second phase of my flying career, before I left the OCU, my pilot instructor dashed my hopes and desire to be the best. 'The best,' he retorted, 'You will never be better than bog average.' I was to prove him wrong, but that would be long after he retired.

Interesting, after I myself retired, under the Freedom of Information Act, I applied to the Royal Air Force for copies of all my annual and flying reports. They make quite interesting reading. Time and time again, I was to prove my assessors wrong in their predictions. By and large, I am sure that they were accurate in their assessments of me at the time, but predicting the future is not so easy. Whatever, the Annual Confidential Reports made fascinating reading. One can clearly see a characteristic running through some thirty-nine years of development. I am still the chap who joined the RAF in 1964, but boy have I mellowed—and changed in places too.

If only I had access to them way back in the '60s. One particular report stands out. My squadron commander, who obviously disliked me, wrote it. He disliked me because he was very much a 'died in the wool' transport pilot of limited flying ability and I was the cocky ex-fighter pilot, decorated by Her Majesty for bravery. But he was the boss. I should have flattered him and made him look good; stupidly, I did the opposite and got what I deserved in that report. Ah well, they do say that hindsight is a wonderful thing and none of us are born with wisdom!

Thus I entered the world of 'co-pilot', that lowly breed, capable of screwing up everything, keeper of the imprest, and at the beck and call of 'His Holiness the Captain'! The imprest: that was a briefcase of money, loads of money, which was used to pay all the bills encountered when circumnavigating the world. From hotels bills to fuel bills, from laundry to landing fees. Few agencies in the third world accepted credit cards; most of the time, only US dollars would suffice. This therefore was a huge responsibility for me, more so for the usual 'wet behind the ears' co-pilot. Moreover, such a vast sum (a million dollars sometimes) should not be tucked under ones pillow, but some fools did. It had to be left in the hotel safe deposit box. That posed problems. On more than one occasion, later as captain, my co-pilot would inform me that he had left the imprest in the hotel safe. Sadly now, we were thousands of miles away on the next leg of our flight to yet another continent. In time, I devised a plan to avoid this embarrassment for the co-pilot and mega problems for the crew. In short, I ordered the co-pilot to place his uniform shoe in the safe deposit box along with the loot. When he dressed to depart for the next sector of our voyage, he would wonder where his shoe was. Then the penny would drop.

Such were indeed the joys of being a co-pilot, which I had to endure for three whole years. I got my ears clipped at times, but I learnt that the path to success was to make the captain look good. Not difficult for me in the early days as my landings were not as smooth as they should be. Indeed, I suspect that many crewmembers might say that they were more like 'arrivals' than landings. However, they improved. Much later in my career, when landing at London Heathrow in quite inclement weather, with Margaret Thatcher as Prime Minister on board, I pulled off one of those 'once in a lifetime' landings when none of us knew we were back on *terra firma*, it was so smooth. The Prime Minister popped her head around the flight deck door as she departed and remarked 'That was the best landing I have ever experienced'. But it took me quite a while to get to that standard and, overall, flying the 'Big Jets' was not as easy as I had originally thought it would be.

Today, some thirty years later, I no longer fly the 'Big Jets'. It certainly was an experience, as you will gather if you care to read the following few chapters compiled from several 'in-house' magazine articles written by me over the years. Amazingly, it was not until ten years after I retired that the VC10 was finally pensioned off, after fifty years of service. I suppose that was partially due to the fact that it was built so well in the first place. Today, when profits count for everything, the Vickers VC10 would not stand a chance of even getting off the drawing board.

The early years of my time on Shiny Ten was just like being an airline pilot. All we did was fly passengers from 'A' to 'B'. War was a long way off and I was told categorically that I should put all thoughts of 'operational' flying out of my head. It would do me no good at all. We flew in uniform and flying suits were definitely not required. Three times a week, we flew to Washington DC. At least twice a week, we flew to Cyprus. Twice a month, we flew to the Far East, and the rest of the time, we transported soldiers to Germany and anywhere else they wanted to go to play their war games.

The author as captain of VC10, No. 10 Squadron, RAF Brize Norton. (*Author's collection*)

The schedule to Washington was called the 'red eye' on account of the fact that we invariably took off at about midnight. Sometimes, however, departure was at lunchtime. Such luxury. We flew out to the USA, stayed there for a week, then returned the following Friday. Occasionally, we were required to take a VC10 down to Belize in Central America, which was a jolly day out, but that was relatively rare. So the crew enjoyed a whole week in DC on a quite generous food allowance. Some wasted it on drink, the stewardesses spent their allowance mainly on goodies from the huge department stores, and I spent some of the money on food and what was left on getting out and seeing the great USA.

Despite Washington DC enjoying the nickname 'Death City' as there were often up to five murders per night, only one of our crew was ever mugged. I often walked across the city late at night and even carried a spare wallet packed with out-of-date credit cards and a few dollars. If I had been waylaid, I would have handed it over promptly, but I never was even approached. Americans never walk anywhere, so perhaps the bad guys assumed that anyone walking across DC late at night must be broke, mad, or an idiot. Perhaps in those days, I was all three, but I survived.

I also remember walking across Dupont Circle to my hotel at about midnight when I was accosted by a lady of the night. I excused myself by saying 'sorry, dear, I only have a dollar'. When I arrived at the hotel, my matronly lady loadmaster was in reception and said, 'Oh, thank goodness, Captain, you are here, would you escort me across the Circle to the drugstore, I need some paracetamol'. That I did and when we reached the ladies of the night, one said loudly, 'See what you get for a dollar!' I did not explain that to the loadie.

For seventeen years of my life the 'Ten' gave me enormous pleasure. During that time, I saw every corner of our rapidly shrinking world. I flew my enormous craft down the slopes of the Himalayas into Kathmandu airport and I flew the IGS (Instrument Guidance System) into the old Kai Tak airport at Hong Kong, now closed as it was too dangerous. This approach often resulted in many a disaster due to a 70-degree right turn immediately before the runway. I even went to war in a VC10, though while training, the 'Old Guard' had told me the VC10 would never venture close to a war zone. I refuelled aircraft in flight. I taught embryonic transport pilots to fly and to learn the tricks I had learnt. I even flew members of the Royal Family and Heads of State.

Our sorties to Nepal were much looked forward to, not least for the amazing scenery. Actually, many pilots preferred the weather to be awful as then they were unable to note how close the aeroplane came to the mountainside as they made their approach into Tribhuvan International Airport. Though possessing a mighty long runway, Kathmandu airport needed it. The airfield was situated high up in the Himalayas, at nearly 6,000 feet. Worse still, it was built in a bowl between 15,000-foot mountains, and thus, even on a good day, the approach was always fraught with danger. Worse still, however, was the 'go-around': if the approach was unsuccessful, the pilot overshot and thus had to turn sharply to avoid hitting enormous mountains. He then had to continue the turn through 270 degrees to fly the only means of escape route down a very narrow valley. Some did not make it. At the time, the VC10 was the largest aircraft to land at Kathmandu and we all had to have our wits about us. Pilots were not even allowed to try until they had flown it with another pilot who had done it before. This was even despite a few trial runs in the simulator before setting out for Asia.

Even on the ground, crews were not safe. Stomach disorders were the norm and one drank the water at one's peril. Even handling bank notes then putting one's finger in one's mouth would result in agonising stomach pains and a lengthy time spent in the bathroom. One such navigator fell afoul of the dreaded Kathmandu trots and spent the entire flight back to Hong Kong in the aircraft forward loo. His navigation suffered, though we managed as he sat attached to a very long intercom lead and some help from the flight engineer with switch manipulation at the navigator's station.

Of course, food poisoning was not the only danger faced in Kathmandu. One day, my erstwhile (and rather rotund co-pilot) challenged me to a rickshaw race. Ambushing residents outside our hotel often occurred by a plethora of rickshaw owners. They were an intrusion into our drinking plans, so one day we hailed two and gave our destination as the Hotel Annapurna. I suppose the look of surprise on their faces was understandable as we were standing immediately outside that very hotel. My chum briefed them that we wanted to race up the high street, around the monument, and then back to our hotel. The first one back got a sizable bonus. The rest of the crew assembled to watch the spectacle, however, I do not think we actually managed to reach our destination as we collided with each other as we sped around the monument at literally breakneck speed, then both fell out of the rickshaws amid gales of laughter, only to fall right back into a local bar to nurse our bruises.

Shortly after overcoming significant prejudice by virtue of being an ex-fighter pilot, I was 'elevated to the peerage' and promoted to captain. Within a few weeks, I was invited to join that very elite set of aviators who were privileged to fly VVIPs (Very Very Important Persons). Though enormously fulfilling, the task was not immune from stress.

23

Air Force One: British Style

Here is just a sample of what I got up to, written for my column entitled 'From the Sharp End' for an in-house magazine in early 2000:

Have you ever wondered how easy it is to drive passengers around the blue skies in a large four-engined airliner? Your views will possibly range from 'glorified bus driver' to 'I could never do that'. Passenger transportation is just one of the many aviation roles we RAF aircrew were privileged to be able to do. One of the honours I was awarded during my time with No. 10 Squadron was being appointed as a VVIP captain. Only a few rose to such giddy heights. Though I was particularly pleased to receive this honour, it gave me particular pleasure and a smack in the eye for the instructor who originally said that I would never make the grade. Well it proved that one should never say never. Not only did I make the grade, but eventually I rose to the top of the pile!

Thus I started my additional career as personal chauffeur to Royalty and Heads of State. Many people have asked me if I regretted my duck strike accident and thus a change of career. Of course, I did in a way, but certainly being captain of a prestigious flight, with perhaps Her Majesty as principle passenger, was something that the vast majority of pilots never got to do. It was truly a great honour. Prestigious flying is perhaps the pinnacle of professional transport flying and one also met some very interesting people. In fact, I once flew an old chum to Saudi Arabia shortly after he had been promoted Air Chief Marshal and having being appointed Air Officer Commander-in-Chief, RAF Strike Command. As young officers, we had served together on Jaguars many years previously. Certainly Air Chief Marshal Sir Charles John Thomson could be considered having reached the top of his tree. During the long cruise to Riyadh, Sir John visited me on the flight deck to chat about old times. I congratulated him of his promotion, but in typical fashion of an RAF fighter pilot, he replied that it was I who had the better job. Sir John meant what he said.

Most VIPs popped into the flight deck, partly out of curiosity, partly out of boredom on a very long flight, but also to thank their chaps for a service well done. Prime Minister Margaret Thatcher was very good at that and always appeared incredibly interested in what we did. One other Prime Minister was not so charming. Whatever, personally meeting Prime Ministers and Royalty and chatting to them casually over a period of time

The co-pilot's main task was to ensure that he had sufficient loot, in multiple foreign currencies, to cover all eventualities. Bearing in mind that the VC10 required over 88,000 litres of fuel and that the co-pilot may have needed to pay for that in cash, he required a mighty big bag—even bigger than the captain's wallet! The air engineer liaised with both ground engineers and squadron engineering flight to ensure that we were provided with one of Her Majesty's finest and perfectly reliable VC10s. Though engineering and role preparation was beyond the scope of this article, suffice to say that many man-hours were required to bring the trusty VC10 workhorse up to standard. This all culminated in the final aircraft inspection attended by station commander, squadron commander, senior engineering officer, and, of course, me, the captain.

Preparation was paramount, and without the hours of hard work, we would all have been in trouble. However, sometimes the best laid plans of mice and men count for little and things could go horribly wrong. Though safely, smoothly, and on time are key words in the VVIP world, flexibility is indeed the key to air power. One must be ready to tear up the script and ad-lib.

As usual, our little adventure was to prove to be something of a challenge. Maps of Milan were studied and then discarded when the plot changed. A route to Helsinki was arranged, until we were told that the airfield was on strike. Finally, our first port of call became Arlanda outside Stockholm. This was purely a night stop for our principal passenger and his staff, who were anxious not to waste too much time there. However, the crew would have a major problem with this program. Whereas our passengers would disembark from the VC10 and could possibly be in their hotel half an hour later, we had work to do. The aircraft had to be cleaned and serviced by the crew for the next day, the washing-up had to be done, and the aircraft then moved to a secure place. Moreover, not for us the police escorted limo to the hotel. Good old crew bus for us. Additionally, we needed to be back at the aircraft some three hours prior to departure to move the aircraft, study the weather, decide on fuel, check the 'notices to airmen', supervise the catering on-load, refuel, de-ice, and complete the plethora of other vital checks. Normally, with the luxury of fourteen hours between flights, this is not a problem, even if the hotel is quite some distance from the airfield. However, due to this itinerary, we were only going to have just over ten hours between flights. This, unfortunately, would leave us a mere five hours at the hotel. What with registration, a couple of showers, and breakfast, we would probably at best get four hours' sleep. Authority for a reduced crew rest period was sought and obtained, so that dilemma was negated. As the rest of the route seemed to be a doddle, we were deliriously happy to accept this arrangement. The final itinerary evolved as this: Brize Norton–London Heathrow–Stockholm–Murmansk–Moscow–Sochi–London Heathrow—Brize Norton.

So what happened in the event? Did it all go smoothly? Did it heck!

Here are extracts, slightly doctored in the interests of good journalism and state security, of the official story of Flight 1104.

Brize Norton to London Heathrow

This simple leg normally presents few problems for the crew. That said, however, everything is always simple if you do it often enough. Departing in a very noisy military aircraft without exceeding the strict airport noise limits is almost impossible. More importantly, if you ring 'the bells' you get a hefty fine! Consequently, we always achieved the impossible and never exceeded the noise limits. Additionally, on this particular day, just a few hours prior to chocks the departure from Heathrow was delayed by over two hours. As most of the crew was already at work, this delay resulted in a significant increase in the crew duty day.

Heathrow to Arlanda

Due to circumstances well beyond the crew's control, the aircraft departed slightly late on the revised itinerary from the Royal Suite (the VIP terminal at Heathrow). Now I am not going to blame our principle passenger, but they were often late. That went with the job. Shortly after departure, the co-pilot's main gyro failed, thus giving me the excuse to have to do all the flying. Well I did need an excuse. Though we landed exactly on time at Stockholm, we opened the doors late due to a last minute change of parking position. Everything then went well until we reached the hotel. Despite being booked into the Arlanda Hotel, on arrival, it became clear that this was not the case. No room at the inn was the cry and our luxurious five hours of kip went straight down the tube while the loadmaster attempted to find accommodation for us within 100 miles. Luckily, the crew was subsequently directed to another hostelry some 5 miles distant. However, as there was now insufficient time to do anything other than collapse into our bunks, we slept like babies and woke without hangovers. What a strange sensation!

Arlanda to Murmansk

The stage to Murmansk went well and the aircraft touched down exactly on time. Nevertheless, due to snow and considerable ice on the runway and manoeuvring areas, door time was a little late. More importantly, on arrival at the parking area, ATC requested that the aircraft auxiliary power unit (APU) be kept running as, despite previous assurances, no ground power or air start equipment were serviceable. A pity as our APU was also unserviceable. It was not our day. So it was decided to keep No. 4 engine running until such time as the APU could be repaired. Luckily, after maintenance in sub-zero temperatures, it started on the seventh attempt. We kept our fingers firmly crossed for the next five hours. If it subsequently failed again, we would be stuck there forever, together with our VVIP. As the Prime Minister's visit was to discuss how to minimise the effects of large numbers of obsolete military nuclear reactors at Murmansk, the crew were keen to proceed on the next leg. None of us wanted to be fried.

Murmansk to Moscow

The Principal Passenger was over an hour late boarding the aircraft and, as the route to Moscow Vnukovo Airport was more or less in a straight line, little opportunity was available for time to be recovered. Despite putting on all speed, the VC10 was late on chocks at Vnukova. Shock horror! However, the main thing I really remember about that flight was that I broke the second law of VVIP. The Prime Minister's wife insisted on having her lunch as we took off. Sadly, the runway was rutted with snow and the take-off was as rough as a ploughed field. As a result, the large glass of vintage claret tipped all over her beautiful white dress.

Moscow Stopover

This proved quite interesting and certainly not what I had expected. The Hotel Baltschug Kempinski was superb, but I was later told that the only reason we were accommodated there was that it was the only hotel where we would be safe from large numbers of beautiful Russian girls seeking our hand in marriage. Spoil sports! By the way, accounts, that £35 you gave me for the whole day's food paid for exactly half of the dinner from the hotel budget menu. Of course, I could have gone out into the Russian winter night in search of goulash, but I remembered the ladies waiting to prey on my vulnerable body. Discretion thus became the better part of valour and I stayed in and read my aircrew manual. Actually, I lie. We went to an Irish bar. Imagine that, an Irish bar in Moscow. However, like Red Square, Lenin's tomb, and other tourist attractions, the pub was completely deserted.

Moscow to Sochi

On this leg, 10 Squadron was also greatly honoured with the task of conveying the Russian Prime Minister to Sochi together with our principal passenger. This was the first time that both British and Russian Prime Ministers had travelled together in the same aircraft. Though no problems were encountered on this leg, as usual, it was necessary to reposition the aircraft whilst on the ground. This caused considerable vexation and some amusement because the Russian tug was not compatible with the VC10. Improvisation saved the day as always. I would reverse the aeroplane and I was one of the very few captains who were trained to do just that. The reason why was that such a process was fraught with danger: there was a huge risk of the nose wheel (which was definitely not designed to go backwards without a towing arm attached) castering through 180 degrees and thus snapping the aircraft steering mechanism. Our poor VC10 would then be dead. How embarrassing. Worse still would occur if I applied the brakes while moving backwards. The VC10 would tip on its tail and that would again be the end of that VC10, and me. However, VVIP captains had been advised that 'where needs must', so with both pilots holding the steering tiller very firmly, I reversed our trusty steed backwards, making sure the toe brakes were not touched. Simply selecting forward thrust instead of reverse thrust would stop the aircraft. Luckily my deft touch succeeded and we were ready for the next adventure.

Sochi to Heathrow

The principal passenger was again late boarding the aircraft; however, much of the time was made up during the transit. Just as well, as my cockpit side window shattered in the night sky above Poland. I, of course, was worried that I would be sucked out, just like that other BA captain some years previously. However, the kindly navigator put my mind at rest when he said such a thing was impossible. I was much too fat to fit through the hole.

No problems were encountered on the final leg. I think the VC10 knew its way home. Finally, as always, it was wonderful to arrive at Heathrow right in the middle of the rush hour and go straight to the front of the queue. Obviously, it must be the way I ask for landing clearance. Safely back at the Royal Suite at Heathrow, our principal passenger departed with the encouraging words: 'I could not have done it without you'. Conceitedly, I thought how right he was. We certainly were all rather tired but pleased that, as always, we had got the job done despite the proverbial slings and arrows. As far as the passengers were concerned, and despite constant changes to the itinerary and aircraft unserviceabilities, everything appeared to go exceptionally safely and smoothly, though not always perhaps exactly on time. However, as is often the case, a totally different picture was seen behind the scenes. However, that is what prestigious flights are all about.

The above was written for *Gateway* magazine a long time ago. For political reasons, I obviously never mention the disasters, but of course there were many. One such event took place in 1993. I was flying the Prime Minister around Europe with another VIP captain (sometimes two VIP captains were stipulated) and we did leg and leg about. A night stop was planned in a European capital famous for its nightlife. Both pilots got to bed fairly early in anticipation of the busy day ahead. However, the other captain was rather a partygoer, and though he had turned in before midnight, the stewardesses had other plans in the hotel disco. When they realised that the captain had gone to his room, they sent a delegation to drag him down to the disco. Whether he protested or not, I do not know, but he finally got to bed a little worse for wear.

Unfortunately, it was his leg the following day. I sat in the left-hand seat and he operated from the right (we were both qualified to operate as captain from either seat). All went fairly well until the approach when his fatigue got the better of him. Maybe I was not monitoring this very able captain sufficiently or not, but the first thing I knew that something was very wrong was when the stall warning sounded, followed immediately by the stick shakers. Of course we recovered the situation very quickly and landed safely, albeit a tad firmly, but to stall an airliner with the Prime Minister on board was not a good idea. To crash would have been far worse, but at least we would have become famous—or should I say infamous!

24

Balkan Adventures

This little adventure could possibly be called 'A Life in the Day of' or 'Tales of Daring-do from the Balkans'. However, here goes, but first a little history.

By 1991, the Serbian politician Slobodan Milošević gained power in Yugoslavia through inciting Serb nationalism. Along with growing nationalistic feelings in the other parts of Yugoslavia, the day came when Slovenia and Croatia declared independence from what they saw as a nation dominated by Serbs. The Yugoslav Army attempted to prevent the breakaway republics from leaving, but soon failed. Serbs living in southern and western Croatia then attempted to break away and form a new nation called Krajina. In 1992, Bosnia also broke away from Yugoslavia, precipitating yet another war. In southern Yugoslavia, the region called Macedonia broke away to form an independent nation. In August 1995, Serb mortars cause thirty-seven civilian dead in Sarajevo, which led to major NATO airstrikes against the Serbs beginning on 30 August.

In a previous chapter, I suggested that the life of a VC10 transport crew was long periods of boredom punctuated by very short periods of excitement. However, I do have a worrying habit of proving myself entirely wrong. Nothing illustrated that more than a sortie to Skopje one day late in 1995 to support the Balkan war effort.

Do you not always know when the day will not go well? It starts badly and then just gets a whole lot worse. I should not really have even been on this trip in the first place. The Prime Minister had wanted a lift to somewhere quite exotic and insisted that his favourite pilot flew him there. However, some conflict preoccupied our leader's mind and the jolly was off. Consequently, and especially as I was running out of credible war stories (are any of them credible?), I volunteered for a mission to the front line. As it turned out, I nearly wished I had not, especially as I broke my father's golden rule: 'Never volunteer for anything'.

The first warning sign appeared in the form of the crew list: only one steward. Surely there must be a mistake, I thought. We need three for an aeroplane full of gorgeous Amazons off to war. 'No,' said Operations, 'you just have cargo.' My mind flashed to the film *Top Gun*. What did that line say? Something about demotion to lugging cargo out of Hong Kong. Except this was not out of Hong Kong, and this would be a far cry from flying royalty to peaceful destinations. Worse was to come. The cargo was 35,000 lb of high-explosive artillery shells needed for our friendly peacekeeping force. I felt all wobbly and tried to think of an appropriate line from *Black Adder*. A bullet with my name on came to mind.

Anyway, after the usual pre-departure problems, in the small hours we departed for Macedonia, only a few hours late. All was sweetness and light until we crossed the Adriatic. Not that I was really worried about flying through the 'No-Fly Zone', nor skimming the mountain tops to avoid pilotless cruise missiles inbound to Serbia, nor the threat of the nasty thunderstorms ahead. However, an important fact had just come to light. We only had rations for six hours' flying. How could I possibly cope with so little food? Did this justify the transmission of a Mayday call? I decided to pull myself together and concentrate on picking out the nastiest storms on the weather radar.

A glance at that radar confirmed my worst nightmare. A mass of terrible ugly blotches on the screen stretched for as far as my eye could see. As I started to blub, my wise old navigator calmed me down by telling me that the blotches were merely mountaintops and we were just 2,000 feet above them. That was the maximum height allowed due to the cruise missiles above us. Moreover, I could affirm his statement by looking out of the window. What luck having a window seat. Nevertheless, I would have to pick my route through the bubbling cumulonimbus clouds with care and especially those clouds with a very hard centre (a mountain top). Suddenly a jagged fork of lightning launched at us out of a dark ominous cloud. Without so much as a 'You piss me off' call from above, we were hit. The plane shuddered and filled with a strong acrid smell of burning. Instantly I thought, 'just as well we are not carrying passengers'. Then I remembered the timid air stewardess who was afraid of flying, who I had invited to sit on the flight deck jump seat to observe just how routinely safe everything always is! Then I also recalled we were carrying 35 tons of high explosive.

Apparently, the fireball from the lightning strike rolled down between the high explosives and exited the aeroplane by the tail. Now I too had a fear of flying and my wobbly lip became a blur. Still, I thought this would make a good scenario for my next simulator sortie—assuming I survived. Moreover, we would now qualify for an additional laundry allowance.

Of course, prudence dictated we divert to somewhere less hostile than Macedonia and so we pointed the VC10 at a jolly nice holiday airport in Greece. Once safely on the ground, the engineers ascertained the damage (not a lot, just a few charred bits and some holes) and without too much serious trouble, we resumed our odyssey to Skopje.

Arrival at the front line was totally uneventful, apart from a surface-to-air missile being fired at us. After landing, my mobile phone rang. Was mother calling to wish me happy birthday? Was it the boss ringing to give me a hard time for making a mess of my logbook (not my fault my computer adds up in error) or was it just in-flight catering wanting to apologise for starving me to death? No, it was none of these, just HQ telling me that air-to-air missiles had been fired at aircraft inbound to our destination airfield. We were not to pass 'Go', nor collect '£200'. I am not sure what his thoughts were when I replied that 'yes, I know, the surface-to-air missile had been fired at us and actually we are already on the ground having a cup of tea!'

After some hours of negotiation (let us face it, transport crews do not want to spend the night sleeping in tents), we managed to persuade HQ to let us come home. Something to do with the fact that refugees were still departing in their civilian airliners and also the suspicion that the sightings were miss-plotted anyway. So, as the long day drew to a close, we lifted off, not for home as planned, but for Germany. The other airliner inbound had fled on hearing of possible violence (the cowards) and we were left with the task of taking his passengers to Brüggen. All went well (apart from the usual co-pilot landing) until after shut down when we checked in with HQ. 'You have been on duty for over 18 hours and are now grounded' came the order. Worse was to come. By the time we got to the hotel, the bar was closed (after all it was 2 a.m.), so we staggered off to bed happy in the knowledge that a jolly good job had been well done. Tomorrow was another day and obviously it would go completely smoothly, as usual.

Postscript: the next morning, as we lined up for take-off, the Army colonel, who I had invited to sit on the jump seat, remarked to me: 'I heard that you had a difficult day yesterday'. My reply went along the lines of 'Yes, but that was really exceptional. Today we will run on rails'. Two minutes later, the colonel's faith in my predictions was rudely shattered by the flight engineer's call of 'Abort Abort, Fire, Number 1 engine!' Ah well, I cannot always be right. Good old guardian angel must have been on double time that day.

At least the bar was open when we got back to the hotel.

Later, another chapter of my life in the Balkans opened when one day my boss called me into his office to give me some bad news. 'Derek,' he said, 'What are you doing next week?' I replied that I was on leave and visiting my sister in California. 'Ah,' he replied, 'well, you are off to the sun, but not in a westerly direction, more southerly. We need you to command the RAF detachment at Ancona airport on Italy's Adriatic coast.' Apparently, we had three Lockheed Tri-Star air tankers based there to refuel the NATO fighters operating over the Balkans. To support the three huge aeroplanes required a team of some fifty men and I had been selected from a cast of thousands to command that detachment.

Despite protesting that I knew nothing about in-flight refuelling (that was a lie as I did it while flying Jaguars), I found myself the very next day on an Alitalia commercial jet inbound to Bologna in northern Italy. From there, I was picked up by one of my staff in a rather nice BMW and transported at speed to my hotel in the seaside town of Senigallia, my accommodation for the next few months.

It was wonderful accommodation: my team occupied the whole hotel and indeed another close by. Naturally I was assigned the entire top floor penthouse suite. I even had a balcony that looked out over a crystal clear Adriatic. Was this the way to fight a war? I appreciated my quarters even more so when I recalled what my accommodation had been during the First Gulf War. So I gratefully accepted the luxurious facilities in the knowledge that this was payback time.

It was even better to find out that I would only work mornings. Brilliant. Even more wonderful, I discovered that my unit had hired fifty BMWs to enable my staff and the aircrew to drive to Ancona Airport each morning. Apparently, our work was so varied we could not rely on public transport and the cost of taxis was prohibitive. Well who was I to argue with that. We could also use our personal vehicles at will for leisure activities in the afternoon and at weekends. Though I would not be flying, and had lost a paid-for holiday to the States, life in the Le Marche region of Italy was not going to be too much of an imposition.

The following day, after touring my Empire, I met the airport manager and other dignitaries. They were naturally very hospitable, given that my fleet of tankers uploaded millions of gallons of aviation fuel from the nearby oil refinery every week. Sadly, though, due to the draconian RAF regulations pertaining to the receiving of gifts, I could not enter into the Italian custom of being 'sweetened up'. However, life was hardly minimalistic as our allowances came from a NATO fund and more than covered our food and accommodation.

I passed a happy few months in La Marche, was able to make several Italian friends, and spent many a happy time exploring the beautiful countryside around Senigallia. I actually was rather sad to return home at the end of my time, though my homecoming was blighted somewhat by the news that my wife was suing for divorce. Perhaps I had had rather too good a time, or was it that 'the mice do play whilst the cat was away?' Either way, I was about to start a new chapter in my personal life.

25
Fighter Pilot or Truck Driver?

Many of my civilian friends asked me: 'What is the difference between a fighter pilot and a transport pilot?' I was often tempted to say that it is the cost of the laundry of the underclothes. However, it was not really as simple as that. True the fighter pilot's life involves lengthy periods of excitement coupled with very short periods of boredom, whereas the transport pilot's life is long periods of boredom coupled with short periods of excitement. I remember years ago, when I too was a member of the SEFJMR (Steely Eyed Fast Jet Master Race), I spent many a day getting airborne from my home airfield, flying to a beach, dropping a bomb on a target in the sand, missing, then flying back to the same airfield I departed from. Then off to the bar for tea and medals.

However, it is not true to say that either job is any more difficult than the other. Similarly, it would be inappropriate to suggest that a Red Arrows pilot has a more difficult life than that of the SAR helicopter pilot. Certainly there are fundamental differences in techniques and skills, but it is accurate to say that neither could do each other's job, nor is either job any more important than the other.

One could even make a good case for proving that the 'truckie' has a harder life than his FJ counterpart (hush my mouth). From my experience, when a fighter four ship attends met briefly for night flying, if the weather is poor then a stack to the bar is the only sensible course of action. Unfortunately, if when down route, a truckie crew discovers that the weather for their destination is terrible, they invariably launch regardless. Occasionally, we ended up somewhere completely unexpected. Perhaps the dissimilarity between jobs (operations apart) is that many fast jet sorties are merely practice flights. However, transport crews do it for real all the time. Should difficulties arise, they have a set strict set of rules to ensure that the task is always completed safely.

Fighter cockpits are tight jumbled little places—room for a map and stopwatch and that is about all. No loo, no galley, nothing but you and the aeroplane. On the other hand, flight decks are also stressful places. They are full of past memories soaked in sweat, stress, boredom, and sometimes fear. Sometimes they are wondrous environments, especially on a clear starry night when the view resembles an inverted city at midnight. Snow-capped mountains thrusting through low cloud or a tropical sunset blinding one's vision as the aeroplane sails serenely onwards. Such pleasures are there to savour on a flight deck; not so for the single-seat fighter pilot who has little time to view the scenery.

Perhaps the dissimilarity between jobs, with the exception of operations since the start of the twenty-first century, is that many fast jet sorties are merely practice flights, in contrast to transport crews. Should difficulties arise, passenger crews have a set strict set of rules to ensure that the task is always completed safely. Safer than flying a fighter, though I must remind you again that passenger aeroplanes do not have ejector seats.

Not that our life was all boredom. Contrary to the vicious lies put about by lesser mortals, even captains work jolly hard. Just watch the eyelids of any crewmember driving home after a thirty-hour crew duty day having 'deadheaded' back from Western Canada. Perhaps I should explain 'deadheading'. To save money, once the crew reached Calgary in Alberta (after an incredibly long flight via Newfoundland), they were told to sit in the passenger compartment and fly all the way back to Blighty. This saved Her Majesty a few pennies in hotel bills, and if you think that a 'jolly' to Washington with thirty-one hours off is a good deal, many such recent trips were prime examples of just how little sleep one got. For example, we often crewed in at 2 a.m. having had precious little sleep beforehand. You try sleeping in an officers' mess during the afternoon or early evening. Even at home, the telephone rings, visitors arrive, or the kids refuse to tiptoe around the house. Arrival in Washington fails to bring any respite from fatigue. Knowing that sleep in a hotel during the day is impossible due to constant housekeeping visits, incorrect wake-up calls, mini-bar checks, spurious fire alarms, other guest's arrival and departures, or merely the eight-lane highway immediately outside your hotel room, one stays awake until the evening. The following day, one awakes at 7 a.m. UK time. Unfortunately, this is only 3 a.m. in the USA. Following a few hours of scanning the ninety-nine TV channels, one wastes a few hours showering and shaving. Have you ever noticed just how clean crews are down route. Now you know why. After breakfast and a short wander, one tries to get some sleep before the call, but that is impossible for the reasons previously explained. In fact, most crewmembers get about six or seven hours during the three days away; an average of two hours per day. No wonder fast jet pilots travel to Red Flag during the day, then have a couple of days to acclimatise. They must be pretty smart.

Life rarely went smoothly those days. A trip to Florida demonstrated this admirably. The trip out went fairly well and some less well-informed crewmembers looked forward to fourteen hours off in a small hotel on the Florida Keys. Unfortunately, our hotel was over one hour's drive from the base. Having taken over an hour to taxi in, bed down the aircraft, book met and catering for the next day, wait for transport, then drive 40 miles to the hotel, only eleven hours remained before take-off. As three hours of this time was needed to drive back to the base and prepare for flight, this left just eight hours off for crew rest. That would never have been allowed if the crew belonged to a major airline. Remember when I once arrived at the hotel to be informed that there was no room at the inn. When we eventually found an alternative we just got five hours' crew rest.

Anyway, back to our trip to Florida. The following day, while on route to Gander, our vintage VC10 decided to shed its load of hydraulic fluid all over the Carolinas and a hasty diversion was made to Washington, the nearest suitable airfield. After 30 tons of aviation fuel and many gallons of hydraulic fluid were dumped on the USA, we headed for the safety of earth. Following a few thrills trying to get a rather insubordinate undercarriage to lower (it helps with the landing), we ended up blocking part of the taxiway when the brakes and steering finally gave up.

On our way home the following day, we proved yet again that the simulator is superfluous. We really did not need to practice emergencies—we often had real ones. Halfway across the pond, and with the crew really looking forward to a landing at Kinloss at 2 a.m., with a 30-knot crosswind, in blowing snow, our trusty steed again came to the rescue and gave us a little red light to look at just to help curb the boredom. Unfortunately that little red light told us that the top rudder had quit and, as it was a good idea for it to be working when we landed on snow in a gale, especially as the gale was at right angles to our landing direction, we had an outbreak of cowardice and headed for Brize. Once again that yellow streak on our backs shone brightly.

On the approach, it became uncertain whether we would be able to land at Brize as here also the winds were now out of limits. Moreover, we had no fuel to go anywhere else unless, of course, we settled for the grass at South Cerney. In the event, ATC was smart enough to stop announcing the wind speed over the radio once a small lull between gusts occurred. So all was well that ended well and we landed in one piece back at home, very much looking forward to some well-earned and desperately needed crew rest. Wrong!

At 2 a.m., as we dragged our exhausted bodies into Ops to sign off and fall into our beds, the jolly pleasant operations officer 'invited' us to prepare another aircraft, fly the passengers to Kinloss, then come home. After such a polite 'request', how could we possibly refuse? So three hours later than the schedule (sorry, beg your pardon, one day and three hours later), we landed in a snowstorm in northern Scotland, waved goodbye to our ever-so-grateful passengers, and returned to Brize to practise the droopy eyes method of driving back to our loved ones.

Yes, we did work hard, occasionally. Unlike our fast jet colleagues, we had little say in what we did. Their practice bombs in the sand can wait. Our customers cannot. The task must get done and we always ensured that it did. Safely, smoothly, and mostly on time. It was so easy we actually did it in our sleep.

26

Far Eastern Suarez

It has been said that whoever ignores sound advice does not deserve it in the first place. Well, my late father gave me three pieces of advice on joining the RAF:

1. Eat as often as you can because you never know when you will again.
2. Stay away from loose women (cannot think why he of all people should say that).
3. Never volunteer for anything.

The first I always put into practice. The second, well, all I have to say is 'fat chance'. The last was possibly the best advice and I totally ignored it by agreeing to write the 10 Squadron monthly articles for the RAF Brize Norton in-house magazine. So during a well-earned crew rest (only a sixteen-hour crew day the previous day), I put pen to paper (or at least bytes to hard disc) and produced my first article for the station magazine. It would have been nice to have received a handover from my predecessor, but he went looking for penguins in the South Atlantic (Falkland Islands) without so much as a 'you have control'. To make matters worse, the only advice I got from my boss was 'get a grip, produce it by yesterday, and woe betide you if you upset the Stn Cdr'. Consequently, upon that ominous note, this is what I wrote:

I have been told not to make this article too 'in-house' so I will not be mentioning that Squeaky (the nickname for a pilot on the squadron) was hit by a moving building the first time he was released as a brand new captain (the airport finger collided with his VC10). Moreover, I most certainly will not mention that a fellow Flight Instructor left his keys behind in flight planning and travelled the length and breadth of Canada trying to get into his locked suitcase. That said, however, little of note has happened on 10 Squadron that will rivet the attention of the average person in Supply or Admin wings. I note from the October edition of *Gateway* that car parking on the grass is an offence, that it rained when 101 Squadron visited Muskrat Falls and that the mean number of days with air frost in October is one! Consequently, it would be pointless trying to match such important information. Suffice to say that 10 Squadron, despite insufficient spares, insufficient manning and a runaway airport pier, has quietly achieved the task as always. Elsewhere in this edition of *Gateway* there are 2 articles describing how several slightly mad individuals from 10 Squadron walked across Australia for charity and other mad fools walked up Pen-Y-Fan in Wales. Other than that, little of note has occurred. Away from base most of us have had our 'adventures' and I do recommend that all of you who have little knowledge of the 'the sharp end' try and procure a 'ninth seat' on one of our foreign jaunts. You may just discover that life down route is not always 'jolly' and can sometimes be really hard work.

As a good example, by then I had become a flight instructor (FI), and despite initial euphoria, a planned voyage to the Far East to complete the training of a couple of new crews completely demonstrated just how agreeable and also how unpleasant a route could be. Now you would think that a 'jolly' to the Far East would be great fun. A 'trainer' normally was. However, if things went pear-shaped, it could be rather hard work for the captain, and on this occasion, I had drawn the short straw. We were tasked to take an Army unit to Aqaba (an airfield in Jordan), fly on to Bahrain for a night stop, stop-over in Sri Lanka, collect passengers and freight in Brunei, then, after night stops in Brunei and Bahrain, return home via Akrotiri in Cyprus. Five fairly easy days, which sound really jolly, does it not? The following was what really happened.

Day 1

We were one hour late departing due to spares not being readily available (duty storeman on call). We had a good flight to Aqaba, but it was nothing like expected as Italian, Greek, Israeli, and Jordanian air traffic all tested our ability to stay flexible. Then onwards to Bahrain. On arrival, a brake failure on landing ensured that the ground engineers (GEs) had something to do for a change! Following a change into civilian clothes at the airport (local anti-American factions are plotting to blow up us Western military personnel), we proceeded downtown to the hotel. Later that evening, our GEs return to inform us that the hydraulics are knackered, that spares would arrive the next day, and that we could be serviceable by the third day. Thus the saga commenced and the prospect of a day's delay did not, at this time, appear to be anything other than 'WHOOPEE!'

Day 2

The day was spent by the pool studying our bible of regulations, while the GEs had a wonderful time playing with all their toys and getting XV105 ready for its new bit. Then, after Evensong, our illustrious engineers return to say that the initial problem was fixed, but additionally we now required further parts as they had discovered more complications! Ray, one of the crew, who was expected to be home by the end of the week to be best man at a wedding, began to wish he had not taken the risk of a Far East trip. Still, no major problems at that stage as we could always fly direct to Brunei with just a refuelling stop in Sri Lanka and thus make up for the lost day.

Day 3

More time was spent buying presents for Operations for sending us on such a wonderful holiday. However, a telephone call from our GEs ruined our day as they informed us that the spare from the UK had been lost. No one on the crew owned up and another spare was despatched from the UK together with a specialist engineer to fix the aircraft. At this stage, the ladies on the crew achieve a world record for shopping.

Day 4

However, before the second spare arrived and before we got totally fed up with a five-hour instructor's conference arranged by a rather enthusiastic new pilot instructor, the missing part was found. There is no truth in the rumour that it was discovered in the RAF handling agent's office. After much wringing of hands and an incredible amount of hard work by the captain (me) who had been presented with a myriad of trivial problems such as expiration of diplomatic clearances, a revolution at our next port of call and a mutiny from two co-pilots who refused to go anywhere until they had finished their homework set by the keen FI, Auntie at Operations issued a new revised itinerary that would put us back into Brize only three days late.

Day 5

The GEs worked solidly for almost twenty-four hours to get our vintage aircraft serviceable and we started engines as the sun set over the Persian Gulf. Clearance for start and pushback was rapidly followed in turn by clearance for pull forward and shut down. We had sustained yet another major technical failure. It seemed as if someone was trying to tell us something. After some high-speed rectification and rapid calculations of crew duty day left remaining, we chocked out with a couple of minutes to spare for our five-hour flight to an island torn by revolution and then onwards for another five hours to another island where alcohol was banned. We wondered why some of the crew were getting rather despondent.

Day 6

After flying through the night, surviving monster electrical storms, eating the world's worst in-flight breakfast, and keeping the student's morale up with a practice ditching drill, we landed at our destination, Brunei, some sixteen hours after arrival at the aircraft the previous day. Little happened here, though the GEs struggled for twelve hours to close the freight door. This was a common problem with the VC10, which often resulted in crews having to taxi round the airfield while the GEs continued to try to solve the problem. Apparently, the motion of the aircraft helped to get the locks to move into place. The rest of the crew collapsed into their beds in non-drunken stupor (remember that place was dry) and we slept for over twelve hours. Unfortunately, the loadmaster was now suffering from flu and the flight engineer had conjunctivitis.

Day 7

We were up at 4 a.m. and set off to the airport. Goodness me, so this is what a non-hangover felt like! We actually felt well (except the loadmaster who was now full of flu). However, terrible news awaited us. There was only a limited supply of Diet Coke available. On a much lesser note, we receive a message informing us that a terrorist group calling itself Ellalan Force would try and assassinate the passengers and crew when we arrived at Colombo airport. As this was less of a threat to our health than the co-pilot's flying ability, we ignored it completely and pressed on. *En route*, we again experienced monster thunderclouds, St Elmo's fire, and severe turbulence, but after many hours, we arrived back in the comparative safety of Bahrain. Sadly, the flight engineer still had conjunctivitis.

Day 8

By then, Ray had missed his duty best man slot, the loadmasters' flu was a corker, I had missed a free day at the races, the co-pilot was desperately trying to make the imprest tally after being talked into financially looking after the passengers, the navigator had missed his wife's birthday, and people still thought we were on a swan. However, day eight promised to be a piece of cake as we had a full ten minutes spare before our Egyptian diplomatic clearance expired. Additionally, despite its restricted operational times, RAF Akrotiri agreed very reluctantly to stay open to allow a refuel, but unfortunately the weather forecast for Brize was for thick fog. Following a one-sided discussion with the duty controller at Brize, everyone agreed that despite the fact that our arrival back home would clash with an inbound Tri-Star aircraft, our reputation will suffer more if we had to divert to Prestwick, so we were allowed to return home. Eventually, after several more near disasters, we arrived back at Brize as thick fog rolled in. We were only three days late and the loadmaster felt like death. The drive home, in the dark, in 15-metre visibility was going to be particularly unpleasant, so the navigator, who had not been home for over a fortnight, sensibly decided to spend the night on base. The rest of us were too cowardly to hide any longer from our partners and drove home in the pea soup. So ended yet another leisurely week in the life of a 10 Squadron crew.

The author on the beach at Beer Devon, *c.* 1947. (*Author's collection*)

Plt Off. Derek Minden Sharp (Uncle Derek), *c.* 1939. (*Author's collection*)

Copy from 44 Squadron's Operations Record Book, June 1943—'Last Flight'. (*IWM*)

A Slingsby T21 Sedbergh glider, the same as one flown school CCF. (*Su Khoo*)

Above: Avro Anson as per the author's first flight. (*Su Khoo*)

Opposite: Notice of the author's RAF Commission, 2 April 1965. (*Author's collection*)

MINISTRY OF DEFENCE
Adastral House, Theobalds Road, LONDON W.C.1
Telephone: HOLborn 3434, *ext.* 7547

Please address any reply to
MINISTRY OF DEFENCE
(AR 1(RAF)   )

and quote: AF/OP 4232596/1/AR 1(RAF)
Your reference:

2nd April 1965

Sir,

I am commanded by the Air Force Board of the Defence Council to inform you that approval has been given for your appointment to a Direct Entry Commission Type A, as a pilot in the General Duties Branch Supplementary List of the Royal Air Force in the rank of acting pilot officer and on the conditions of Air Ministry Order A 146/1963 as amended. The commission will take effect from 2nd April 1965, and you will be discharged concurrently from service as an airman. An announcement of your appointment will appear in the London Gazette in due course.

2. You will be required to serve on the Active List until your thirty eighth birthday although the Board reserves the right to retire an officer prematurely or to retain him beyond the normal retiring date, should either course be necessary in the interests of the service.

3. The retention of your commission will be subject to the satisfactory completion of training and to your character, conduct and efficiency being fully up to the standard of a commissioned officer.

4. The Commanding Officer of the Initial Training School will supply you with a copy of pamphlet Pam(Air) 106, which contains information about the issue of pay and allowances, and a memorandum showing the scale of uniform which officers are required to possess. An outfit allowance as laid down in AMO A 24/1963, paragraph 8, was issued to you on entry to the School and you are not entitled to any further payment on appointment.

5. You will retain your present personal number, 4232596, which should be quoted in all official correspondence.

I am, Sir,
Your obedient Servant,

H E Langley.

Acting Pilot Officer D. J. Sharp
Royal Air Force

A Folland Gnat Course, 4 FTS, RAF Valley, 1966. (*Author's collection*)

Above: A Folland Gnat, 4 FTS, RAF Valley. (*Ray Deacon*)

Opposite above: The author and his crew at Hal Far, Malta, 1968. (*Tony Carter*)

Opposite below: Canberra weapons, RAF Akrotiri, 1967. (*Author's collection*)

RAF Akrotiri Strike Wing Canberra B.15. (*John Sheenan*)

Jaguar pilots Royal International Air Tattoo, 2016. (*Su Khoo*)

Farewell to 6 Squadron RAF Coningsby, 2007. (*Steve Buckby*)

Jaguar GR1 at night RAF Coltishall, 1979. (*Steve Buckby*)

Sepecat Jaguar, RAF Coltishall, 2005. (*Steve Buckby*)

Sepecat Jaguar at work low-level. (*Author's collection*)

The author at 6 Squadron RAF Lossiemouth in 2017, with fin from a Jaguar. (*Su Khoo*)

BLINDED AT 500 mph

Hero pilot tells of battle to land jet damaged by a duck

Sharp .. hit by duck

By MICHAEL CHARLESTON

RAF FIGHTER pilot Derek Sharp told yesterday how he was blinded at 500 miles an hour . . . but still managed to bring his plane down safely.

The life-or-death drama began when Derek's Hawk jet hit a wild duck over the East Anglian countryside.

The bird shot through the plane's one-inch thick windscreen as if it were tissue paper—and smashed through the visor of Derek's helmet.

Squadron Leader Sharp, 37, was left blinded.

Blood

His left eye had been knocked downwards from its socket. His right eye was closed with bruises, blood and, as he put it, "mashed duck."

For 10 minutes Squadron Leader Sharp, of RAF Chivenor, North Devon, flew

A Hawker Siddeley Hawk

blind as a colleague sat almost helpless behind him in the dual-control plane.

Flight Lieutenant Les Pearce, 28, is a navigator, not a pilot.

Squadron Leader Sharp could not talk to ground control because of the noise in his shattered cockpit — although he could still hear instructions in his radio headphones.

With Flight Lieutenant Pearce acting as radio communicator, ground control talked the two fliers down to within 200ft of the runway at RAF Wittering, near Stamford, Lincolnshire.

Then Squadron Leader Sharp's battered right eye, washed by tears, managed to pick out the ground — and he made a perfect landing.

For a fortnight, as he had three eye operations at the RAF hospital in Ely, the RAF kept quiet about the incident.

But yesterday, back in his married quarters near Barnstaple, Devon, with his wife Anne and their two young sons, Squadron Leader Sharp told the incredible story.

He is still blind in his patch-covered left eye and sees only blurred shapes with the right.

But he still hopes to fly again. . . . "I should be good for another 19 years' flying—this was my share of the bad luck," he joked.

The hero pilot said : ' We hit the duck near Peterborough. There was no pain—just this great bang, and I couldn't see.

"My cockpit was the noisiest place in the world. It was three times the force of a hurricane — we were doing 500 mph.

Spoil

"I have been flying years without a prang or an ejection and I wasn't going to spoil my record."

He added : " A 500 mile an hour duck does more than black your eye. I would have been dead if I didn't always fly with my visor down."

Flight Lieutenant Pearce said of the happy landing: "It was an exceptional job. Derek is my favourite man."

Above: A national newspaper article regarding the author's duck strike, 1983. (*Author's collection*)

Opposite above: The author at RAF Chivenor, 1983. (*Author's collection*)

Opposite below: Air-to-air gun kill Hawk *v.* Hawk gun camera film, 1982. (*Author's collection*)

Above: McDonnell Douglas RF4C, Alabama, 1983. (*Author's collection*)

Below: The author's last VC10 flight, RAF Brize Norton, 17 June 2003. (*Author's collection*)

27

Easy Life being a Captain

The previous chapter illustrated just how much administration a captain could be lumbered with, especially if things started to go wrong. Things usually did go wrong and here is yet another prime example described in an article I wrote for the base in-house magazine in June 1998.

Well, there I was yet again on the Cyprus schedule steaming up the Med on a warm late May evening, desperately trying to stay awake! We had been up since 4 a.m. and a combination of warm sun and a tummy full of flight crew curry was a wonderful cure for insomnia. How could I keep awake? The flight deck were fed up of my war stories, in fact they were not even being polite about them anymore. No magazines to read, though I noted that the co-pilot had the latest copy of *Maxim*. However, as he had only just learnt to read, he obviously was going to take some time with it. The flight commander navigator was doing ACRs (annual confidential reports) so I suppose I could help. Only trouble was, it was mine he was writing! The engineer was doing an 'engine trend', whatever that is, so he was too busy to swap gossip. That only left me with the next edition of the base magazine: *Hey Ho*.

Somebody once asked me what I did for a living. Typically I returned their question with another question: 'Have you ever seen that TV program *Only Fools and Horses*.' 'Well,' I continued, 'That's what I do. I'm in import/export and drive a three wheeler.' In fact, it was a really easy job being a captain. You never have to do any work at all. The autopilot flies the aeroplane, the co-pilot watches the autopilot, the navigator writes those little notes to the passengers telling them where they were an hour ago, the flight engineer makes sure that the cabin is too cold for anyone to sleep, and the loadmaster sleeps despite the temperature. Oh yes, I have almost forgotten the chappie who works almost as little as the captain. He, of course, is the air steward. All he ever does is make tea for the loadmaster and sometimes helps the captain off the aircraft if his Zimmer frame is broken. That leaves us with the captain. All he has to do is write letters of apology to the boss after the trip. Even then, the really experienced captains have lots of standard letters, thus do not even have to spend much time on this chore. And, to cap it all, they get paid much more money than they can spend.

So how does one get to be a captain? Quite simple, really. Firstly become a co-pilot; all you have to do is to be able to switch on an autopilot (i.e. find the on/off switch). Then you have to bribe a panel of ex-captains with lots of dosh and persuade them that you are worthy of such an incredibly high honour. Finally, you have to buy the flight instructors gallons of beer, promise to always land more firmly than them, and above all listen in awe and hero worship to all their amazing war stories.

Of course, I exaggerate just a little. Very occasionally, a captain has to land the aeroplane when the co-pilot has fallen asleep listening to your war stories. This procedure, of course, is very easy, otherwise the co-pilot would not be able to do it. Even women can do it! All that is required is to wait until the autopilot positions the aeroplane in the right place, pull back on the control column thingy to the count of one-two, and then wait for the crunch. Additionally, but only very rarely, the autopilot has a wobbly. If this coincides with the co-pilot falling asleep, you have to steer the aircraft. If one can see the sky, this is very easy. If not, then wake up the co-pilot and say 'You have control.' If the autopilot is duff and you are in cloud and the co-pilot is unavailable, you are in trouble, big trouble!

Of course, the secret of most things is to cheat. I know a special way of stopping the aircraft from turning upside down in cloud. It goes as follows:

'The Cat and Duck Method of Blind Flying'

Although captains are usually modest, we are forced to admit that we are considered experts on certain phases of instrument flying. Only recently, I have done a considerable amount of research on the 'Cat and Duck' method of blind flying.

You are probably familiar with this 'Cat and Duck' dodge, which sounds like simplicity itself. All it takes is a cat, a duck, and you on an instrument flight. The cat is placed on the cabin floor, because in theory that a cat always remains upright; he or she is used for the flight instruments. Merely watch to see which way the cat leans to determine whether a wing is low. The duck is used for instrument landing. Because a duck will not fly in cloud, all you need to do is throw it out of a window and follow it to the ground.

After several experimental flights, however, I find this system has some serious pitfalls, and the pilot using 'Cat and Duck' for the first time would do well to observe some important rules:

Cats:

1. Get a wide-awake cat. Most cats do not want to stand at all at any time. A large, fierce dog should be carried to keep the cat at attention. It can also be used to bite the co-pilot if he dares to touch the controls.
2. Make sure your cat is clean. Dirty cats will spend all their time washing. Trying to follow a washing cat usually results in a tight snap roll, followed by an inverted spin. You can see this is very unsanitary.
3. Old cats are best. Young cats have nine lives, but an old used-up cat with only one life left has just as much to lose as you have and will be much more dependable.
4. Avoid stray cats. Try to get one with a good pedigree. Your local vet can help you locate a cat with a good character. Or try a breeding farm. Or, if in the city, try any reputable house for cats.

Ducks:

1. Be sure the duck has good eyesight. Near-sighted ducks sometimes fail to realise that they are on the gauges, and will go bogging off into the nearest hill. Very near-sighted ducks will not realise they have been thrown out at all and will descend straight down in a sitting position. This is hard to follow in an aeroplane.
2. Use land-loving ducks. It is very discouraging to break out and find yourself on finals for a farmer's pond, particularly if there are duck hunters around. Duck hunters suffer from temporary insanity when they are sitting freezing in their hides and will shoot at anything that flies.
3. Choose your duck carefully. Many water birds look very much alike, and you may get confused between ducks and geese. Geese are very competent fliers but are seldom interested in going the way you want to go. If your duck heads off to Canada or Mexico, then you know you have been given a goose.
4. Beware of cowardly ducks. If a duck discovers that you are using the cat to stay upright, she will refuse to leave the cat. Ducks are no better on instruments than you are.

So there we have it. As you can see, it is an easy life being a captain. Of course, that really was a stupid statement to make, but made for effect. Part of the task of a captain is to command. I found that to be the hardest part of my job as no matter what I decided, some senior officer would criticise me for it. Sometimes I had to make difficult decisions, like the one I made *en route* to Sardinia one day.

One task I was ordered to do was to fly a Jaguar squadron to Decimomannu in Sardinia for an air weapons detachment, something I had personally done many times whilst serving with No. 6 Squadron at Coltishall. While flying the engineers of the squadron down to Sardinia, the Air Load Master (ALM) popped into the flight deck to report that one of the stewardesses had discovered a fire in the waste bin in the rear toilet. This obviously could have had disastrous consequences, but she reacted calmly and professionally and the fire was quickly extinguished. Apparently, the idiot low-life had decided he could not wait any longer for a cigarette and had entered the rear loo to smoke. Knowing that the smoke alarm would sound, the fool immobilised it. Luckily, the stewardess went in shortly afterwards and discovered the waste bin on fire. I then sent for the Senior Engineering Officer (SENGO) and requested the name of the miscreant. Not surprisingly, a name was not forthcoming. I then let it be known that if I did not get a name before landing, the entire squadron would suffer. Still a name did not arrive and, as we came to a halt after landing, one can imagine the 'think bubbles' in the cabin when three very large black Italian police riot buses pulled up at the aircraft and transported all the passengers away to jail. Needless to say, a name was forthcoming before the buses reached the gates of the air base. Three weeks later, I got the short straw to collect the engineers after the detachment. To my surprise, they were as good as gold, but I realised why when the ALM told me he had informed them all who the nasty aircraft captain was.

I had many incidents of impending disaster while flying the VC10. None were more dangerous that when I flew an apparently innocuous mission to southern Africa.

I had been tasked to fly to Gaborone, the capital of Botswana. I cannot remember exactly why, but I suspect it was to pick up troops who had been on exercise there. Given the limited range of a VC10 (about 5,500 miles), we needed to refuel *en route* and obviously at a friendly airfield. The powers that were decided to save money and arrange a refuelling stop at that tiny island in the South Atlantic: Ascension. Easy for them to decide but less easy for us to plan. For a start, we had to carry what was known as 'island holding fuel' as once there we would have insufficient fuel to divert to any other airfield should Ascension be subject to bad weather or the sole runway blocked by another aircraft. Another problem, which was subsequently going to become a significant hazard, was the total lack of reasonable communications. In short, we would be getting airborne without knowing the weather at our destination. This totally contravened all regulations and was also contrary to all aspects of flight safety. However, it was a necessary evil if we wanted to complete the second leg of our journey.

On that trip in question, we found that little outpost of the British Empire without too much trouble and landed at Ascension late in the afternoon. Early the next morning, we attempted to get a weather report for our destination and were incredibly lucky. Not only did we manage to get a proper met forecast for Gaborone, but also for our main diversion of Johannesburg. It naturally was imperative that we had a cast-iron diversion in case our destination weather was not as advertised. As always, I had to remind myself that the VC10, unlike fighter aircraft, was not equipped with ejector seats. Consequently, the captain of a large passenger airliner needed to be 100 per cent sure he had somewhere he could land. We also obtained a BBC civil forecast for the area as a whole, so I was happy. Though the forecast predicted the usual occasional thunderstorms, we had plenty of fuel to orbit our destination for a couple of hours, thus we were OK.

Anyhow, off we set across the Southern Atlantic bound for Africa and ultimately Botswana. This area was particularly hazardous as no air traffic service or even procedural co-ordination was available. This was purely a 'see and be seen' part of the world. Aircraft were encouraged to transmit 'blind' radio calls so that any other aircraft in the vicinity would be aware if they were on a collision course with the aircraft transmitting. This did not always work and there was at least one mid-air collision about this time between two aeroplanes.

Of course, there was always the high frequency radio (HF). Sadly, many things, including not least sun spot activity, which affected HF! Of course, this day our luck was out and the HF did not work.

Nevertheless, we continued eastwards trusting in fate and God that we would reach Africa and an air traffic service. At last then we would be able to obtain reliable and up to date meteorological reports for our destination and emergency diversion, should we need it.

Eventually we did reach Africa, spoke with ATC and requested an aviation forecast and details of the actual weather. Straight back came the information that Sir Seretse Khama International (Gaborone's airport) was experiencing an exceptionally heavy and violent thunderstorm. When asked how long it was expected to last, we were told 'for the rest of the day!'

As we did not have fuel for waiting until the next day, we requested the weather for our alternative airfield, Johannesburg. Unfortunately, back came the same reply. When asked what Pretoria was like, we were told 'no chance'. Now we had a major problem. No airfield within range had weather suitable for a safe landing. We had no choice but to continue to the nearest airfield (our destination) and have a look. With the ejector seats removed from our aeroplane and anyway I suppose we had to look after our passengers, continuing to an airfield where the weather was duff was the best of a bad job. No landing meant death, simple as that. Fighter pilots invariably and arrogantly consider their task infinitely more dangerous. Of course, they are right—95 per cent of the time—but they always have the opportunity to return to earth by parachute. Even if I had one that day, I doubt if the passengers would have been pleased to spot their captain nonchalantly walking down the aisle towards the back door, donning a parachute at the same time. So it was a landing or nothing, despite the weather being totally unsuitable.

We droned on across deserts and vast expanses of uninhabited territory until eventually we flew into radio contact with Gaborone. We did not like what they told us. Apparently the mother of all thunderstorms was still sitting right over the threshold of the runway in use. No chance then of an approach. Wind shear, that dreaded killer of aeroplanes, would force the VC10 into the ground and there would be little we could do about it. Even with full power, we would still be going down. In short, the air would be descending much faster than we could go up!

No chance of a landing—or was there? I had an idea. Antiquated though the VC10 was, it was equipped with a reliable inertial navigation system. Though ATC were quoting the wind from the southwest at 30 knots, which normally would preclude a landing on the reciprocal runway to that in use, it was worth a look. I briefed the crew that we would monitor the surface wind on the approach and if it exceeded 15 knots of tail wind, we would overshoot and think about our options. This of course was a risky business because it would necessitate flying into the bad weather. However, I calculated that an immediate hard turn to port might just ensure we stayed clear of the thunderstorm. If the wind was less than 15 knots, the navigator calculated that despite touching down at high speed, we would still stop before the end of the long runway—just!

We had to try. We had no other choice. Of course there were risks in this strategy. Big risks. The humungous cumulonimbus cloud could move closer to the centre of the airfield and engulf us as we touched down. Or our inertial navigation system might be inaccurate and we would land with a big tailwind. This would mean our groundspeed was too high and we would not stop before the end of the runway, but we had to try.

But then the angel appeared once more. As we started the approach to the north-easterly runway, with ATC informing us that the wind was very much favouring the reciprocal, the navigator informed us that the wind was actually 180 degrees different to that quoted by Air Traffic. Was their equipment incorrect? Was ours? Or had some divine force merely changed the wind through 180 degrees. It mattered not, we were going for it. As we touched down, with my experienced eye, I could see that the wind indeed considerably favoured the runway we had chosen, not the runway in use.

But the story did not end there. This day, the angel saved not only my life and the lives of all those on board my VC10, but also all crew and passengers on a British Airways Jumbo about to depart for [the] UK. It had been cleared to take-off from the runway in use, the very same runway that allegedly had a 30-knot headwind. With only ATC information to go by, the captain of that aircraft would have attempted an impossible task. His aircraft, heavy with fuel and passengers, would never have reached flying speed and all would have perished. Naturally, on landing, I dropped this bombshell on the poor unsuspecting pilot who wisely decided to pack it in for the night and head back for the hotel. We were accommodated in the same hotel, thus I did not need to buy any beers that night.

28
Winter Adventures

One of the many pleasant aspects of semi-retirement is that one can pick and choose what one does. Now that I am semi-retired, I have awarded myself a 'Blue Card'. In the early days, RAF pilots were awarded a credit size card of an appropriate colour. 'Master Green' was the highest award, unless of course you were a god, namely a command instrument rating examiner (CIRE). Now I merely hold a 'Blue Card' and say each day to myself 'If the colour of this card is the colour of the sky, then I can fly'.

I did not have that luxury when full time. We flew in all weathers. What worried us the most were winter operations. Planes either failed to reach flying speed, with terrible consequences, or, just as bad, failed to stop before the end of the runway. Sometimes they just fell out of the sky. Quite simply put, aeroplanes do not like ice and snow.

So it was on a very chilly morning in North America I learnt more about winter operations. I had been returning from New Mexico in a VC10 with a 'special load' (that is, the one where we had to wear Geiger counter badges, if you get my drift), which necessitated what was known as a 'Military Operating Standards'—that is, we were permitted to take off at 15 tons overweight if it was really operationally necessary. As long as nothing 'went wrong', we were quite safe, and within an hour, we would be down to maximum operating weight.

We arrived at the VC10 to find it lightly covered with hoarfrost, at a temperature of minus 20 degrees centigrade with a brisk northerly wind blowing. No problem; I ordered the de-icer truck and requested that I wanted 100 per cent de-icer fluid at a temperature of 140 degrees Fahrenheit. This would ensure that the light covering of frost would dissipate and the aircraft would stay clear of ice.

Now for those who have never de-iced a 350-ton airliner, here is an explanation. Lift makes the aeroplane fly. Wings produce lift. If a wing is covered with rough ice, the lift is destroyed. No lift, no fly. Consequently, if one does not fly, one goes straight to the scene of the accident without the option of pulling that little yellow and black ejector seat handle that will ensure you live.

To preserve that lift, we remove the ice by applying de-icer. Simple—or is it? Well, unfortunately not. Sadly, de-icer only lasts for a while, is not very environmentally friendly, and is also quite costly. One needs to put sufficient on to solve the problem, but not to break the bank or destroy the local ecology. Hence, the captain decides how much and what percentage of de-icer fluid is mixed with hot water.

On this occasion, I calculated that I needed 100 per cent de-icer fluid and actually watched the chap select only the de-icer tank. Great!

VC10 Bardufoss, Arctic Circle. (*Author's collection*)

On application to the wing surface, great clouds of steam were produced. Great joy! On completion, I was personally satisfied that the hoarfrost had melted, having personally felt the surface of the wing. Now to get airborne. No problem.

However, there was; unknown to the flight deck crew, what had been sprayed on the wings was pure hot water and not, as requested, de-icer fluid. Thus the combination of minus 20 degrees centigrade and a brisk wind ensured that the water rapidly turned to ice. What no one knew was that the de-icer fluid tank had been filled with water by mistake, so both tanks contained only water. Consequently, we were about to attempt a take-off, not just at overload weight, with no margin for safety, but actually some 6 tons over even that limit. We would not have made it and I would not now be writing this story.

Luckily, the gods were on our side that morning and my loadmaster was the proud holder of a Commercial Pilots Licence. He knew that icicles hanging from the trailing edge of the wing was a sure recipe for disaster and informed me of this fact. So we lived to fight another day!

Actually, I rather liked those 'special' hot load missions, which we hauled to New Mexico for the Atomic Weapons Research Establishment (AWRE). We often then flew up to Nellis Air Force Base in southern Nevada. You may recall that in an earlier life, I had operated from there flying the Jaguar. It was also quite an interesting experience sampling the bright lights of downtown Las Vegas where we stayed. I do not believe I ever had to purchase any food, but then again, I never won a fortune on the tables. The highlight of the entire trip was of course 'The Canyon Tour'. In the late '80s, it was permissible to call Las Vegas ATC to request a tour of the Grand Canyon. Needless to say, this was very busy airspace, full of puddle-jumpers flying tourists up and down the canyon, so permission was necessary to avoid a mid-air collision. Whenever we called, I am sure ATC were unaware that we were hardly a 'puddle-jumper'. Due to the size of my four-engined airliner, I never had the courage to venture down deep into the Grand Canyon, but it was a very spectacular tour for the crew nevertheless. Sadly, nothing like that is now allowed and tours of the Grand Canyon are highly regulated. Quite right, too.

Should I say that we lived to experience yet another near disaster? On one trip returning to Dulles International Airport, Washington DC, from Belize, we very nearly made world news. The weather in the Caribbean was, as usual, very beautiful. We had earlier that day departed DC for the usual run down the American East Coast, round Cuba and into Belize to rotate the British Garrison there. After a sweltering three hours on the ground, we took off for Dulles. The forecast was not good with low cloud and drizzle all along the East Coast from Charleston to New York, but it was good enough. I had enough fuel for the trip, a couple of approaches at Dulles Airport, plus a diversion to Boston if necessary, so all was well.

The trip went to plan and we arrived overhead Washington bang on time. Dulles airport were giving very low cloud and poor visibility, but it would be legal for our approach. We flew down the electronic glide path in thick cloud, purely 'on the dials'. It was certainly a dark, dismal, bumpy night, and we were all looking forward to a wind-down beer and some sleep. At about 1,000 feet, we were cleared to land and I expected no further problems. The cloud base was reported at 200 feet, so again we were still legal. As per the procedure in very poor conditions, the co-pilot flew the approach as I peered into the inky blackness to pick up the lead-in lights to the runway. If I could not see the runway at 200 feet, I would order a 'go-around', the co-pilot would overshoot and we would have another go. If I saw the runway, I would take over and land. We had just sufficient fuel for just one more attempt, then we would have to divert to an airport to the north where the weather was much better.

The co-pilot called '200 above', giving me warning that we were now just 200 feet above my decision height, then he later called '100 above'. At 200 feet above ground, he called 'Decide'. We broke cloud and I could see the runway lights twinkling in the mist. Sufficient for me to land safely. I called 'Landing', signifying I had control, could see the runway, and was going to land visually.

Then, almost immediately, I spotted something on the runway. Another aeroplane—a fucking big aeroplane—right on the spot where I needed to touch down. I immediately hauled back on the controls and slammed all the throttles wide open. Four mighty Conway engines burst into full power and we shot back up into the cloud. We must have given the passengers and indeed the crew in the aeroplane on the runway a huge fright as they heard our noise, but I think our own hearts were also pounding at that stage. We had very nearly landed right on top of what we later were told was a huge Jumbo Jet carrying 400-plus passengers. The death toll would have been in the region of 550 and we would have of course made international headlines. Not that I would have been around to read them. My radio call to the tower that night was rather interesting, hopefully polite.

ATC gave us priority for our next approach as we were by now running very short of fuel. Later, we were told that the Boeing 747 had been given permission to take-off, but had delayed his roll to investigate a technical problem. His cardinal sin was not to tell ATC, and as they could not see him in the murk and dark, they assumed he had departed Dulles Airport. Hence my permission to land; right on top of him!

We later enjoyed our beer that night. Flying fighter planes can be hazardous; the same could be said for airliners. Lucky such incidents happened only very rarely.

29

Rules and Regulations

Of course, RAF peacetime flying, especially in a large airliner with a plethora of passengers, is necessarily governed by a variety of rules and regulations. For example, a necessary one governs the consumption of alcohol before a flight. Even stricter than the UK limit for drink driving, crewmembers were not allowed to drink any alcohol within ten hours of flying (bottle to throttle) and even then, consumption had to be moderate within twenty-four hours of flying.

Crew fatigue was also regulated. RAF crews were constrained to just sixteen hours on duty, which actually was quite a long time when operating at high workload or in adverse weather and especially at high temperatures.

Sometimes, however, a captain had to use his discretion and turn a blind eye to the regulations. A very good example of this was when I was rostered to fly to West Africa to recover three badly injured SAS soldiers. This at face value seemed to be a simple task and I was very experienced in casualty evacuation missions. We set off from the UK with a full complement of doctors and nurses, together with all the medical equipment they would need for the long flight back to Blighty. This included a full operating theatre.

After a lengthy flight to Banjul in The Gambia, we landed in bright sunshine in the middle of the day, tired but looking forward to a rest in a local hotel. After dispatching our medical team to the hospital, where apparently our three SAS were, we set about bedding down our VC10 for the night. Before that, however, we were mandated to pay our landing fees, naturally in US dollars. Before I had even finished the aircraft shutdown checks, a local official arrived uninvited on the flight deck, demanding cash for the landing. That in itself was not a problem, but when he demanded that we pay $5,000 for use of the landing lights, I became annoyed. The landing had been performed in bright sunshine in daylight and more importantly the landing lights were not only inoperative, but were stated in NOTAMs (Notices to Airmen) that they had been broken for many months. However, given that this local gentleman was waving a gun in my direction, prudence dictated that we should pay him.

Worse was to come. Before we were able to vacate our aeroplane, I received a telephone call from the senior doctor to say that our three patients were not only in a very bad way, but given the filthy hospital conditions and total lack of facilities, it was quite likely that they would die before we had completed our necessary crew rest.

So, despite the fact that we all had not only been on duty for some fourteen hours, the temperature was in excess of 40 degrees centigrade, and the flight back to the UK would mean that we would have been on duty for some thirty hours, I agreed to return to the UK without crew rest. I knew that as the lives of our patients depended on it, my crew would agree and they did. However, the story did not end there.

It took our medical team several hours to stabilise the patients and get them to the airfield. I cannot actually remember the planned flight time back to the UK, but unfortunately due to the severity of the patients' injuries, I was informed by the medical team that cabin altitude had to be kept at sea level throughout the flight. That meant that we could not fly above 20,000 feet and thus our return trip would be at least two hours longer than scheduled.

During the flight, one of our patients died, but due to the skill of our medical team, was resuscitated.

Then, after a very lengthy flight back to the UK, we were then confronted with the harsh reality that our destination, RAF Brize Norton, was out in fog. Nevertheless, after a few lengthy phone calls to various hospitals, Manchester Royal Infirmary accepted our patients. Actually that was an interesting phone call. The doctor at the hospital was not quite sure where in the UK 'Abeam Gibraltar' was, and I took a while to explain that I was not calling from an ambulance halfway up the M6. We eventually landed at Manchester Airport some thirty hours after departing the UK. To say we were tired is perhaps an understatement.

Even then, we had a confrontation with Her Majesty's customs, who insisted that no one was to leave the aircraft before it had been comprehensively searched for drugs. However, once I pointed out to the senior customs officer the carnage down the back of the VC10, he realised that he too had to waive a few regulations that day in order to save a few lives.

Subsequently, I heard that two of the three soldiers recovered, thus justifying us breaking the rules on that flight that day.

Understandably, I declined the instruction to fly back to Brize Norton when the fog had cleared and thus we headed for the nearest hotel.

Another very long flight occurred just one month later. Once again, we were tasked with transporting SAS soldiers, though this time they would be fully fit and definitely well-armed.

After a very busy day in the office, I drove home and settled down to relax in the evening. Later, when just turning in for the night, I got a call about midnight. 'Be prepared for a very long flight' I was told. I replied that I was about to go to bed and enquired about crew duty regulations. After a very long day, I was already rather tired. I was told in no uncertain terms that there was only one rule applicable to this mission: there were no rules. However, I could sleep in flight as I would be augmented by a second crew.

So I hurriedly gathered some clothes together and arrived at Base Operations within thirty minutes. I should not have rushed, as diplomatic clearance for our flight was less straightforward to obtain than finding a double crew. Even then, the duty officer at the Foreign Office failed to obtain all that was necessary.

It appeared that the task would involve a very long mission, perhaps as long as thirty-six hours, but on this occasion we were forewarned, and just like our passengers, forearmed. Consequently, my team would consist of two full crews and I was nominated as mission commander. My team would fly the aircraft to the destination (which we would only be informed of an hour before departure), and the other crew was to fly the aeroplane back to a safe haven not too far from the danger zone to await the outcome of the Special Force's risky operation. The second crew could sleep on the long journey to our destination.

I was then personally briefed by the Intelligence Officer that British Embassy staff in the capital of Colombia had been captured by terrorists. Our mission was to get the SAS to Bogota, in secrecy in the shortest possible time, wait close to Colombia, then bring the hostages and SAS back to the UK. Obviously, the fast military VC10 was the right solution.

By the time the majority of the essential clearances had been received, the Hereford Hooligans had arrived together with a substantial amount of equipment. Additionally, the route was decided (straight line across the Atlantic Ocean via Lajes Field in the Azores) and by then the rest of my crew had arrived looking rather bleary eyed, together with the second crew, equally comatose. As previously mentioned, due to seniority, I was nominated mission commander, and as it seemed impossible to fly direct to Bogota without sensible fuel reserves, I decided to nominate the second crew to fly the first outbound leg of the mission to Lajes to refuel. After a quick turn round, my own crew would then take the VC10 into Bogota International and then back to our parking slot in Puerto Rico, while the second crew slept. From there, when instructed, we would return to Colombia, collect our passengers, and then would all proceed home via a military base in Florida and RAF Goose Bay in Labrador.

All went well on the first leg and, personally, I had hoped to get a little sleep as many of the seats had been removed and replaced with camp beds. However, once airborne in the small hours, I had to resolve a conflict between my air loadmaster and the macho SAS team. They would not part with their plethora of guns, toys, and explosive devices, and my ALM insisted on regulations pertaining to such items in flight. I eventually sorted it all out and the SAS won. Most of us then snoozed on the long haul down to Lajes Field, though I noticed that most of the SAS team spent the time cleaning and adjusting their weapons. Do they not ever sleep?

After a quick refuel in the dead of night, we subsequently departed Lajes Field with myself at the helm and set course for South America. Everything was fine until we passed close to Cuba, a country that had not granted us diplomatic clearance. Though we were slightly unsure of the strength of their air force, and as we were an unarmed airliner, we chose to fly by that country without radio communications with their air traffic control. That was risky business as I judged an argument with Cuba over our lack of diplomatic clearance would possibly provoke a scramble of their rather obsolete fighter aircraft, or worse still, a missile launch. Good night VC10! But the job had to be done. In the event, we sailed past unnoticed in the pitch dark. Perhaps their fighter controllers were fast asleep. Either way, we got away with it, but a more serious threat awaited us.

Initially, there followed a pleasant and rather uneventful flight over the Caribbean Sea, leading to a landfall at Puerto Escondido, then a quiet leg down to El Dorado International Airport itself. Now, unfortunately, El Dorado is surrounded by very high mountains and is itself 8,361 feet above sea level. Given the many black clouds that sit on the mountains in that area, an approach is always fraught with danger, particularly so if the weather is worse than normal.

As luck would have it, the weather that day was worse than usual. Typical! However, despite the high altitude of the airfield and thus a significant lack of thrust from our four mighty Conway engines, an instrument approach would see us OK. Notwithstanding the fact that we would be in cloud for the majority of the approach, I had every confidence in my crew. However, I noticed that the other captain could not sleep and had perched himself on the flight deck jump seat for the approach. If we were going to die, he wanted to be the first to know about it.

We made radio contact with El Dorado control, which vectored us towards the airfield. It was just as well that we could not see the high peaks around us due to the bad weather. Moreover, it was extremely turbulent and there were occasional flashes of forked lightning, but we pressed on.

After a while, we received the very welcome radio call from air traffic to tell us that we were cleared down to 10,000 feet and also direct to the Bogota beacon. Good, I thought, that would save time and I pressed the appropriate buttons on the autopilot. We started our descent and turned for the airfield.

Suddenly, the navigator awoke from his slumber. 'Where are you going,' he asked. 'Oh buck up, Nav,' I replied as I levelled the aeroplane at 10,000 feet. 'Direct to the beacon.' 'Oh,' he said. 'Are you aware that there is a mountain in the way that goes up to 11,500 feet? Make sure you stay above 14,000.' Gulp; best I climb, and climb quickly I thought!

Which was just as well as, after we landed safely, we later heard on the news that the aircraft that was behind us for landing was given the same instructions. Sadly, his navigator slept through the resulting crash. You see, some clouds have very hard centres!

We discharged our cargo and breathed a big sigh of relief. However, it occurred to me that we still were not even halfway. We had to return and do it all again. Nevertheless, was it going to be 'once bitten, twice shy?' In the event, we said goodbye to the Special Forces and returned to Puerto Rico to await further instructions. Of course, we encountered strong crosswinds on the approach (never pleasant when the operating pilot is exhausted) and a 50-mile drive to our hotel, but by then we had grown used to bad news. On arrival at our accommodation (I will not flatter it too much by calling it a hotel), I checked in with the MOD in London to find that for us the war was over. The operation was not going very well in Bogota and we were to return, via the USA and Canada, to RAF Brize Norton. I am not sure what the result of our adventure was, but suffice to say we got home just a little tired.

Most of the time, life for us on the 'Shiny Fleet', as we were sometimes called it in the early days, was a life of luxury. We often stayed in five-star hotels and this earned us a bad reputation. Nonetheless, it was imperative that we were accommodated with our passengers, though for several reasons, we would rather not have done so. However, as the co-pilot was responsible for payment of all bills, it was imperative that we all stayed in the same hotel. This meant we often needed accommodation with at least 100 spare rooms and only the larger hotels could guarantee that number. Moreover, I as captain needed each and every one of my crew to stay safe. If anyone was hospitalised through mugging, we went nowhere. That resulted in extra nights at the hotel, so it was obviously far cheaper to stay in a larger better-quality hotel that offered security.

Yet sometimes there was no accommodation and we either slept on the aeroplane or extended the crew duty day, thus breaking our own rules yet again.

One such trip was the previously mentioned mission to West Africa. We had planned to stay there overnight, but for reasons previously mentioned, that was not possible. We also made several trips to West Africa, none more interesting than those to Sierra Leone during its civil war. As this was a war mission (the rebels were armed with surface-to-air missiles), we declined the suggestion that we sleep on the aeroplane and ensured we had sufficient fuel to make it back to our staging post of Dacca in Senegal. Not that we were at all bothered with the surface-to-air missile threat as our procedures negated most of that threat. Malaria was the big enemy.

Unfortunately, the particular strain of malaria in West Africa was most unpleasant and almost always led to death. Moreover, as we were unable to operate our flying machinery and at the same time take the approved prophylactic drugs as they produced hallucinogenic reactions (hardly a good thing when flying an aeroplane), we wore special flying suits soaked in a certain chemical and we stayed in the aircraft for most of the time we were on the ground. That produced other problems as the temperature on the flight deck often reached 50 degrees centigrade. But perspiration inside our anti-mosquito suits was infinitively preferable to dying of malaria. Unfortunately, death by malaria or being shot down by rebel surface-to-air missiles were not the only problems. Communication with Sierra Leone was, at best, poor. Consequently, we often took off not knowing what the weather would be like at Freetown's international airport. It was situated on the coast and subject to fog and sudden wind changes. Often we touched down with a slight tailwind. Now this would not be a problem at London Heathrow, but on a short runway, barely long enough for us to stop with a headwind, we had problems. While I was there, I witnessed at least one airliner, smaller than a VC10, burn out its brakes, catch fire, and block the only runway.

There were many 'minor' incidents that occurred during my time with 10 Squadron. Seventeen years of global flying, often to third world countries with few facilities and often in bad weather, at night would surely have produced a few adventures.

One such minor incident occurred in Alaska in early 1998. During our stopover, we experienced an earthquake of magnitude 6.9 on the Richter Scale. This was no minor tremor. Not that the co-pilot even noticed as he was prone to the shakes early morning. I too was shaving at the time when the image in the mirror went rather blurred. Strange, as the previous evening I had only drunk a couple of small beers. However, once I descended to the lobby, the talk was all about the 'quake. Buildings had fallen down in the city, but luckily our earthquake-proof modern hotel suffered little damage. However, given that this was the first earthquake I had ever experienced, it was somewhat alarming.

More problems were to await us at the airport, though nothing to do with the earthquake. We had planned to fly direct to the UK from Alaska, but were going to be rather short of fuel—it is rather a long way. However, we would have an opportunity to refuel in Iceland if necessary. In the event, we only got as far as our hotel. Circumnavigating the globe is child's play when it comes to circumnavigating some of America's huge airfields. The problem was that the RAF in its wisdom did not see fit to equip us with the necessary charts to find our way around all airfields, especially at some American Air Force bases. Such charts were expensive. On this particular occasion, we started up and called for taxi clearance. No reply from Air Traffic. This was not unusual at a large airport, as radio reception was often compromised by large buildings. So I elected to move forward some hundred yards to facilitate good communications. That was achieved and we received our taxi clearance.

We followed the instructions to the letter, but eventually came to a dead end on the taxiway.

Bugger, now what do we do? We could not turn round as the taxiway is a mere 50 feet wide and we needed three times that. We could not reverse—airliners normally cannot do that—so the only solution was to request a tug to push us back the half mile to the main taxiway. Trouble was, no tug was available! We were stuck until one could be delivered from a nearby civilian airport. That would take at least a day and our crew duty would have expired by then. So it was back to the hotel while the engineers sorted that one out. The passengers were not amused! Whoever decided not to issue us with the appropriate charts, just to save a few shekels, never got to see my enormous hotel bill.

Our flight the next day was rather uneventful and the passengers did not seem to be too rebellious. After all, they had had rather a good night in the bar at Her Majesty's expense. Our return voyage took us way north over the Arctic Circle, past majestic Mount McKinley, down over the vast Greenland ice cap, through a night when the sun never set, down to the Iceland Sea, then onwards to Blighty.

So what went wrong at that American Air Force base? Well it seems that Air Traffic assumed we were still in the original parking place, so their instructions started from that original spot. Sadly, their directions thus included on extra turn left, which led us down to the dead end. Of course, it was my fault. It is always the fault of the captain. The buck stops with him. That resulted in yet another trip to the boss's officer with my hat on and a metaphorical copy of the telephone directory down my trousers.

Life was not all major problems, though sometimes it seemed like that. As I progressed up the seniority ladder, from lowly co-pilot, through instructor, route-checker, and eventually the dizzy heights of senior training captain, life became a little easier and most of the initial prejudice I had experience by virtue of the fact that I was an alien fighter pilot seemed to dissipate and respect for my ability grew. Sadly, though, the days of the mighty VC10 were numbered. It was beginning to become very costly to maintain and spares were becoming difficult to find. Any VC10 in the main maintenance hangar became a donor for short-term spare parts and was affectionately called 'the Christmas tree', in RAF speak.

Later, the numbers of students moving through the OCU (Operational Conversion Unit) diminished and the highlight of the course, the Global Trainer, was very sadly abolished. Luckily, previously on the squadron, as senior training captain, I had still been able to plan these wonderful 'holiday' trips. But all good things come to an end and they, too, along with the OCU 'jollys', were abolished. However, I was granted one last 'swan song' and set about planning the grand finale.

Using the British Airways holiday guide, I planned the trip of a lifetime, never to be seen ever again. Let us face it, modern airlines do the majority of their training in the simulator, so the very prospect of a 'Global'—i.e. a trip right around the globe with a couple of crews under training—was not exactly cost-effective or cheap, especially as aircraft manned by crews under training were not allowed to carry passengers.

My RAF pilot logbook for March 1992 shows that I flew Brize–Akrotiri–Bahrain–Colombo–Singapore–Hong Kong–Surabaya–Singapore–Bahrain. Prior to departure, my station commander asked if I would take one of his chums, a retiring Army colonel, and his wife with us to Hong Kong. Though we were not allowed to take passengers, by making the colonel and his wife 'crew', no rules were broken.

When we landed at our second stop, where we had planned to stay the night, the colonel was surprised to be asked what he and his good lady wife would like to eat the following day. When told that we were staying the night in Bahrain, and would do so also in Singapore, he was amazed, but not displeased. He had naïvely expected to fly direct to Hong Kong. In fact, when we eventually arrived in Hong Kong, at the old Kai Tak airport (now there is a story), he and his wife had enjoyed the odyssey so much he asked me if he could stay with us all the way back to Brize Norton. That wish was granted, and when we finally touched down on English soil, he and his wife promptly ordered a taxi to take them to Heathrow to catch the next flight back out to Hong Kong to resume his holiday. Such was the fun of those 'Globals' that they had stayed with us for the duration, despite the cost in time and money.

approach in the dead of night, not only without airfield lighting, but also without using our landing lights. However, by judicious use of our Inertial Navigation (IN) systems, we were able to find the runway and perform a reasonably smooth touchdown, turning our landing lights on at the very last minute of the approach.

Actually, the problem of landing an airliner at night at a desert airfield, without landing aids or lighting of any sort, paled into insignificance when we were confronted with what our American friends threw at us. The dreaded 'blue on blue' problem. Unfortunately, as already stated, we were scheduled to arrive pre-dawn, which regrettably coincided with what later became known as the 'Scud shower'. As we overflew the mighty Dhahran Air Base, the Scud shower invariably began. These Soviet-built ground-to-ground missiles posed a significant threat to the coalition forces and were naturally aimed by Iraqi forces at large targets. Dhahran Air Base was just that, a very nice juicy and large target for the fairly inaccurate Iraqi missiles. Fortunately for the personnel on the base, extremely sophisticated anti-missile defences were in place in the form of the advanced Patriot missile defence system.

Regrettably, on a least two occasions, my crew and I were on the receiving end of such potent American firepower. After a fairly quiet and sleepy flight from our base in the UK, as we reached the Arabian peninsula, things hotted up. Sensibly, all civil air traffic had been banned, obviously for their own safety, but did anyone care about the safety of us in our rather elderly and defenceless airliner?

Having satisfied the plethora of rules, regulations, and complex procedures to ingress the Coalition Air Defence Zone, we ploughed on with trepidation. As I personally had come from an offensive background, namely strike/attack fighters, I was well tuned to offensive operations and the makings thereof. Not so my young female stewardess who was not long out of school. Her eyes were larger than my tummy.

As we approached overhead, the target of Saddam's missile attack, Dhahran (now called Dammam to avoid confusion with a city of the same name in the west of Saudi Arabia), the Scud missiles arrived *en masse*. The US response was immediate, potent, and effective and several Patriot missiles were launched in defence. Sadly for us, we presented a larger and vulnerable target than a Scud. Other military aircraft in the warzone possessed a defence against this form of 'blue on blue' in the shape of a specific IFF (Identification Friend or Foe) system. Though the VC10 was indeed equipped with IFF, our 1960s equipment did not contain the all-important Mode 4, necessary to alert the automatic tracking mechanism of a Patriot missile that we were indeed friendly. Hence we were a sitting duck and at least one of these huge missiles locked on to our aeroplane.

We watched this huge missile spiralling up towards us, its rear end emitting a red-hot plume. We had minutes to live! My co-pilot froze, but a frantic radio call from me to the American air traffic control seemed to do the trick. Some 1,000 or so feet below us, the deadly missile exploded in mid-air. We felt nothing other than a slight bump, no more than a little clear air turbulence, and we all expelled a sigh of relief. Yet another reason that day to fill in our laundry list.

On one occasion, we almost blew our own trusty VC10 to pieces. Fighter planes often carry missiles. Attached to each missile is a safety pin designed to ensure that the ordinance does not fire or explode before it leaves the aeroplane. Attached to the pin is a red flag with the words 'remove before flight' printed on it. Immediately before take-off, the fighter aircraft's ground crew remove the pins. On one occasion, I flew some 600 air-to-air missiles to the battlefront. Immediately after take-off, the air loadmaster came onto the flight deck and asked what he should do with all these safety pins. He had actually removed them before flight! Well that is what it said on the tin, so that is what he did! Unfortunately, the missiles were now live and due to certain conditions being met, might explode. I stopped the climb and ordered him to put the safety pins back in, very quickly! I then ordered a cup of tea and a rag to mop my fevered brow.

Yet it was not all excitement. VC10 crews were often billeted at RAF Akrotiri on the island of Cyprus in the eastern Mediterranean—a base I knew well from my early days. Here we were able to unwind and imbibe of a few pints of the local beer. Unfortunately, we got little sleep, as our wooden hut was situated not far from the extremely active runway. Akrotiri became the busiest RAF airfield in history and heavily laden transport aircraft, fighter jets, and refuelling tankers would take-off every few minutes around the clock. Sleep was impossible, unless of course one had taken a few sleeping pills. For myself, and definitely a few others, we preferred that well-known sleeping draught, namely KEO beer. I am not sure if we would have passed the UK breathalyser before flying, but at least we got some sleep. Well, I say 'some', as often our little hut was full and a few aircrew were forced to sleep on the veranda or indeed in the bushes outside the hut. No problem for them after a few glasses of sleeping draught! Still, that was so much better than a tent in the desert. That was the only accommodation available if we were tasked to fly to Oman. As Thumrait was rather too far to complete the task and return home in a day, we slept fifty to a tent—men and woman and a few nasty camel spiders. Camel spiders are not deadly to humans (though their bite is very painful), but they are vicious predators that can visit death upon insects, rodents, lizards, and small birds. They were just one of the hazards of the Gulf War. Consequently, we tried very hard to return to Akrotiri, the noise, and KEO rather than subject ourselves to tents, camel spiders, and, oh, I forgot, no beer in Oman. So sometimes our working day was rather protracted.

But lack of sleep was not the only problem we encountered. Long working days were the indeed the norm. An airline pilot's duty day can be as short as twelve hours. That means, from reporting for duty to getting in the crew bus to go to the hotel must not exceed twelve hours. RAF rules before the Gulf War allowed crews to stay on duty for sixteen hours, 30 per cent more. During times of conflict, crews could operate for up to twenty-one hours and more if necessary.

Consequently, our mission planners, faced with impossible tasks, planned us for the maximum. Their planning assumed that everything went smoothly, but in war, it never does. We captains of aircraft were thus left with a dilemma: if we reached our operational destination late we would certainly exceed our twenty-one-hour limit on the return journey. Naturally, we could not stop in flight on the way home—i.e. pull into a lay-by for ten minutes of shuteye—but conversely it would be very dangerous to stop at our operational destination. For a start, there was no room to park our aeroplane and often we operated a cab rank system for fuel, sometimes being number twenty in the queue. Moreover, apart from a slit trench by the side of the runway, there was absolutely no accommodation, not even a tent infested with camel spiders. Additionally, our VC10 was desperately needed back at base to be turned around for yet another operational flight. Those VC10s hardly ever stopped flying and RAF Brize Norton set records for the number of flying hours achieved in a period. Finally, each and every one of us would rather break crew duty regulations and fly home than camp at President Saddam's main target for his Scud missiles. Hence we sometimes lied about the crew duty timings so that we could avoid the hazards of the desert in a warzone.

One other way we got round the long crew duty days was to fly faster. The VC10's normal peacetime cruising speed was 0.84 Mach (84 per cent the speed of sound), normally about 350 mph depending on the aircraft's altitude. The maximum speed allowed was 0.866 Mach above 32,500 feet. We flight instructors were allowed to take the VC10 up to 0.96 Mach purely for demonstration purposes during initial training flights. This was merely to show our embryonic student pilots the dangers of flying too close to the sound barrier. In truth, the VC10 was relatively benign even at and beyond the speed of sound, though one false move and I suspect that the elderly tail would fall off due to years of corrosion hidden inside. After all, one would never purchase a 1920s Bentley, then drive it all day flat out. Well, not for long anyway.

One dark night, two instructors (me being one of them) got airborne from different UK bases to fly their cargo of high explosive to the Kuwaiti border. Independently, we both had decided to fly at the maximum permissible speed (for instructors) to ensure we would be able to return to the UK within the crew duty day. I listened to my colleague chatting to French air traffic control and calculated that he would arrive before us at Al Jubayl. This would mean that we would be further down the queue for fuel and, thus, as the VC10 needed some 20,000 gallons for a top up, it would result in a significant delay.

Nothing for it then but to fly just that bit faster than my friend. We won the race. On arrival at Al Jubayl, he queried my cruising speed. I replied 0.96. When he raised his eyebrows, my navigator chipped in with the comment, 'Oh, we climbed above the recommended cruising altitude and found a fantastic tail wind.' My fellow VC10 captain then turned to his navigator and criticised the poor fellow for not doing the same as we had done.

None of us were interested in spending a night in a slit trench, well within range of Saddam's missiles, so some of us came up with a plan to effect a safe take-off even if an engine refused to start. There was already a standard operating procedure to allow a take-off if one engine refused to start, but understandably the caveats for that were rather restrictive. A long runway, no passengers, weight, and weather restrictions were just a few. Even then, the crew had to be specially trained and adopt a technically demanding procedure.

One of the problems of getting airborne with one engine inoperative was that rudder authority was insufficient to keep the aircraft straight on the runway. With one engine out, the aircraft was subjected to asymmetric power and would naturally turn towards the dead engine. By use of the special procedure, in some circumstances, a safe departure would be possible.

Part of this procedure would be to start the take-off roll using only the two engines that produced symmetrical thrust. Later in the take-off, when sufficient airspeed had been reached for the rudder to become effective, it would be possible to increase power on the third engine. I suggested that if the aircraft was light enough, take-off would even be possible using just two of the four engines. Of course, one would only try this if the enemy were at the gates of the airfield.

Another potential problem we encountered was later to be called 'Gulf War Syndrome (GWS)' otherwise known as 'Desert Storm Diseases' or simply 'Gulf War Veterans' Illnesses'. This is a collection of symptoms reported by veterans following the First Gulf War. While I was never exposed to nerve gas or other toxins (well not to my knowledge anyway), I was injected with a plethora of drugs. I have already mentioned the taking of 'uppers and downers', drugs to send me to sleep or to keep me awake, but I also received several inoculations, some of which I believe were not fully tested. More importantly, I very much doubt the cocktail of drugs were tested together to discover the combined interaction within the human body.

Troops sent to the Gulf were given a large cocktail of vaccinations in a short period of time. In total, I received as many as seven different vaccines, including live vaccines (polio and yellow fever) as well as experimental vaccines that had not been approved (anthrax, botulinum toxoid) and were of doubtful efficacy. In the UK, the MOD has declared only ten vaccines given, but reports from veterans and official documents seem to tell a different story. A large 2002 study of 900 veterans found a strong correlation between the anthrax vaccine and subsequent ill health. The study indicated that those who received anthrax vaccines reported more adverse reactions than those who did not receive the anthrax vaccine.

Now, in 2018, I suffer many of the symptoms mentioned in the many medical studies of GWS. Tinnitus, arthritis, muscle pains, skin disorders, insomnia, and short-term memory loss. Though none of these symptoms are life-threatening or incredibly serious and could be put down to just the process of growing old, they are nonetheless rather a pain.

That said, our trusty VC10 was relatively quiet, cool, and comfortable. Unlike my old fighter colleagues, we could take some rest in flight. Moreover, we were well fed, unlike many of the other combatants in the Gulf living on hard rations.

We invariably stocked up on little luxuries before the flight and I distinctly remember one air loadmaster buying strawberries and cream from the NAAFI before flight. On arrival at Al Jubayl, close to the forward edge of the battle area, we totally ignored any threat of incoming Scuds and laid the crew table with a gingham tablecloth and proper cutlery. We then invited the crew of the USAF transport aircraft, which had parked next to us, to afternoon tea—cucumber sandwiches and strawberries and cream, served beautifully by a couple of our air stewardesses. Given that the American crew were living off 'meals ready to eat', long-life rations at their very worst, you can imagine their faces when they sat down to dine. We, of course, explained that this was quite normal for Brits to go to war in this way—there are standards!

Following the war, Charles Allen wrote a definitive book on the subject. In the index at the rear of the book is a list of participants. It goes like this:

Saddam Hussein—President
Schwarzkopf, Norman—General
Sharp, Derek—Squadron Leader

Fame at last!

31

New Tricks:
Air Tanker Blues

When I first joined 10 Squadron, it was a purely strategic transport squadron, very much an airline. We wore uniforms and only flew to lovely big airfields. Our catering from foreign airports was the same as British Airways, though the in-flight catering from RAF Brize Norton was also fine. We carried suitcases and rode in taxis to glitzy hotels. We were even given a modest allowance to tip hotel porters, do our laundry and eat well down town.

With the advent of war, that all changed. We needed to be multi-role. There already was a sister squadron at Brize, 101 Squadron, who were more military. In fact, their main task was air-to-air refuelling (AAR)—a black art to most 'truck-drivers'. So, eventually, our transport VC10 C1 aircraft were also all modified to be able to dispense fuel to other aircraft and refuel ourselves. That was no small modification. Our role now had changed. We still flew passengers to nice places, but we also had to do our share of in-flight refuelling of fighter aircraft. Additionally, given our take-off weight restriction at small airfields, we would sometimes have to refuel ourselves from a 'buddy' VC10 tanker. This required new skills to be learnt.

Consequently, all crews had to be retrained. We would now have to learn the plethora of rules, regulations, and disciplines of the black art of AAR. In theory, I should have taken this like a duck to water. After all, all it entailed was flying along, trailing our hoses and watching while my old fighter mates plugged in and took on fuel. In theory that was simple, but given that we often had to control a sizeable number of impatient fighter aircraft, the task became complicated and crews needed above average situational awareness.

I had done the plugging in bit before in the Jaguar, so thought it would it be like learning old tricks—not a bit of it. For a start, one had to fly in formation. Now I was good at that, very good, but only in little aeroplanes like the Jaguar that were light and responsive. Moreover, the view from my plush VC10 armchair was significantly poorer than that from my Jaguar ejection seat. Flying the VC10 in formation, with its unresponsive controls and enormous inertia, was akin to trying to formate on a F1 racing car while driving a 60-ton articulated lorry. What made matters worse was that I had to operate the throttles (something the flight engineer normally did) and thus had to fly the VC10 one-handed. That was not a problem in the Jaguar as it had a little stick, but the VC10, like all airliners, had a huge yoke—i.e. spectacles—thus one always had the moment arm of the control column to overcome. Yet it was the very inertia of 'the beast' that posed the biggest problem. A pilot had to anticipate a rate of change and make corrections as soon as possible as the effect of his input was seriously delayed. In short, flying the VC10 in formation was difficult, and if you thought that difficult in broad daylight, try it in the middle of a black cloud, late at night. Part of our task was to escort my previous colleagues to exercises on the American continent. Though, as previously suggested, the fast jets had the harder task and at least I could pop down the back for a comfort break, I sometimes had to formate on other tanker aircraft, in all weathers, day and night, to top up my fuel prior to giving it away.

Planning for that detachment to the other side of the world was relatively easy and not done by my crew. Moreover, it was well orchestrated; it needed to be as there are no diversion airfields mid-Atlantic if errors were made by tanker or 'chick'. However, managing over thirty fighter jets over enemy territory was always a planning nightmare and that required much mental agility. This was where I, in my middle age, failed to do well. Luckily, I had a good team around me who carried me through the more difficult parts.

Between Gulf Wars, we, along with other NATO forces, maintained a presence in Turkey at the Incirlik airbase. Our mission was to protect the Kurds from Saddam Husain's air force. Regularly, we would launch with two VC10 tanker aircraft and dozens of attack or reconnaissance aircraft. Managing that Balbo took skill. It also was not without risk. Over Iraq, we were within range of surface-to-air missiles. To provide us with minimal protection, we planned to fly higher than the range of their anti-aircraft guns. Unfortunately, we could not fly higher than what would be a suitable height for the fighters to refuel at, but we were told that 20,000 feet would be safe, as shells would only reach 18,000 feet. I then pointed out to our senior planners that the ground height over which we were flying was at least

VC10 air-to-air refueling with Tornados. (*Author's collection*)

10,000 feet and thus we were well within range of the enemy guns. Luckily, I was not shot down, otherwise this book would not have been written—well, at least I would have had to write it without my toenails.

Today, tanker aircraft are fitted with very sophisticated computers to control the Balbo, but back in my day, we had to use our brains. Yes, we had specific procedures to prevent the 'chicks' from bumping into each other as they arrived and departed. Worse still was the possibility of a fighter bumping into us. It did happen once when a Buccaneer collided with a Victor tanker aircraft of 57 Squadron on 24 March 1975 while refuelling. The Buccaneer struck the Victor tanker's tailplane causing the tanker to pitch nose down beyond the vertical, and out of control. Only one crewmember managed to escape using his ejector seat. The VC10 had no such escape mechanism. Consequently, due to the inherent hazards of this procedure, comprehensive management and control were important; however, I did witness a few near disasters in my time as a tanker pilot. One was when a Lightning fighter called up for fuel. I told him to join the queue only to hear him report that he had just three minutes of fuel remaining. I allowed him to jump the queue.

The bulk of my tanker flights were over the North Sea and passed without any incident. Only once did we have a problem when the hose would not wind in. That gave us a problem on landing, as you can imagine. There often used to be a crowd of spectators on the public road immediately before the threshold of runway 26 at Brize Norton. On our approach, our hose would be hanging below the jet and likely to hit anything close to the runway. That day, I elected to land a bit further up and from a steeper approach to avoid spectators being clobbered on the head with a heavy basket. In fact, it took normally two people to even lift it. In the event, no one was hurt, though the hose made rather a spectacular display of sparks bouncing down the runway behind us. On inspection, it was hardly fit for the scrapyard.

32

The Last Forty Years
Have Flown By—Literally

However, in a busy world, full of rules and regulations, there was still one place where pure flying could still be had: the Falklands. The following article was written by me during a typically wet and very windy day on that incredibly remote island. It was my final article for the base's in-house magazine before my retirement in 2003.

This article was written some 3,200 miles south of the Equator on that group of islands so similar to the Outer Hebrides it would be easy to fool anyone from the BBC series *Two Thousand Acres of Sky*. I was, of course, referring to the Falkland Islands. As part of my RAF career 'swan song' I had been 'volunteered' at very short notice to begin my resettlement there in sleepy hollow. Great if you fancy sheep farming. Over 300 hundred years ago Dr Samuel Johnston described the place as:

> What a bleak and gloomy solitude, an Island thrown aside from human use, stormy in winter and barren in summer: an island which not even the southern savages have dignified with habitation: where a garrison must be kept that contemplates with envy the exiles of Siberia.

Actually, it was not that bad. In the alcohol free environment (we hard-done-by aircrew are on standby continuously for 3 weeks) in the RAF it was as close to being a health farm as one gets.

For those of you old enough to remember my *Gateway* articles entitled 'The Sharp End' you will recall that I was old even then. I am now very much in the twilight of my lengthy RAF career so, after more than forty years in the saddle, the time has come to hang up my rather oily flying helmet.

The Royal Air Force I joined a very long time ago was vastly different. As the great Bob Dylan once sung:

> Come mothers and fathers
> Throughout the land
> And don't criticize
> What you can't understand

Your sons and your daughters
Are beyond your command
Your old road is
Rapidly changing.

The times unquestionably were rapidly changing during the last decade of my service career. Though it would be very easy to say that it was considerably better during my early days, I'm not tempted to use that cheap phrase. Why not? I suspect you are asking. Surely it is the prerogative of my generation to remember only 'The Good Old Days'. Well, despite the fact that my memory is fast deteriorating, I can remember more difficult times. Conversely, there were good times too. Hopefully there are still good times to be had for the youngsters that still serve.

So what are my memories of the last forty years of RAF life? What do I miss? More importantly, what would I rather forget about! Has anything really changed at all?

Well of course it has. Partly for the better, but also quite a lot for the worst. I suppose for me the most important change is the additional crewmember in the cockpit/flight deck. I don't mean a navigator or engineer; I refer to the Accountant who sadly rules everything these days. He sits beside us incessantly counting the beans. When I was an unprofessional hooligan 'budgets' was not a word in our dictionary. The only thing that mattered at all was 'the pursuit of excellence'. We were the best (well at least we thought we were). Now, the policy is 'How cheap can we do it?' This naturally affects morale and ultimately operational efficiency. We possibly are still a 'can do' breed of aviators, though I suspect less so than in yesteryear.

Though the previous comment indicated (in my opinion) how life for us in the Royal Air Force has deteriorated over the last forty years, there have been many major improvements. Possibly the most significant change is the massive increase in the professionalism of all of us. This has been brought about partly by increased discipline and a quantum leap in the amount of rules we now must obey. Perhaps you might think that I find this to be a negative aspect of our current life. Whatever you or I may think, one particular fact is true; we enjoy a significant decline in aircraft accidents, and more importantly, a far greater reduction in fatalities. That must be a distinct bonus.

However, for me the fun seems to have mainly evaporated. We have a job to do and a serious one at that. Forty years ago our Air Force was very much the archetypal flying club and we enjoyed enormous Esprit de Corps. This was definitely true of my Near East Air Force Squadron. Rules were indeed few and far between, we were not very professional, medals were non-existent and operations were something we only practised for. Of course we were happy despite a distinct lack of facilities and amenities. There was no such thing as personal computers, microwave ovens, Internet, e-mails, iPads, iPods, digital cameras, mobile phones, DVDs, satellite TV, VCRs, PDAs, station exercises, MOTs, breathalysers or drink/drive regulations. GPS and inertial navigation systems were fitted only to Sputniks. Hence navigators were a necessary evil (only joking).

We were also a far larger Air Force. There were actually well in excess of fifty or more operational RAF stations in the UK than there are today. We were indeed a large outfit, happy though naive. As our expectations were low we were quite satisfied with few possessions, limited facilities and primitive accommodation.

That is not to say that we did not get the job done. We did, but little was expected of us compared with today. Our tasks were relatively minimal. Wednesday afternoon was always sports afternoon. More importantly, few restrictions were placed in our way. Remove the quadruple problems of Targets, Finance, Standards and Macro Supervision and I defy anyone not to enjoy and achieve. Our mission was infinitely easier and I am convinced that many of my colleagues would not survive in today's harsh world.

I realise that some of my generation have been heard to mutter that the youth of today are far inferior to us when we were young. I think not. Our present generation of toddlers have far more skills and basic qualities. A simple example of this is the hand–eye co-ordination skills of youngsters, who are totally used to playing computer games. What my generation sometimes forget is that we received incredibly lengthy training. Certainly quantity, if not quality. However, despite this, we still died in our hundreds. Point made.

Would one of today's generation recognise the RAF if transported back in time? Of course he would, as many of the pre-war buildings still exist. However, let us follow this fictional officer's arrival process on his first day at a fictitious RAF station.

Firstly, our brand new baby pilot would drive straight through the main gate without being challenged. There would be no armed guard; in fact no guard at all! As for registering his car (though it is doubtful that he even owned one), that would certainly not be necessary. The Officers' Mess would be open 24 hours a day and, amazingly, staffed continuously. Having warned in, our new pilot would be shown to his room by his personal batman who would proceed to unpack for him and even suggest what to wear that evening! Naturally, he would be asked what time he would like to be woken next morning and what type of tea he preferred. Looking round his bedroom, he would spy a wardrobe, a washbasin, a single 2'6″ bed, a bedside table and light and only one electrical socket. If he wanted a shower, a bath or the loo, he would have to wander down a draughty corridor to the communal ablutions.

Subsequently, prior to dinner, he would meander down to the bar to find it fairly full, especially if his arrival coincided with a weekday. Of course the bar staff would be comprised almost totally of RAF personnel. More importantly, no money would pass over the bar, nor would our man be asked to fill in a chit for his beer. The barman would definitely know who he was and enter his purchase in his personal bar book. Later that evening he would collapse in his bed, having left his shoes outside his door to be polished by his batman.

Dining of course was definitely not self-service. The experience started on entering the dining room when one would collect one's own linen napkin wrapped in a silver napkin ring. Upon sitting down at a long oak refectory table, one would be confronted with a plethora of silver cutlery. Within minutes a Mess Steward would arrive, resplendent in white tunic, to show you the comprehensive menu. Silver service was commonplace. This ritual happened at every meal, not just at the elaborate and ceremonial dining in nights.

Incidentally after the meal, unless our pilot repaired to the Mess bar, nightcaps were out of the question for our young pilot as one had to be a Flt Lt over the age of 30 to keep alcohol in one's room. As our chap was probably only 19 yrs old and only just been promoted to full Pilot Officer, fat chance of that. Not that having a few drinks late at night would bother him as there were no rules governing drinking and flying. Incidentally, if he popped out to the pub for a few beers, that would not bother him either as it was years before the breathalyser.

The following day, having been gently woken by his batman, our chap dons his No. 1 uniform, leaves what clothes he wishes to be pressed on his bed and strolls down to breakfast. Obviously waiter service is the order of the day at all meals. After brekkie he presents himself at Station Headquarters (SHQ) to commence the minimal arrival procedure. The majority of this process was completed there, with the exception of the bicycle store! Apart from the three operational flying squadrons and Station Sick Quarters, the only other unit on the station was EPAS (Equipment, Personnel, Accounting and Supply Squadron). This tiny unit, headed by a Sqn Ldr, did everything that our present day Admin Wg, Security Wg and Supply Wg do today. Moreover, there is no such thing as Engineering Wg or Operations Wg, as those functions are indigenous within the operational Sqns. However, my memory fails me as to who owned ATC, but in my defence we are talking about another world.

Following his visit to SHQ our young man would perhaps call on Mrs Station Commander to leave his calling card. Well, according to that well-known book entitled 'Customs and Traditions of the Service' by Gp Capt. Stradling, issued to every newly commissioned officer, he should do so as soon as possible. He definitely would have plenty of time to fit this in as there was no such thing as operational defence training or fitness tests. Gas masks were a thing of the past, so no requirement to collect one of those.

However, much would be familiar to our young cherub, but he would be confused with the uniforms. He would be wearing his No. 1 and would not understand the total absence of RAF woolly pullovers. They would come years later. Most chaps wore battledress; the airmen's were made of a rather hairy material and naturally the officers were made of finer fabric. Still, officers were not allowed to draw uniform from stores, but purchased it from their bespoke tailors in London. Many of us can remember when we flew in uniform, but few can perhaps recall when VC10 captains always wore their No. 1 uniform for flight (after all, the captain was a deity). Indeed he put his SD hat on to walk through the cabin. Moreover, as the forage cap had been discontinued after the Second World War, the SD cap is the only headdress he possessed.

Before I forget, we are talking about a time before the advent of the Military Salary. That arrived in 1970, so don't feel bad if you cannot remember its introduction. So our intrepid pilot would get his food and accommodation for free. Moreover, he would be paid 'ration allowance' when on leave, and of course be allowed four free railway warrants per year. Interestingly on reaching the ripe old age of 25, he would actually be entitled to 'marriage allowance' when he tied the knot. There had to be a good reason for that fatal mistake. Not that many chaps were actually married, as it was not encouraged until a chap reached 25. Sadly, if a chap were foolish enough to do so, he would not be entitled to marriage allowance, married quarters or indeed take his wife with him on the many overseas tours available to him.

Our junior officer would also have to personally manage 'pay parades' for the airmen as they were always paid in cash. Another duty would be Orderly Officer. Not Station Duty Officer as that was the responsibility of the Grown Ups. The Station Orderly Officer saluted the Flag and other such vital tasks such as inspecting the food in the Airmen's Mess and performing stock checks of rations. Another world indeed.

But what of aircraft and operations. Well our intrepid young aviator would not comprehend this present world of ours at all. Firstly he would not 'enjoy' the dubious facilities of a simulator. They had yet to be invented, but the advantage of that was more real flying training. Furthermore, there was no Aircrew Manual Flying, merely a pocket size 'Pilots Notes' that would fit comfortably in a flying suit pocket. Not that we needed huge instruction manuals as the aircraft were really quite basic. Anyway, one would require a separate manual for each individual aircraft as no two aeroplanes were the same.

Our man would not have had the use of a calculator, but would either use his fingers, a slide rule or the ubiquitous Dalton Computer (no, that is not an electronic computer, merely a circular slide rule). Compulsory Basic Training Requirements (BTRs) were a thing of the future as indeed was the dreaded Tactical Evaluation (TACEVAL). Low flying was exactly that. No limit was placed on minimum height, which is perhaps understandable when the correct height to drop napalm (Oops, sorry, petroleum jelly) was a mere 50 feet. Climbing to get over a railway train WAS great fun.

Crew duty was just a gentleman's agreement, not that we worked very long hours anyway. As for flying and drink, well I'll leave that subject to your imagination. Suffice to say that we were sometimes not too Sharp (excuse the pun). Perhaps that was one of the many reasons why our mortality rate was so high.

So you see it was a vastly different world, but I am on balance not totally convinced that those carefree days were superior. One example was the standard of married quarters (MQs). Though not significantly worse than the MQs of the 21st Century, the married quarters of the sixties did not have central heating as coal or coke stoves were the order of the day. Garages were also in short supply, but as motorcars were rare, that was no problem.

However, and here is the rub, the average Joe Public's home was also almost certainly rented and of a similar or possibly lesser quality than the military equivalent. Conversely, batting extended to officer's married quarters and the average Flt Lt could expect a batman to clean his quarter and look after children etc on at least 5 mornings a week. So on balance, I suppose our junior officers were better off. Pity that all went with the military salary.

Nevertheless, our young aviator did not join the Royal Air Force to live in married quarters, enjoy a huge salary (my first salary was £5 per week gross), or even get drunk. He joined to fly and see the World. And see the World he did. Apart from the many UK Commands: Flying Training Command, Signals Command, Fighter Command, Bomber Command, and Coastal Command to name just a few, he had the choice of Germany (2ATAF), Gibraltar, Malta, Cyprus (NEAF), Bahrain, The Gulf (MEAF), Gan, Singapore (FEAF), Hong Kong and many lesser outposts. Akrotiri boasted seven flying Squadrons (commanded by Sqn Ldrs) and an equal number of Gp Capts. As for 2ATAF, the number of operational squadrons was too numerous to remember.

Our youngster would almost certainly have been posted overseas on his first tour, especially if he was red blooded and opted for Day Fighter/Ground Attack (DFGA). RAF Airfields with names such as Akrotiri, Tengah, El Adam, Sharjah, Kai Tak, Luqa and Halfar, to name but a few, conjured up romantic images of far off sunny climes, dusky maidens and duty-free motor cars.

My first tour was indeed east of Malta. Despite the hot climate, my room had no air conditioning and just one electrical socket, but I cared not. My sole possessions were a second hand sports car, a battered transistor radio and a brownie box camera. How times have changed! But I was in heaven.

But why did I earlier suggest that some of the fun has evaporated? Well, I have painted a picture of a chap, mad keen to fly, who almost certainly did not own an automobile and was paid very little. So what did he do for fun? Firstly, there was always the opportunity to take one of the Sqn jets home for the weekend. Yes really! Just sign it out. Our young blade could easily enlist the services of a like-minded navigator and set off for Singapore for a few days on their own. Just for R&R. I did just that. Inspect my flying log and check the date. Additionally, most RAF stations had what was affectionately termed the Station Flight. Any pilot, even those on a ground tour, was allowed to sign out the station hack, normally an Avro Anson or similar light twin and set off home for the weekend.

As recent as the late '80s, 10 Sqn planned and flew global trainers to the Far East without the burden of passengers or freight. I flew the very last one in 1990 and the itinerary was taken completely from a British Airways holiday brochure! We flew Brize, Akrotiri, Bahrain, Colombo, Singapore, Hong Kong, Surabaya (I am sure that you know that is in Indonesia), back to Singapore (to pick up the imprest left there by the co-pilot), Mauritius, Bahrain, Akrotiri and home. It took us two weeks with plenty of time off for rest. The only passengers we had were a grand old army colonel and his wife who thumbed a lift to Hong Kong. When we arrived there they had had such a great time they asked me if they could stay with us all the way back to Brize. On arrival home he and his lady wife got a cab to Heathrow and took the next Cathay Pacific flight back out to Hong Kong! As for the crew, we certainly learned a lot about flying on that trip.

What of today's young blades? What other differences would they have noticed different if they cadged a lift in Mr Well's time machine and whizzed back forty years? Well firstly our university graduate would not have entered the RAF with the rank of Fg Off as they do today. He would have started at the bottom with the rest of us. Subsequently an officer had to pass five promotion exams to reach the exalted rank of Flt Lt. After all, Flt Cdrs were Flt Lts and the incredibly senior rank of Sqn Ldr, commanded squadrons. What was it that someone recently said? 'The dilution of the rank structure'; we will be having Gp Capts commanding Sqns soon. Come to think of it, didn't one recently command 101 Sqn? More importantly, our modern hero would perhaps rapidly become confused by the fact that in the early sixties many of the pilots and navigators were non-commissioned officers (NCOs). Certainly, the rank of Master Pilot was common.

I mentioned earlier that supervision was far less prevalent forty years ago. No doubt supervisors think that was a bad thing and the young bloods otherwise. Perhaps we do need more supervision today compared with then, after all the mortality rate was totally unacceptable. However, oppressive supervision can be counter-productive. The advent of computers and hi-tech communications has enabled leaders to keep a very close tab on what lesser mortals are up to. Nevertheless, responsibility and trust breeds reliable and trustworthy personnel. Treat people like children and some will behave like children. Give them responsibility and most will behave responsibly. There are thus two sides to this argument and maybe there is a happy medium, but it is a fact of life that subordinates are now much more closely supervised than previously.

Having said that, rules and procedures are necessary. Though crashes would be eliminated if all the aircraft were permanently locked up in the hanger, what is equally certain is that we would not get the job done. No one is suggesting that our leaders adopt that policy, though over the last forty years I have noticed a definite change in flavour in management style. Gone is the Douglas Bader approach to leadership; remember when he declared his Sqn non-operational because it lacked spares? And that was during a real war. Today, we often attempt to get the job done regardless of whether we have the materiel or personnel to do it. Though this is perhaps a laudable 'can do' approach, our finance orientated masters seize this as an opportunity to save money. Thus it is sometimes sensible and, like Bader, brave to draw a line in the sand.

I earlier suggested that the Accountant is now an essential part of our team. In our halcyon pre-budget days, on his travels around the Station, our chap would have given scant attention to the state of the Base. He probably would not have noticed that the grass was in excellent condition and recently manicured, nor the fact that the curb stones were painted white. The old axiom,' If it moves, salute it, if not paint it white' would have been a familiar phrase to him. More importantly, the very fabric of the buildings was in almost perfect order. Windows did not stay broken for long in the '60s. Though Married Quarters were basic, they too were in faultless condition.

Medical facilities were also readily available and waiting times, either for primary care or beyond, unheard of. A serviceman would be seen very quickly and at a Service hospital close to his base. This, if nothing else, ensured that personnel took the minimum time off to recover. It is stating the obvious to say that modern medical skill is worthless if not available.

Perhaps more importantly, aircraft were invariably in good working order. This was not just down to availability of spare parts and uncomplicated aircraft, but also due to the fact that both aircrew and ground crew had a fierce pride in the Service. Yes we played hard, but chaps worked hard also because they wanted to. Despite the limitations, the combination of ample spares and keen well-trained personnel resulted in a well-honed, efficient and capable outfit.

Don't get me wrong, I am not suggesting that the modern Air Force is neither efficient nor capable. Today we are obviously far more cost-effective and infinitely more capable. We jolly well ought to be, given the level of the Defence Budget. However, just think how much better we would be if we had a less restrictive budget, pursued excellence, had sufficient spares, if morale was sky high and personnel were as keen as mustard. Perhaps we cannot re-invent the wheel nor turn back the clock, but just maybe there are lessons to be learnt by our Lords and Masters. Unfortunately everything seems to come down to money. We now live by the 11th Commandment 'How cheap can I do this task'. Though perhaps a necessary evil, this policy fails to promote good morale. Will that ever change? Unfortunately, I think not.

So in conclusion, much has changed in my lengthy service career. Sadly, but possibly out of necessity, our Royal Air Force has evolved into a cost-conscious company. We make no profit, but conversely are hidebound by cost constraints. In my opinion this has had a serious affect [*sic.*] on morale and consequently on operational effectiveness. Truly today we are far more professional, but at the expense of fun and Esprit de Corps. Though our young Pilot Officer would certainly recognise most of the modern Air Force, I doubt if he would like it.

On returning from the Falklands, I cleared my desk and locker. I said my goodbyes to colleagues and the commanding officer and flew my last mission from Brize Norton. Traditionally, on most RAF strategic transport squadrons, one had the choice of plum trips. Perhaps even a global or at least a week in the United States. My final sortie in the RAF was simply an air-to-air refuelling trip over the North Sea, thirty-eight years, six months, and ten days after that momentous trip down to RAF South Cerney. Having started my career all those years previously flying offensive support aircraft, I ended it given away fuel to the very latest fighter aircraft in the RAF's inventory, namely the Typhoon. Perhaps that was appropriate, the 'Old' giving way to the 'New'. On 17 June 2003, fittingly a day of torrential thunderstorms, I flew VC10 XV102, dispensed some 20 tons of aviation fuel to my successors in the fast jet world, and returned to RAF Brize Norton to be greeted by the station commander and my wing commander, my colleagues (many of whom I had trained), and a bucket of bubbly. We had come a long way from old-fashioned 'map-and-stopwatch' flying, and I was glad to be hanging up my trusty old flying helmet. Thus ended my military flying career.

33
Time to Go

They say that old soldiers never die, they simply fade away. This one was not for fading. However, most people stay longer than their 'sell by date'. Throughout my professional flying career, I had noticed elderly pilots staying in post long after their motor faculties, memory, and reactions had passed their peak. However, these pilots still had much to offer the youngsters: composure, maturity, experience, and knowledge are but a few of the essential attributes necessary for a pilot to survive until a ripe old age. The axiom 'there are no old, bold pilots' is still as valid today as it was when I started my career. Trouble is, we young upstarts rarely listened to the old fogies and I often thought that such pilots should be put out to grass.

Nevertheless, when I became an ancient aviator, I did at least remember some of the thoughts that buzzed through my head as a JP (junior pilot). Better to quit when on top than halfway down the hill. I most certainly did not want to become a burden to my fellow aviators and definitely not a figure of fun. Having reached the very pinnacle of my career and having been awarded not only the highest grade available, the fabled 'A' Category, but also having been appointed by the Honourable Company of Air Pilots as a Master Air Pilot, there was only one way my career could go—downwards. Moreover, with my forthcoming bi-annual flying tests scheduled for a few months' time, I was convinced that I would fail the ground school part of the exam. Yes, I would perform to an exceptional standard in the air, but in the classroom my memory would fail me. Consequently, having reached the top of the tree, I could not bear the humiliation of failure and thus decided to quit.

So with some two years left of my contract, it was with not too much soul searching that I tendered my resignation after thirty-nine years of service in the RAF. After all, that was not a bad innings. This was accepted immediately by their Airships, thus confirming that I had made the correct decision. I left the RAF without any doubts and have had none since. I left at the right time, not too early or even too late, but the RAF was not what I had joined all those years ago. Yes, it was safer, but partly due to considerably more rules and regulations—sadly, the fun had gone, the accountant ruled, and I was glad to go. The RAF was (quite rightly) no longer a flying club, and pilots now knew how much their salary was, something in the beginning I never bothered to find out.

Thus Her Majesty's RAF and one of her most trusted servants bade farewell to each other and on 31 August 2003, I finally retired. This was part of what I wrote in my Letter of Resignation to their Airships:

It is with considerable sadness that I announce my retirement. I have served continuously for 39 years. It seems a lifetime, perhaps because it was! However, though I have many reasons for taking this decision, I am fully aware that we all have to quit one day. I would like to fade away whilst I have some skills left. That time has come.

I had achieved most of my ambitions and thus I was happy to leave an Air Force that had changed out of all recognition since that cold December day in 1964 when my mother drove me in her old Morris Minor down to No. 1 Initial Training School at South Cerney in Gloucestershire. It was perhaps prophetic that where my RAF career started, my flying career would end.

Having started with low assessments, and on more than one occasion being told that I would never be very good, I was particularly pleased to finish my service with the very highest of assessments an RAF pilot can achieve—the coveted 'Exceptional' rating. The final comment in my RAF logbook, written by my squadron commander, read thus:

Assessment of Ability: Exceptional.

Remarks: Derek—what can I say? You have given so many years of dedicated service to the Royal Air force. On behalf of all your previous 'Bosses', thank you for your professionalism, loyalty and hard work. I enjoyed my few trips with you—there was never a quiet moment on the flight deck. Thank you.

That assessment, gained just two years before retirement, together with the Award of the Air Force Cross, being made a Master Air Pilot by the Honourable Company of Air Pilots, and becoming UK Man of the Year in 1983 laid to rest the justifiable criticism of my flying ability in my younger days. I thus retired gracefully, but determined that my flying career was not completely over just yet. I had handed in my notice, but had not hung up my flying helmet.

34

Solo Again

They say that flying is a bit like riding a bicycle—you never forget how to do it. I am not sure if that is true. However, what is true is that when the bicycle stops, you fall over. So it is with flying. So the solution? Well, it is obvious really; do not stop.

Thus on a clear late summer morning in Oxfordshire, I once again ascended the luft on my own. It had been over twenty years since I had flown by myself and, not surprisingly, the occasion held some significance for me. Having been informed by the dreaded medics, some two decades previously, that I would almost certainly never fly again as pilot in command and most definitely never fly solo, this event gave me a certain amount of satisfaction. As a concession to the Civil Aviation Authority, I carried 'protective spectacles' just in case I wished to perform inverted aerobatics. Fat chance in my docile steed, a Piper PA28 Warrior of the Brize Norton Flying Club.

My little trip was quite uneventful. Its purpose was to rekindle those light aircraft skills I had learnt so very long ago so that I would be up to speed during my 'Skills Test' necessary to obtain my civil pilot's licence. I need not have worried. After a lifetime of flying, the 'skills' came flooding back and I was reminded of the old axiom of 'riding a bicycle'!

However, the sortie started badly. I could not even start the engine. After a number of attempts, I suddenly realised that there was little wrong with my aeroplane, merely a measure of carelessness on my part. The mixture lever had been sent to 'cut off'; in short, the fuel was off and in my eagerness to fly, I had overlooked this important item.

However, once I got the show on the road, all went surprisingly well. As the poem written by John Gillespie Magee Jr described, I truly slipped the surly bonds of earth, danced the skies on laughter-silvered wings, sunward I climbed and joined the tumbling mirth of sun-split clouds and did a hundred things that I personally had long forgotten. I really did fling my eager craft through footless halls of air, up into the burning blue I topped the windswept height with easy grace where never lark or even eagle flew. Indeed, it was quite a surreal and spiritual experience knowing that I was one with the elements and indeed only I alone would be able to bring my craft back to earth.

So did I survive without a crew? Of course, I did, and as for the experience, well it was almost spooky flying without the help of co-pilot, navigator, and flight engineer. Though their services are vital when venturing far from home in 350 tons of heavy 4-jet, this day, in my little 'puddle jumper', I was relatively safe on my own. Well, as safe as I could be given that the weather was perfect and few others were cluttering up my sky. Perhaps they had been warned of my auspicious event.

On landing, which I thought most conceitedly was quite perfect, I felt great. One small step for mankind, once giant stride for Bluntie. I really did feel wonderful.

Great as those initial early flights in the Warrior were, I soon felt something was missing. Moreover, though RAF Brize Norton was a busy military airfield and it had all the facilities a pilot could wish for, I was made to feel like a second-class citizen. Furthermore, following a Jumbo down the approach path was fraught with danger for a puddle jumper like me. Such wake turbulence from their massive wings would flip my little craft upside down in a millisecond. Not a pleasant experience and certainly terminal if it occurred close to the ground. Consequently, it was eminently sensible to give these enormous leviathans of the air a very wide berth.

More importantly, I felt my flea-sized craft was an encumbrance to that busy airport. I spent far too long orbiting downwind to allow the more important gentlemen of the sky to land. After all, they had crossed continents to reach their destination and were no doubt fatigued. The last thing they needed was for me to cause a go-around.

Finally, the lure of more adventurous flying called me. I needed to cast off the shackles of my present 'family saloon' form of flying and once again fly upside down. Hence I came to Kemble in search of more excitement. In a way, back to my roots.

I first looked at the new breed of light aircraft, the Light Sports Aircraft (LSA). Both the futuristic Flight Design CT and the more conventional Evektor Eurostar appeared to offer exciting flying without wallet-busting problems. Though nimble and efficient, this breed suffered from one major problem: in order to achieve a Civilian Aviation Authority (CAA) certification, their weight was restricted to a mere 450 kg. Whereas this did ensure sprightly performance, it did preclude much equipment, especially given my portly frame. Moreover, neither was certified for bad weather flying or aerobatics.

So on the day I was supposed to part with more than just a month's pension to secure a share in one of these aircraft, I by chance spotted something from my past. A Scottish Aviation Bulldog, ex-RAF, fully aerobatic, built for bad weather, and looking like it had my name on it. Here was my chance to turn upside down once again.

Another opportunity came my way. While the majority of Assistant Flying Instructors (AFIs) work at flying clubs merely to gain flying hours so that they can get a foothold in the door of an aviation career with the airlines, I did not need such experience. I had more hours than everyone else put together at my club. Moreover, unlike the typical twenty-two-year-old AFI, I fortunately did not need the money. By now, no mortgage, no wife, no kids at university meant that my outgoings were minimal. Additionally, when the opportunity to set up a Ground School Facility arose, few AFIs rushed forward to take on that task. It paid badly and produced zero hours for the flying logbook. Giving just a little back to 'budding would-be-aviators' appealed, as this was a project I could get my teeth into. So I immediately accepted the challenge with much enthusiasm. Forty years of flying experience, ground training, and computer skills would come in handy in the months ahead.

More opportunities came my way. My club concentrated on postgraduate training: formation, aerobatics, and air racing. My boss appointed me to the exalted (and unpaid) position of Director Post Graduate Training. From then on, many weekends would find me at Kemble or North Weald running courses in formation flying. Quite scary really, as my pupils did not benefit from the formal and lengthy training I had enjoyed some forty-odd years previously. Consequently, my motto became 'Flight Safety is Paramount' and the sole aim of our training was to occupy the same piece of sky, enjoy oneself, and come back in one piece. That we miraculously did.

Nothing further illustrated this than the fortieth anniversary of the Beagle Pup. Our flying club had been invited to provide a formation flypast at Shoreham Airport, home of the Pup. On a beautiful Easter Sunday in 2007, a mix of five Bulldogs and two Pups launched from Shoreham and amazingly produced a very creditable and professional flypast. I led that formation and should have been worried as up until an hour before departure, I had no idea how many would take part or who they were. Consequently, fag packet planning was the order of the day, but we lived. Maybe that guardian angel flew as Number 8 on that Easter Sunday.

Even flying little aeroplanes was not without risk. Previously I had written 'three years teaching youngsters to fly passed without much incident. After all, no one was shooting at me, though I often thought my student was trying to kill me and himself'. I suppose all things are relative. During my time as a RAF flying instructor, I suffered a few engine failures, all of which were far from high drama, especially the engine failure in a Chipmunk when I omitted to call Mayday.

I learnt a little from that incident. Many years later, having got airborne from Kemble in a Beagle Pup 150 on an instructional sortie with a student on his very first flight, I suddenly heard a very large bang and could no longer read any of the instruments as the vibration was too severe. Following those magic words 'I have control', I took over and just about managed to coax my stricken craft back to Kemble, losing height all the time. We accomplished a safe landing on the runway, though had to avoid another aircraft taking off in the opposite direction. Of course, I had elected to land the wrong way; it was either that or the ploughed field.

Later, on telephoning the owner to inform him that we had saved his Pup from almost definite total destruction and that it was all in one piece, I was slightly miffed to listen to his annoyance that he would now have to shell out for engine repairs. I pointed out that not only was the aeroplane in one piece, but so were we.

From then onwards, I often told myself that the previous ultra-high standard of maintenance enjoyed by RAF pilots did not necessarily apply to general aviation. Flight safety was no longer paramount, but that economics and budgets played a more important part. Private pilots had to pay for a very costly hobby; RAF pilots more or less were handed blank cheques. Well, that was at least true until about 1990.

35

Air Racing

Earlier in my career, while instructing on Chipmunks, we instructors had races back from our relief landing ground at RAF Rufforth to RAF Church Fenton. Just a little bit of fun to make up for some of the boredom and routine of teaching embryo naval officers to fly.

Since the dawn of aviation, pilots have sought to compete and perfect their skills. Aerobatics is perhaps one of the ways to improve pure handling skills, but air racing brings together planning and handling. Air racing and the setting of records came to the fore from the earliest of times, although it was not until the 1920s that it took on a formalised and more spectacular form. In Britain, royal patronage for air racing came with the annual King's Cup, first awarded by George V in 1922 and hotly contested to this day. In the 1980s, the spirit of seaplane racing was rekindled with the rebirth of the famed Schneider Trophy. The Schneider Trophy originally was a trophy awarded annually (and later, biannually) to the winner of a race for seaplanes and flying boats. The Schneider Trophy is now kept at the Science Museum in London and is an enormous trophy.

In 1912, Jacques Schneider, a French financier, balloonist, and aircraft enthusiast, announced the competition and offered a prize of approximately £1,000. The race was held twelve times between 1913 and 1931. It was intended to encourage technical advances in civil aviation but became a contest for pure speed with laps over a triangular course. The contests were staged as time trials, with aircraft setting off individually at pre-agreed times, usually fifteen minutes apart. The contests were very popular and some attracted crowds of over 200,000 spectators. Both the King's Cup and the Schneider Trophy, together with a series of other prestigious events, go to make up the modern day handicap air-racing season. Generally, these present races comprise four or five laps of a course of some 25 miles centred on an airfield, with again a staggered start based on handicap and designed to produce a simultaneous finish. Spectators, therefore, are usually able to see both the start and the finish.

In June 2007, a good friend said to me, 'Derek, don't you think it is time to slow down, put your feet up, call for your slippers and pipe and take it easy?' My answer? I took up air racing. Not that silly 'round the pylons stuff, one at a time'. No, I wanted a slice of the famous Schneider Trophy. So it was on a lovely Friday afternoon in August that a friend and I set off for Bembridge on the Isle of Wight to be part of the business. My chum had won the race a number of times and actually in the Beagle Pup that we were flying that day. Regrettably, however, he had just had a quadruple heart by-pass operation and had temporarily lost his licence. So it was up to me to chauffeur him to the race. Think about it, a pilot with a quadruple heart by-pass being supervised by a one-eyed pilot. You could not make it up.

The weekend was fun and I was asked to navigate for a Spanish pilot in a sporty number called a Cap 10. This was my chance. Now for the majority of readers who have little idea of air racing, the Schneider Trophy has been running for a very long time. This in fact was the seventy-fourth annual event. What makes it so much fun and possibly dangerous, too, is the fact that most aeroplanes can enter. As mentioned, they are handicapped so that the slowest start first. A bit like the tortoise and the hare. It is quite amazing to be still drinking one's coffee on the terrace of the pilot's club watching the first aircraft take-off, knowing that you had to get back before them. Consequently, given that five laps of the course are required, much overtaking occurs. This naturally leads to some interesting moments, especially as, unlike motor racing, one can overtake on the left, the right, above, or below. Four eyes are definitely necessary. Pity in my aeroplane we had only three.

On the day of the race, God smiled upon us and the weather was set fair. We took off and did exceptionally well, coming in a good fifth out of about forty-five entrants. Not bad for a beginner. Air racing was now in my blood and though the season drew to a close, I resolved to take part myself the following year in the Bulldog.

Sadly, that did not happen. For reasons various, as you will subsequently read, it was a very long time before I purchased a Bulldog. Moreover, financial constraints precluded me from this rather expensive aspect of flying. Maybe also I was just getting old; so touring was to become the preferred option. Whatever, any form of flying is good fun. Moreover, as you will see, it still can produce a few spills and thrills, as I too was to discover to my cost, both financially and to my pride.

36

Full Circle: Chalk and Cheese

Almost fifty years to the day when I first took to the skies as pilot in command my aviation experiences had come full circle. Chapter 1 described my exploits and first solo flight at the controls of a T38. Sadly, this was not the jet trainer as used by the USAF, but a modest Slingsby T38 Grasshopper glider. It would, of course, be using rather too much artistic licence to call it a sailplane. This rudimentary aerial machine was based on the pre-war German SG-38 *Schulgleiter*, and was used by Air Training Corps Squadrons and Combined Cadet Forces between 1952 and the late 1980s.

The Grasshopper had absolutely no instrumentation what so ever. One judged one's height by Mk 1 eyeball and speed by the wind in one's face. This was hardly scientific and definitely inaccurate. Though my one solo flight in the machine was reminiscent of the Wright Brothers' first flight, I shuddered to think of the consequences of being launched off the side of a cliff. Mad fools actually did that in this glider.

However, late in 2008, I decided to purchase my own aeroplane. As at the time I was flying Scottish Aviation Bulldogs, teaching a little formation flying, doing a little touring, and sometimes turning upside down, it seemed a good idea to buy my own craft. I identified a suitable example and set about the process of procurement. However, the more I learnt about the cost of maintenance, the more I got cold feet. As someone said to me at the time, the sure-fire way to bankruptcy would be to buy a vintage aeroplane. Someone else told me how to become a millionaire, start off as a multi-millionaire, and then buy an aeroplane. So discretion being the better part of valour, I changed my mind.

Nevertheless, earlier in the year, an old pilot chum of mine and I visited an Aviation Expo and were considerably interested in an incredibly modern single-engined aircraft. What impressed us was the avionics suite and in particular the glass cockpit instrumentation. This was a mighty fine four-seat touring machine with every creature comfort and facility necessary for flight in all weathers. The only trouble was that it cost an arm and a leg. 'Jolly nice' we both said and just about left it at that.

With the demise of my plan to purchase a Bulldog, I revisited the idea of this ultra-modern aircraft which had a name: a Cirrus SR20 GTS. Its major selling point for me was the glass cockpit dash fitted with a comprehensive and fully digital avionics suite. A pair of Garmin 430s provided GPS navigation, conventional radio navigation, and radio communications, so hopefully getting lost would be a thing of the past. I was also intrigued by the safety

The author in the cockpit of Cirrus SR20. (*Author's collection*)

systems, least of which was the Ballistic Aircraft Parachute System, a large parachute that could be deployed in an emergency to lower the entire aircraft and its occupants to the ground safely. Finally, a good autopilot ensured that my brain, slowed by advancing years, would keep up with the aeroplane while I fathomed out what everything did.

In short, this futuristic aircraft was a far cry from my elderly Bulldog and light years ahead of the Grasshopper that I first flew fifty or so years previously. I explored a number of options and eventually decided to join a group who had a share for sale at an airfield not too far from me. The shared ownership plan would save my hard-earned pension and appeared not to stop me flying when I wanted to. Moreover, 'my' aeroplane would be kept tucked up nice and warm in a hangar, pushed out and refuelled when I needed it. No more for me the battling with aircraft covers in a force 9 gale. I was obviously getting very soft in my dotage. Just before New Year, I parted with a sizeable sum and for the first time became a joint-owner of an aeroplane.

However, this short adventure with the future nearly ended in tears. It is true to say that I was totally seduced by Cirrus. The glitzy glass cockpit, the performance, the sleek lines, and the abundance of toys to play with all convinced me that this aircraft was for me, but perhaps it was like the proverbial Italian mistress, beautiful to look at and went like the wind itself, but there was a sting in its tail. Maybe I should have stuck with my good old dependable English maid: the Bulldog.

After a year of flying the Cirrus, I thought I had conquered its idiosyncrasies. It flew some 50 per cent faster than the trusty Bulldog, yet only had the same engine power and indeed used only the same amount of fuel at 160 mph as the Bulldog used at 110 mph. Yet there

The author's toys: Cirrus, Ferrari, and Porsche. (*Su Khoo*)

was a cost for this efficiency: it was tricky to handle due to its advanced design. After one year, I was to learn yet again that aeroplanes can, and do, bite.

One day, late in October 2009, following a near-perfect approach to the little airfield where I kept my Cirrus, I bounced on landing. This was an easy thing to do, but I was to later learn that in a Cirrus this too could be an expensive error. After landing I did my usual cursory inspection of my steed and to my horror discovered that the ends of my propeller were slightly bent. Worse was to come.

As is usual with any incident where the propeller strikes something (in this case, the runway), the engine has to be removed from the aircraft and inspected for shock loading internal damage. In addition to this, on inspection of the rest of the aircraft, minor damage was discovered to the nose wheel assembly. Lucky for me that my lovely Cirrus was insured for this sort of incident as a prop strike will be expensive.

For the record, my own experience of a damaging bounce came from a totally stable, normal approach with roundout perceived at the correct height. This was no reckless or cowboy approach, merely a normal careful approach to land. Weather conditions were perfect: good visibility, no precipitation, and only a few knots of wind from the left. Yet the aircraft bounced and I corrected, only to experience an even greater bounce. I went around, not suspecting for a moment any damage had occurred, but it had.

Apart from damage to all three blade tips, there was some evidence of a heavy landing. That could have occurred with a previous pilot, but it was discovered on my watch and thus down to me. It just goes to show that any aircraft can bite, even with an experienced pilot. I still do not know to this day why it happened. All I can think is that perhaps I rounded out a little too high and took all the power off. From the initial small bounce, I suspect I overcorrected and must have subsequently landed on the nose wheel, during which time the prop contacted the runway.

This was a serious incident. I had never screwed up a landing in my life that had damaged an aeroplane. This time, my aeroplane was indeed damaged, but it could be repaired. Not so my pride, but they do say that pride comes before a fall. Though no one was injured, I felt really terrible after this incident. My reputation was in tatters; after all, how could a very experienced flying instructor damage an aircraft while landing in perfect conditions? Moreover, I felt that not only had I let myself down, but had let down my fellow syndicate members. Now I had to seriously consider my future with this aircraft. The approach had been fine, yet I bounced and subsequently damaged the aeroplane. Would it happen again?

Well not for some time because the aeroplane needed to be repaired. There was more bad news. Actually, in a perverse way, this was good news. Once the engine was stripped to check for shock damage, it was discovered that a piston had a hole in it. This was nothing to do with my misdemeanour, but a previous pilot cruising with too weak a mixture. Unlike a motorcar, because an aeroplane climbs and thus experiences a pressure reduction, once in level flight, the pilot has to weaken the petrol–air ratio (mixture). Sadly, over weakening of the mixture can cause what is called 'pre-detonation'. This is when the explosion of the fuel-air mix in the cylinder takes place too soon. This in turn can cause damage to the engine.

In our case, this had occurred. So actually it would appear that every cloud has a silver lining. If I had not been so ham-fisted, the damage would not have been found. This could have led to disastrous consequences in the future. Was my guardian angel on duty again? Luckily, our engine warranty covered some of the damage and as the insurance covered the engine dismantling, we were not much out of pocket. I merely paid the excess on the insurance.

However, as can be seen from my investigation into why I had been so crass, I was determined to ensure that I never again damaged the aeroplane. I vowed that if a solution were not to be found, I would sell my share in the aircraft. No one was hurt in my little escapade, but next time I might not be so lucky. So I went back to flying school.

I flew with a chap who, though not an instructor, had considerable Cirrus experience. He hit on my problem almost immediately. 'Derek, old chap,' he said, 'you are landing it like a jet.'

Now this was not surprising, as most of my flying had been done on jets. Additionally, that technique worked for the other light aircraft I had flown recently. He suggested that I fly the Cirrus like a tail dragger, an aircraft without a nose wheel. Here you fly the aeroplane to a position ideally a few inches above the runway, close the throttle, and allow the aircraft to run out of airspeed and drop onto the runway on three points, the main undercarriage and the tail wheel.

Of course, having flown tail draggers for over 1,000 hours, this was not a difficult technique for me. I tried it and it worked. Eureka! That day I performed ten perfect landings and was ready for my annual flight test. Four more landings the following day with our group instructor were also immaculate. I had cracked it and my confidence improved with leaps and bounds. We were back in business and maybe that whole incident was a wake-up call. Perhaps we all need one of those from time to time.

Following that debacle, I went from strength to strength and started to use the Cirrus for what it was intended—a gentleman's tourer. With friends and family, I flew to many airfields near and far, though stayed well clear of rutted bumpy grass strips. More was the pity. Nothing I liked better than to emulate the biker who meets his chums at some roadside café for a butty and cuppa. We often flew to interesting airfields merely for lunch, though trips to North Wales usually resulted in some safe mountain flying.

Occasionally, we flew across the Channel to airfields such as Le Touquet, hired a bicycle, and pedalled down to the seafront for *moules marinière*. Such a flight was almost an adventure, though I wondered why someone like me, who had circumnavigated the globe, flown down the slopes of the High Himalayas into Kathmandu, and crossed vast oceans would worry about crossing 20 miles of the English Channel. Maybe the fact that I had just one engine had a little to do with it, maybe I was just getting old.

However, flying a puddle jumper through the UK's 'shark-infested custard' (pilot speak for very busy airspace) requires concentration and skill. I remember, many years ago, flying a Chipmunk in foul weather to another airfield when all of a sudden I saw a very big runway. It was that of a major airport. Through the murk, I then spotted a rather large airliner bearing down on me. I doubt if it saw me though due to the awful visibility. If that had happened in the twenty-first century, I would have been seen on radar and had my licence subsequently removed, assuming of course I had lived. So flying today is far more difficult. Airspace is very crowded and infringements dealt with very severely. Of course, GPS devices help enormously, but cannot be relied on.

Modern glass cockpits are OK, but the Cirrus is like a BMW 7 series motorcar—great for touring, but not that much fun. As time went on, I began to realise that most of my flying was fairly short journeys to little airfields. After my landing debacle in the Cirrus, I became very wary of short bumpy grass strips, the sort of interesting places I really wanted to visit. So what to do? Obvious really, sell my share in the Cirrus and do what I should have done in the first place: buy a Scottish Aviation Bulldog. What better for that Sunday trip than to fly the equivalent of an old Austin Healey 3000 sports car?

37

My Other Love: Motorcars

Talking of sports cars, this book has been primarily about my exploits in aerial machines; some quite fast. Thus dear reader you will not be too astonished to learn that my other true love has been fast cars. Ever since I joined the Royal Air Force I have owned many high-performance motors. Only an excursion into parenthood lead me into the realms of pantechnicons! Most of my vehicles have been two-seat sports cars. The older I got, the faster they went and the slower I drove.

It is not within the compass of this book to dwell on each and every vehicle I have owned, nor what amazing adventures I had got up to in those motorcars. Suffice to say that cars were not my life, but most of the time a passport to friendship and a social life. A prime example of this was my membership of Porsche Club Great Britain. This was my gateway to meeting new friends, general petrol head activities, enjoying excellent touring holidays, and, above all, meeting my gorgeous future wife. Here is an article I wrote for the club magazine, *Porsche Post*.

'The Perfect Pair'

Nope, I don't mean anything to do with the subject of Page Three Girls (assuming you remember that chauvinistic newspaper). What I would like to comment on is my own personal choice of the perfect two cars for a man of a certain age. Of course, we are all different, so I very much doubt if you will agree with me. Unquestionably there has been much debate on car club forums regarding the pros and cons of new versus old, Classic *versus* Modern. At the end of the day it really is 'Horses for Courses'.

But before anyone can decide on which car, or indeed which cars, one should really establish in a logical way exactly what that motor is required to do. That is assuming one is rational! Big assumption. Moreover, for most of us budgets sadly pay their part. That said, some enthusiasts make the mistake of saving money by buying cheap, then spending their life savings on keeping the car on the road. I know of one friend who spends more per year on maintaining his second-hand Ferrari Mondial than he paid for it.

Of course we would all like a multi-role car for all seasons. One for the school run, one for the Supermarket, one for posing, one for Concours, one for that summer afternoon drive through the Cotswolds, one for the race track and one for the fast trip to the South of France, to name but a few. But sadly most of us cannot afford to run seven cars and I am no exception.

As a young bachelor, I had no money, but perhaps I did drive the Perfect Pair. For pleasure I drove a sporty little number called a MG TC *circa* 1946. I paid £40 for it! Incidentally, they now sell for £40,000. My other 'steed' was a Hawker Hunter jet fighter capable of some 600 mph. OK, so it was thirsty, but you dear taxpayer footed the bill.

Then life changed and I acquired a wife and children to support. I then needed two cars and had little money. But before I realised that there is indeed a Porsche to suit all budgets, I had a variety of 'Perfect Pairs'.

My first decent car was a Lotus Elan S4 SE (the 'proper' one, *circa* 1970), which went well with my 1965 Mini. Trouble was the Lotus was about as reliable as, well, a Lotus and we all know what Lotus stands for: 'Loads of Trouble Usually Serious'. At least it lived up to its reputation. Many years later in life I went to look at another old Lotus, peeped underneath, saw how much oil was leaking and walked away, saving myself a King's Ransom. At least the chassis was never going to rust with all that oil on it.

Following the original Elan I went from the sublime to the ridiculous. I chose a Ford Capri GT XLR in Daytona yellow with a black vinyl roof to accompany a VW Caravanette. Actually that made sense. The Ford was sporty (well it looked flashy) and the VW was a great load carrier. Trouble was, the Ford was a heap of shit and the VW could not maintain 60 mph up even gentle motorway inclines. Moreover, with a little air-cooled engine at the rear, I in the front froze.

So I went up market to Saab. Yes I did say up market, as they were brilliant cars in their day when they were real Saabs. In fact I had 16 in all! Not all at the same time you understand. To join them, I also had a plethora of smaller cars, but the Saab always doubled as the runabout. They were indeed great cars of that era and not for insignificant reasons they won countless rallies. Sadly, the company was taken over and quality became much diluted. Worse still, the spectre of declining residuals reared its ugly head and I moved on. Unhappily now the company is no more.

But where to go after Saab? Well, further up market of course. I then launched myself into the 'Mercedes Era'. At the time they were great quality family cars, which held their value. How times change! To accompany the expensive Mercedes estate was a little hatchback, a Ford Fiesta. I rang the changes with that combination more than once, slowly increasing the money invested. No change there then! Then sensible family values departed and I returned to my youth. Was this a midlife crisis? The first of many?

My wife at the time still hankered after estate cars, but selfish me bought her a sporty Mercedes C Class and treated myself to the first of two Mercedes sport cars. Was this the greatest combination possible? Err, well no! Despite collecting the second SL from Stuttgart (my first, but not last visit to that city to collect a new German sports car), the attraction wore off quite quickly. Wonderful though the Type 129 was, it really was an old man's car and I was getting younger by the day. Even today a Type W129 Mercedes SL is a great car, but not a sports car. It is heavy, thirsty, drives like a Panzer tank and is really a car to be seen in, rather than to drive. But it will outlast most modern motors.

So, what to do? Well obviously the new little Mercedes SLK would not suffer from the problems of its heavier sibling. A test drive was imperative. Sadly though, it failed to inspire me. It felt, sounded and drove just like a saloon car. Not surprising really as it really was a saloon car with a sporty body. However, all was not lost. There was an interesting garage just over the road! They sold Porsches.

More importantly, a new model called a Boxster. I ordered one after a quick test drive and for several years never looked back.

But what to mate with this perfect roadster?

Well, I am not a complete chauvinist and my then wife at last had her say, a Chelsea Tractor, in fact a monster of a Chelsea Tractor, a Shogun, worse still it was a diesel! Nevertheless, as the two vehicles were like chalk and cheese they got on, opposites attract and all that. Mrs Sharp was happy and so was I.

But was this at long last the 'Perfect Pair'? A zippy roadster for Sunday afternoon strolls though [*sic.*] the Cotswold countryside and a truck for the Tesco shop? Err, no. Whereas the Boxster was reasonably economical and fun, the Shogun was not. It guzzled fuel like a Saturn Rocket and required servicing every 5,000 miles. It was smelly too! But 'she who was never obeyed' loved it. I never did understand why, though 'she' would say that she enjoyed the driving position, sitting up high, peering over enormous bull bars and feeling as safe as houses. Trouble was it was as big as one!

But just before you think I am an old Softie, letting my wife drive a non-eco-friendly monster of a pantechnicon, we (the Royal we) decided to cut the roof off, change the engine to petrol, put a BMW badge on the front and call it an estate car. In short, we traded the Monster for a BMW 5 series Estate (but not before we bought a second and indeed a third Shogun).

Now we were cooking on gas with the Perfect Pair. A sporty number for holidays and a load carrier for, well carrying a load.

However, all good things come to an end eventually. The wife departed and I found myself single. She had naturally departed with the house, the BMW, the dogs and all other assets, leaving me with just the Porsche. So I got the lion's share!

Now I was down to just one vehicle. Did I now really need two cars? No dogs to transport. No mega shop. No kids. Could I manage with just a Boxster? The answer was 'of course I could', but with just one car, how could I possibly write an article entitled 'The Perfect Pair'. Moreover, I had yet another problem.

My Boxster was almost new, as by now the 2.5 had been recycled into a 3.2 S and represented a sizeable amount of my assets. I did not want to merely use it as a commuter or indeed park it just anywhere. In short, I needed a runabout. Now I have always been good at maths. I calculated (and it is still true today) that I could purchase a cheap runabout and my total motoring costs would reduce, even if I were running two cars. Though I had two lots of road fund licence and insurance to think about, I calculated that I could save on day to day running costs. Moreover, depreciation on the Porsche would be minimal and if I reduced the annual mileage so also would the insurance premium decrease.

But for this cunning plan to work the second car had to be cheap, ultra-cheap. So I purchased a Ford Ka. A brilliant little runabout. Having paid less than £5k for it brand new, fuel consumption at 50 mpg and minimal insurance, what I saved by not driving the Porsche was more than I paid for running this little Ford.

But there was a catch.

Walking is cheaper still! What I mean is that there is more to life than saving money.

By now this little car was my main vehicle and though, for the price, it was brilliant, it did little for my street cred. I could afford better, though that would go against the principle of owning two cars for the price of one.

However, common sense did not prevail and I weakened. I traded the Ka for a new BMW Mini Cooper. Now I (though not my bank manager) was happy! There was also another downside to the purchase! I actually really enjoyed driving the Mini. Those who have a Mini will share my conviction that at the time it was the best small car ever made. In fact it was very difficult to fault. Apart from a rather outrageous initial outlay, it was near perfect. At the time, even the purchase price could be offset by its incredibly good residuals. So was this then the Perfect Pair? A Porsche Boxster and a Mini Cooper?

Possibly yes, but there was yet again a problem. A problem with the Boxster. Shock horror!

By now my main journeys were in the Boxster. Like most of us, to save time, I used the motorways. Anyone who has driven a small roadster on our busy exhaust contaminated highways will have experienced both noise and air pollution. I found on motorways the Boxster claustrophobic with the hood up and noisy with it down. In my humble opinion, top down motoring is for slow speed only. You may disagree. In short a fast drive up the motorway in a small topless car is less than pleasant. Hood up is little better.

But I did persevere with the Boxster/Mini combination for a while, but combining my Sunday cruiser requirement with my long distance reliable rapid transport system did not work well.

So what to do?

Well it was obvious. Buy a glass roof Boxster. Then I would get the great views without the noise or smell. Trouble is, Porsche didn't make a glass roof Boxster. But wait a minute, they did make a Porsche Targa, a glass-roofed 911. So I bought one.

Would a Targa solve my perceived Boxster problems?

Err, no!

The Targa turned out to be just a noisy as the Boxster when the roof was open and then, given that I was looking through two thick panes of glass, the rear visibility was seriously impaired. Moreover, the roof weighed some 70 kg, which did little for the car's centre of gravity and hence its ultimate handling. Trust me: this was not the ultimate track day car.

Pity really as I thought at last I owned the Perfect Pair.

I suppose by now you are thinking something along the lines of 'a fool and his money' and you are probably correct, but in my defence I always told myself, and others, that this was my very last Porsche.

Then came a really stupid decision. Due possibly to my midlife crisis I decided I either needed a chest wig or a Ferrari. The Ferrari won, of course, and a resplendent 360 Modena arrived. I don't regret buying it, but those of you who read my magazine article 'An Italian Mistress' will understand why it disappeared after 1,500 wonderful miles. It was beautiful to look at, went wonderfully well and sounded simply great. But I did not want to marry it.

Anyway, as always Porsche came to my rescue and invented the 997. And so it was that I again parted with my hard earned money and bought a 997C2S Coupe. By now the accountants at Porsche must have been rubbing their hands in glee. Interestingly, just before I bought my first Porsche, Porsche were in financial trouble. Now it is acknowledged that they are the most successful and profitable car manufacturer on the planet. Sure this is all down to me!

Unfortunately, I missed the wind in my hair on those balmy summer Sunday afternoons. So I swopped my Mini Cooper for a Mazda MX5 (my second, but not my last). Was this an inspirational move? The MX5 was certainly a great little roadster and I had the 997 C2S for those long Porsche Club outings.

Err, again no!

My weekly Tesco shop was now confined to purchasing a packet of Polos and one apple. That pretty little Japanese copy of my earlier Lotus Elan was hardly suitable for a supermarket run and was not particularly ideal as a runabout during the winter months.

But I had a cunning plan.

Yet again, Porsche had come up trumps. Though I adored the 997S, I missed the hatchback of the 996 Targa. Then someone whispered that Porsche were going to bring out a Coupe version of the Boxster called the Boxster Coupe. Brilliant. Moreover, it would have a hatch to store all those goodies from Tesco. I had to have one, and slapped down my letter of intent immediately. Years later, when the Boxster Coupe metamorphosed itself into the Cayman, the deposit flew out of my wallet.

Sadly I am unable to tell you whether a Cayman and MX5 were ideal bed mates, as logic at last prevailed and I rashly swapped the MX5 for another cheapo Ford Ka. This definitely was a match made in heaven. A fast comfortable prestigious load carrier for those long Porsche Club outings and a mega cheap runabout for the Tesco run. Unfortunately, my everyday car was yet again a Ford Ka—enough said. Will I ever learn? More importantly, I still hankered after the wind in the hair Sunday drive.

Interestingly, I had for some time flirted with the idea of an old car. An old Porsche or even a Jaguar E Type Roadster. That came much later! Sensibly though (I was ever thus!), I decided against spending every Sunday lying under a vintage motor.

What I needed was a new car that looked old. Then I had a brilliant idea! I would order a brand new Morgan. Well they are just like they were in the 1930s. Reasonable performance, minimal aggro, great looks and minimal service. Apart from top speed the performance was ok as it would out accelerate a Boxster 2.5 and it certainly fitted the requirements for a Sunday Cotswold tourer. Moreover, it looked a million dollars and cost almost as much. In fact this homemade kit car cost the same amount as my original Boxster. Regrettably though it could not double as a shopping car—not a chance. For a start it did not have any luggage space at all. Additionally, it took me all day to clean it, two hours per wire wheel! Hence I was very reluctant to drive it in the wet. Consequently, if I were going to use it as a shopper, I would starve on rainy days.

Unfortunately it turned out to be exactly like a 1930s Morgan. Though it was manufactured exclusively for me in 2006, it had all the warts and problems of a 1930s car: sliding pillar suspension, grease nipples and leaf springs. An ancient Porsche is light years more sophisticated than a modern Morgan and much more reliable.

But the Morgan did look flash.

So by now I had a Cayman, a Morgan and a Ka. That worked OK until I realised that the Morgan was slowly destroying what was left of my tired skeleton. Despite having the easy-up hood, I did think that 19 minutes of getting soaked and 2 fingernails was an excessive price to pay for nostalgia. I also thought that I was getting a vintage car without vintage aggro. How wrong I was. Nonetheless, on paper at least, the combination looked good. A car for summer day cruising, a shopper and a long distance reliable rapid transport.

I did keep all three vehicles for just about one year. With just a double garage guess which car was parked outside?

Finally my patience, back and fingernails expired and the Morgan and I decided to part. On amicable terms as luck would have it. I then had another brainwave.

I'd convert the Morgan and the Ka into a combination of both. A runabout convertible, so what better than a Mini? OK, they are overpriced, but worth every penny. Moreover, I suppose it is not what they cost, but what you lose when you sell. Then a Mini was the best UK car for residual value. And so it came to pass that my garage housed a Cayman and a Mini Cooper Convertible. Absolute perfection! The Mini Convertible was a great little everyday car, comfortable practical and economical and of course I do not need to extol the virtues of the Cayman.

At last, my search for perfection had come to fruition.

Now I'll let you into a little secret. My conclusion is flawed! My Porsche is for long runs and pleasure driving, the Mini is a runabout shopper. Surely it makes sense for the Porsche to be the convertible and the runabout to have a tin roof. Now there is a thought! And who said women were the only ones who are indecisive and fickle?

So finally I conclude there is indeed a better combination. If I cut the roof off my Cayman and stick it on the Mini, it will satisfy all my exacting criteria. So here is the secret, the very best combination of all—the Perfect Pair, the Holy Grail: a Porsche 911 Cabriolet and a Mini Cooper saloon. I challenge anyone to prove me wrong! They sat resplendently on my driveway for quite some time.

Only trouble is, which car to drive for fun? Perhaps there is an alternative solution— stop it, Derek, right now.

Of course, that was not the end of the story; not by far. That combination was indeed the Perfect Pair, at that particular time. Until the next perfect pair came along. That was not much later! I purchased many cars after writing that article and as I write this, I still am buying.

But enough of cars, this book is primarily about aviation. More importantly, cars became less important to me, partly due to my decision to buy my own aeroplane, partly due to the fact that old cars were trouble, and, most importantly, I could not afford an aeroplane and a fleet of cars. I have explained how to become a millionaire—you start off as a multi-millionaire and buy an old aeroplane, but which aeroplane? I previously wrote that the Cirrus, with all its fancy gizmos, was beginning to bore me. Perhaps I should purchase the perfect pair of aircraft? But I could not afford a pair of aircraft, so which one? A Cirrus *versus* a Bulldog is a very interesting comparison—a bit like comparing a modern limo with a vintage sports car. I could afford a Cirrus and hire a Bulldog, but that is not quite the same as ownership. Despite the saying 'if it floats, flies, or fucks, then hire it', the joy of ownership cannot be overstated. One does not really feel that interested in tinkering with someone else's motor. Cirrus *versus* Bulldog? Chalk and cheese. Horses for courses. But when I analysed my requirements, my main joy was turning upside down, throwing aeroplanes around, and landing in little fields. None of which I can do in a mini airliner. So when the chance to purchase a rather untidy Bulldog arose, I grabbed it and ignored the problems that would inevitably arise. Rather like very old cars, old aeroplanes need heaps of TLC. Was I about to ignore the saying, 'buy an aeroplane and become poor, buy an old aeroplane and become bankrupt'? Additionally, I do not do old cars anymore, so should I buy an old aeroplane?

38

How a Bulldog Devoured
My Bank Account

As you have suspected, Cirrus seduction was not to last and the novelty of fancy gizmos rapidly wore off. But try as one might, ignoring the problems of an old aeroplane was not an option. When I initially started my search, a few Bulldogs were available, but they were snapped up speedily. Finally, there were just three left in the entire world. One had no wings and was dead (unlike a car, an aeroplane has a shelf life and when it expires that is just scrap). One had sat in a field for years and was covered in moss and mildew and one was a Swedish model (no jokes please) situated far away in Hungary with a duff engine. Nothing suitable really. I also learnt about the dreaded fatigue factor and found that any Bulldog with a FI (Fatigue Index) of 114 was kaput. I actually found a rather good-looking Bulldog, but that had just hours to live; no good for me as it would become an expensive hangar queen within a year. Just as well, as it was a Swedish model, and due to my previous life, I really wanted an RAF version. Some six years later, it still sits in the hangar looking rather forlorn.

Then one day a mate told me that someone had an ex-RAF Bulldog that he might consider selling. To cut a very long story short and after much negotiation delayed by heavy winter snow, I arm-wrestled him into a deal. Had I taken leave of my senses? I, who never purchased old cars, was now buying a forty-year-old aeroplane. Worst still, I paid more than I wanted and it certainly did require heaps of TLC, but it was mine. This was quite literally going back to my roots. Yes it was mine, all mine, but the pitot-head heater did not work, the handbrake did not work, the ammeter did not work, the lower side of the wings were covered in mildew, and the exhaust rattled. I wondered what else was broken, but having just had its annual service, I was assured it was safe to fly.

By now, I was no longer that brash brave stupid boy who lacked fear and common sense. They do say that 'There are old pilots and there are bold pilots but there are no old bold pilots'. Now I was old, but no longer bold. I no longer took risks, I now recognised a situation before it hit me. There is another old aviation saying: 'Outstanding pilots use their excellent brains to avoid situations where by they may need to use their exceptional skill'. I think I had finally become one of them! Risk taking was now relegated to the bottom of the pile and so when, during my second test flight in the Bulldog, the weather closed in, I beat a hasty retreat back to the airfield. The next time I flew, I made sure I had the necessary maps and radio frequencies to enable me to extricate myself from any embarrassing situation. I certainly was not going to give any of my former navigators any ammunition.

I also realised just how much over the years I had learnt to rely heavily on navigators and modern navigation systems. My Bulldog possessed little of such aids and thus I now had to rely totally on myself. Again. But I get ahead of myself.

Interestingly, the day after I had parted with a king's ransom, I took to the air exactly thirty-one years and six months after I had handed back to the RAF the keys of one of Her Majesty's Bulldogs. A poignant moment. It was as if I had never vacated the left-hand seat. They do say that some things are like riding a bicycle. Flying the Bulldog was just the same. Despite its minor faults, it fitted like a glove and talked to me very nicely. My lovely bird and I flew upside down, looped, and rolled, and when we finally came back to *terra firma*, I had decided that this was for me. I had come home at last. But though that was to be just about the last flight for quite some time, we had much to look forward to. We would eventually land in little fields, turn upside down, fly in formation with other Bulldogs, and whizz low over the green countryside of Gloucestershire. Nirvana!

A few days later, with all the paperwork complete, the aeroplane insured, and money having changed hands, I flew my new acquisition, G-GGRR (quite an appropriate registration number for a Bulldog) or to use its RAF registration, XX614, to Turweston Aerodrome for substantial restorations, followed by a bare metal respray. Even that flight was an adventure for as I got airborne, the one and only radio failed. Luckily, the weather

The author and his Scottish Aviation Bulldog T1, XX614. (*Su Khoo*)

was glorious. The moral of all that was if you are going to have a radio failure, do so on a glorious day. Better still, install more than one radio. That went on my to-do list. However, a low pass by the control tower at Turweston, waggling my wings, warned them of my imminent arrival, and I subsequently taxied to the maintenance shed for what was to be its home for a long time and the start of rather an expensive restoration.

Thus commenced the very long and lengthy process of refurbishment. First up was a total redesign of the avionics. What was acceptable in 1972, when I first flew the Bulldog, was not acceptable in the twenty-first century. The skies above the UK were now like shark-infested custard. Infringe one of the many restricted areas and one risked bumping into something rather large or at the very least losing one licence. In the past, I had often taken rather a cavalier approach to navigation; if I screwed up, who would know? Now I would be tracked by radar and might even be shot down. So my precious but elderly aeroplane needed a decent navigation system together with a modern transponder allowing air traffic control to identify me and subsequently offer help with collision avoidance.

But all this was not going to be cheap. Moreover, once the maintenance team started work they quickly discovered that all was not well. For example, the magnetos had not been refurbished for nine years though it was strongly recommended that they should be every four years. Holes were found in the fibreglass, many rivets were loose and there were more leaks in my Bulldog than in an English Electric Lightning fighter, and those only stopped leaking when empty. Goodness knows how my aeroplane was granted an air-worthiness certificate and passed its annual inspection! More problems were found and the two- to three-week refurbishment dragged on for many months. During this period my learning curve was almost vertical. In a previous life, after landing, I handed over my aeroplane to the engineering officer with a brief comment of what was broken and wandered off to the pilot's crew room. The engineers were responsible for fixing the problem and ensuring that all the paperwork was tickety-boo, but more importantly no one billed me for the work, not even for the fuel. Now I had to pay, so I needed to know what my maintenance team were doing, otherwise my rapidly depleting bank balance would disappear forever and I would be hauled off to a debtor's prison. Sadly, things did not always go smoothly and I was left for many months with a Garmin 430W installed, but with no authority to use it. Eventually, after calling in an independent team, the vital approvals were granted by the CAA (Civil Aviation Authority), but not until more money changed hands.

After a very long and expensive winter, I managed to fly G-GGRR during the summer months. Having got my Bulldog just about safe to fly and with the avionics upgraded to modern flying, I had a great summer, but then, to my bank manager's horror, I then discovered more things malfunctioning, and I made plans to turn an airworthy Bulldog into the very best on the planet. My aim was to produce one even better than when it emerged from the hangar at Prestwick forty years previously.

Part two of the restoration began in earnest in the autumn, and it was not until the spring of the following year that it was complete. Come that winter, I needed the annual check to be done and what I thought would be a few simple repairs, followed by a comprehensive and very expensive bare-metal respray. Well, I got that wrong. Part two of the restoration was to last an incredible six months as the engineers discovered a major crack in an important part that held the undercarriage on; in short, frame 82 was bust. This

A formation of Bulldogs. (*Su Khoo*)

is a very important component and luckily the undercarriage had not collapsed during my ownership. Moreover, it appeared that this fault had possibly existed for over ten years. How on earth had that been overlooked for so long? I then learnt a little about mending aeroplanes. Apparently one cannot just 'fix' the problem; I had to get approval from de Havilland Support (the company who were authorised by the CAA to keep a 'fatherly eye' on Bulldogs) and, more importantly, I had to pay for the repair scheme. Talk about naïve. Luckily, I had the internet and a decent, though decreasing in size, wallet. However, nothing would proceed until I located a new frame 82 and they did not just grow on trees. Unfortunately, my excellent engineer had not done this particular repair before, so we need some outside help.

Luckily, I managed to find a replacement in the USA and that, together with a new exhaust, starter motor, battery, windscreen, elevator trim tab, complete upgraded brake system, wheels, and tyres, were just a few of the things I needed. Mind you, the windscreen took a week to fit as none of the replacement Perspex screens were the right size and my engineer had to cut to fit, drill holes for the screws (ensuring the Perspex did not crack), then make sure all was watertight. No easy quick job that.

During subsequent fuel/water checks, I also had noticed minute particles in the fuel. This indicated that the rubber lining of the four fuel tanks was breaking down and thus would ultimately clog up the fuel filters. So that meant the fuel tanks had to come out and be thoroughly cleaned. No easy job, but at least at the same time I could renew all the interconnecting fuel hoses and investigate why fuel leaked from the aeroplane when the fuel tanks were filled. This apparently was a common Bulldog fault. Eventually, all this was sorted and we found the source of the leaks. The overflow pipes that took excess fuel away from the filler area actually passed through the fuel tanks. Over the years, these pipes had developed holes or cracks, possibly due to flexing during aerobatics. Consequently, fuel was leaking from the fuel tank, into the overflow pipe and thus depositing a tell-tale puddle under the wing. This was easily sorted, but would have been impossible without tank removal.

By then, we could concentrate on the paintwork and upholstery. I went for the 'Rolls-Royce' approach. Everything dismantled, all paint removed and then came the surprise. I had known that the starboard wing had been replaced early in its civilian life when G-GGRR overran a short field and hit a tree. This necessitated a new wing together with prop and engine repairs due to a concurrent prop-strike, but when all paint had been removed from the fuselage, it was discovered that the rear half of the Bulldog had been replaced, almost certainly during RAF service. However, after many weeks, the job was complete and I was delighted with the finished product. I am not so sure my bank manager was very happy though.

Nevertheless, the proof of the pudding was in the eating. Later that year, we flew into the ex-Battle of Britain airfield of North Weald to attend an Air Britain rally and to soak up the atmosphere of vintage aeroplanes. That day we were definitely glad of our twenty-first-century avionics as we had to battle though some awful weather to get there, but got there we did. Two days later, I got a call from the organiser. 'You left without collecting the cup,' he said. Apparently our pristine refurbished Bulldog had been voted 'Star of the Show' and had won the 'A. J. Jackson Trophy' for the 'Concours d'Elegance'. Later, we were invited to display at the Royal International Air Tattoo and incredibly, among an international entry, would end up in the top twenty of the world's best. The following year, we were to repeat this double achievement. All our hard work had not been in vain!

But the work was still not finished. So at the six-monthly check, the following summer, I decided that I sought perfection and was determined to get my beloved Bulldog into a condition even better than when it was originally delivered to the Manchester and Salford University Air Squadron way back in 1974. I wanted a host of new parts to replace items that were OK, but not perfect. So out went the sticky rudder trim cable, the tatty control column leather gaiters, and the noisy flap motor. Then the whole inner fuselage and wings were treated to a special anti-corrosive fluid and a few minor oil leaks attended to, but G-GGRR was still not perfect, a bit of a curate's egg really. For a start, the engine was forty-two years old and I was advised that it was far too elderly to overhaul. So the plan was to replace the engine with a lovely new factory built one and if I was going to do that, perhaps I ought to get the propeller and constant speed unit fully overhauled so that everything was zero life. That also meant replacing all the hoses in front of the firewall and also behind it.

Consequently, later that year, more upgrades were ordered. During the annual maintenance, I fitted a new engine; well, after all, there are no lay-bys in the sky that one can pull into following an engine failure, then subsequently call the RAC. Nope, if the engine stops, one flies straight to the scene of the crash. If one is lucky (and skilful), then a safe landing in a field is on the cards. If not, one can end up upside down in that field,

The author and Su posing with the Air Britain trophy. (*Su Khoo*)

embedded in a chimney pot, or worst of all barbequed like a well-done piece of steak. So it was out with my elderly Lycoming engine and in with a brand new one from the factory in the USA. Moreover, at the same time, the propeller and associated items went off for a complete overhaul, all the forty-two-year-old rubber hoses were replaced, some essential components were tested for hairline cracks, and a fuel computer was installed as fuel gauges in light aeroplanes are notoriously inaccurate. Many a pilot has run out of fuel and ended up in a field or worst still, in a smouldering heap. This little aeroplane of mine was beginning to cost a small fortune. Correction, a large fortune.

Work progressed during the winter period and finally the new engine arrived. What joy! But the euphoria was short-lived. During its RAF life, the original engine had been modified with an inverted flight oil system, so I had specifically confirmed that I would receive one with this modification. A modified engine has a sump with connection for return oil when the aeroplane is inverted, as oil only flows downhill. If the sump is above the engine that would present a problem. I was told by my UK supplier that Lycoming had indeed confirmed I would receive 'like for like'. Unfortunately, on arrival, my lovely shiny new Lycoming engine was discovered to be pre-mod. Oh dear. Now I had a problem. A replacement engine would take time and, if nothing else, would significantly delay return of my expensive core deposit. Any drilling and tapping of the new sump would probably invalidate my new engine warranty. Complete removal of the inverted oil system would probably require CAA approval, but would be a reasonable option given that I do not fly inverted anymore. That might be a good option as aircraft with the Christen inverted oil system tend to suffer from clogged oil lines if that aeroplane is never inverted allowing hot oil to cleanse the pipes. In short, I had a problem. However, Lycoming came up trumps, supplied the correct sump for my engine and it was rapidly fitted by an approved Lycoming engine facility. But I did make a note that due to the fact that I rarely flew upside down for any length of time, my inverted oil system hoses would have to be cleaned every fifty hours or so.

Finally, we sorted everything. Now I thought my precious Scottish Aviation Bulldog T Mk 1 was perfect and I would never again have to replace or repair anything. At least, not in my lifetime. But I was wrong! Aeroplanes are not like motorcars. It is recommended that one changes the oil and filter in one's car once every year or so. Occasionally, it is suggested that a deeper service is done. After three years, it should be inspected for safety. Unfortunately, aeroplanes are governed by far stricter rules than motorcars. Items have to be replaced or inspected either after the aircraft has flown for fifty hours or, for some components, even replaced after a few years even if the aeroplane had not flown.

Shortly after one such six-monthly service, we discovered that the control columns had to be replaced. Apparently they only had a life of ten years. So my prize Bulldog was dead until I found replacements. Not easy, as they were no longer made, but I did locate the only pair in the whole world and we lived to fly another day. My chums, who also owned Bulldogs, could only look on in envy as they too were searching for spare control columns.

But there was a sting in the tale. Shortly after delivering the precious control columns to my engineers, I was told by the CAA that I could not use them as there was no authentic paper trail to prove where they had come from. Nevertheless, and to cut a long story short, after much arm wrestling with the CAA, I managed to convince them that my stick tops had to be genuine and, as they came in sealed containers, had the correct part numbers and looked in perfect condition, I could see no reason why my beloved Bulldog should be grounded. Reason prevailed and she flew again.

39

Return to 10 Squadron

Some ten years after I retired from the RAF and well into my new career as an intrepid Bulldog pilot, I returned to the scene of my VC10 exploits to check if anything had changed. It had, in spades. Here is what I wrote for the base magazine:

Just before the demise of the VC10 and after my old Squadron had re-equipped with the mighty Airbus, I decided to pay RAF Brize Norton a visit in my Bulldog. So on a rare, but bright sunny morning in late May 2013 I prepared to fly into RAF Brize Norton almost 10 years to the day that I last aviated from there. My mission was to evaluate changes to No. 10 Sqn since I left. I wondered what, if anything, had altered. When I left the RAF some 10 years ago, after serving for 39 years, I wrote an article for Gateway magazine, which reflected on the changes that had taken place in my time. Much had indeed changed. So time for an update.

But firstly, how was I going to find Brize Norton without my trusty Navigator? Then I remember that long ago, before Pontius was pilot, I actually did fly on my own. So no problem this time. However there was. On landing, I was instructed to proceed to Stand 63. Stand 63? I didn't remember that? Still, ATC came to my rescue, but failed to understand that whilst numbers painted on the tarmac can been [*sic*.] easily seen from the lofty flight deck of a VC10, they are impossible when your bottom is a mere two feet off the ground. Nevertheless I found it eventually.

Now it was time to discover if the Brize Norton of 2013 is the same as that in 1986 or even 2003. So far it all seemed much bigger, with acres of fresh concrete and many new buildings. I wondered what else had changed. Such is the pace of progress I suspected much had indeed changed since I was that 'not so young' Squadron Leader driving through the main gate to join No Ten Squadron, way back in early 1986. In fact the RAF I had joined in 1964 had considerably more in keeping with the RAF of 1940 than the Air Force of today.

On that day in May 2013, my aerial steed had changed; no longer the venerable Vickers VC 10, but a diminutive ex RAF Scottish Aviation Bulldog. Moreover, the aeroplane now equipping 10 Squadron had also changed; not the gorgeous shiny VC10, but a gigantic Airbus A330 Voyager tanker transport. Back in 1986, my VC10 had no probe to take on fuel in flight, neither could it dispense fuel, though that was to come. Moreover, it was also painted in the resplendent white livery of RAF Transport Command. In short, when I arrived as a fresh-faced youth on Ten Squadron (OK, I was never that!) the lovely VC10 was more or less as it was delivered to the Squadron from the factory at Weybridge in December 1966.

But aeroplanes always changed. That is to be expected and despite the VC10 being in service for many years, becoming almost part of the scenery, like my own ancient body, the creaking at the seams grew ever louder. So time for change. It was ever thus, but what about the fundamental fabric of Squadron life? I saw immense changes from 1964 to 2003. What had changed since?

When I flew into Brize that day in May (with permission from everyone from the Pope to OC Ten Squadron), I parked under the wing of one of the Squadron's brand new toys. Little and large, I think the photo should be called. But that would be an understatement. I had also expected an airman from Handling Flight to meet me, but no, just a civilian from a company called Air Tanker driving a posh car ... no ancient aircrew bus for me then! Off we set across the airfield and, to my incredible surprise, the Squadron was no longer housed in a rickety ancient building whose roof leaked. The new accommodation was huge, palatial, and very modern. In fact the entrance area (sorry Atrium) would not have been out of place in a modern 5 star hotel. Peering through the huge double-glazed plate glass windows of the foyer I spotted a massive brand new car park. Having heard the odd rumour that parking was now impossible at Brize Norton, I decided that one should not believe everything one is told. Parking right outside the Squadron? Never happened in my time!

Bulldog XX614 under the wing of a 10 Squadron Airbus. (*Su Khoo*)

I never got the chance to see if the Squadron Commander was still supplied with a little Mini; perhaps now he has a Mercedes limo?

After introductions, I was whisked upstairs three floors to a briefing room. By lift! Here in an enormous room, complete with overhead projectors and comfy chairs, OC 10 Squadron was briefing visiting members of the 10 Sqn Association on the role of the Squadron. 'The Boss' explained that Ten Squadron still comprises just 'men in blue' but sponsored reserves are employed by Air Tanker Services and come under 10 Sqn's command when mobilised on the military Voyager. In fact Air Tanker supports 10 Sqn by providing associated support services including aircraft maintenance, much of the training, infrastructure, fleet management and ground services. It would ultimately be equipped with 14 of the specially converted A330-200 aircraft. This partnership brought obvious significant benefits to both parties.

Afterwards we were taken to view the magnificent Voyager, which was actually hangered [*sic.*] within the 10 Sqn building itself. The accommodation seemed very modern, very business like and of course it was. The Voyager too was a little more up to date than the ancient VC10. Just a little! It looked enormous and so different from 'The Ten'. Glass cockpit, no seat for a Flight Engineer, not even a Navigator's seat (though there was one for a mission operator) and up to 291 passenger seats facing forwards were just a few of the very many differences. It even smelt new.

Of course I had to inspect the galleys! Once a co-pilot, always a co-pilot and in a previous life I had been infamous for hovering around the galleys. Here I discovered very modern automated equipment. But I wondered if the food had changed. One thing that had not changed, I was told, is that crews are still supplied with 'butty boxes' when they pop off to the North Sea to refuel fighter aircraft.

Later we were shown into the coffee bar; oops, sorry, the cafeteria. No grubby coffee cups full of penicillin here. This was a spotless little restaurant staffed by civilians. The only difference between this and a modern café was the prices. I tucked into a huge plate of fish and chips, the quality of which would have rivalled anything in Rick Stein's famous diner. But Mr Stein would not have approved of the incredibly low prices!

Then we were escorted out onto the ramp for photography. My little Bulldog looked for the entire world like a model aeroplane under the wing of the gigantic tanker/transport. But the two together complimented each other. Little and large indeed. Interestingly, the Voyager was also parked next to one of the few remaining VC10s. It dwarfed it, which I found rather fascinating as, when I arrived on 10 Squadron all those years ago I thought the VC10 gargantuan. But the Voyager is something else. It holds more than twice as many passenger seats as a 'Ten', carries considerably much more fuel, can carry 50% more freight, goes further, weighs twice as much, cost heaps more and can carry more than twice as many stretchers than the VC10. However, it actually does not go quite as fast or as high as my old aeroplane, but of course I still wanted to fly one!

So in conclusion, what do I think of the modern 10 Squadron? Well, it is just that; modern, indeed very modern, efficient, cost-effective, well-equipped and immensely capable. Maybe it and the Royal Air Force in general has lost that 'flying club' tag, but that in this cost cutting age is no bad thing. Do the current members of Shiny Ten enjoy their new toy? You bet they do. Do they work harder? I suspect that too. Is it a better outfit?

Well it's different, as indeed everything is these days. I'm positive that today's aircrew would not recognise the RAF of fifty years ago when I joined as a boy. But I personally still saw fragments of the original RAF, just a little different. The Ten Squadron of 2013 has still the same comradeship, spirit and ethos that pertained way back in 1986. I also doubt if it is that dissimilar to that that [*sic.*] of 1940. Just the buildings and aeroplanes are different. Very different. And of course there is always that dreaded accountant lurking around the corner counting his beans.

And so my brief and most enjoyable visit to the home of No. 10 Squadron came to an end and I said goodbye to my genial hosts. Would I like to be a pilot flying the mighty Voyager? You bet. Would I like to be a member of No. 10 Squadron in 2013? Of course. So I am sticking by my phone for a call from the boss. I know it will come very soon.

40

Don't Rely on Modern Gizmos

In the spring of 2015, after a lengthy restoration, my Bulldog G-GGRR rose from the ashes like the proverbial phoenix. Now she was perfect inside and out and arguably the very finest Scottish Aviation Bulldog on the planet, if not the entire universe. So much so that a fellow Bulldog pilot suggested that she was a really magnificent investment. Well I did have difficulty accepting that comment, given that I had by then spent about twice as much on it as it is worth, but to think that would be totally missing the point. Not only were we going to enjoy our beautiful war bird, but I had to keep reminding myself that we are merely custodians of these very special aerial machines. Hopefully they will still be flying in many years to come and not parked up in some aviation museum for the public to marvel at.

Despite the problems of modern day navigation, I had fun and aviation kept my brain alive. I also kept up my sporty flying with teaching formation flying in the trusty old Bulldog. I enjoyed that more, despite my preference for the ultra-modern technology in my Cirrus. However, I was careful where I flew in my ancient craft, as it did not have the goodies that the Cirrus enjoyed. Nonetheless, when I was not upside down, I enjoyed flying to little grass airfields, having a light lunch while watching other pilots make a mess of their landings on the bumpy grass. The experience was even better if I flew with another pilot. We would pass the day swapping 'war stories' and generally chewing the cud. Happy days!

Nevertheless, modern technology is OK if it works. About a year after I bought my Bulldog and installed a plethora of modern navigation aids, an experienced pilot mate and I decided to fly over to nearby Cranfield airfield to practice some instrument flying, then land and have a spot of lunch. The arrival procedure was a little complicated as it was initially based on a beacon that my equipment could not use, but no worries, there was another beacon on the airfield that I could use and the instrument landing system would be fine. Finally, I had my super-duper modern GPS. I was so confident that nothing could go wrong I did not even bother to switch on my portable back-up GPS. The weather was fine, God was in his heaven, and everything was right with the world.

So these two elderly aviators set off, in good weather, for what was going to be a very simple straightforward trip to a neighbouring aerodrome for lunch. What on earth could go wrong?

We homed perfectly OK towards the airfield, then set off for the other beacon that for some reason we were unable to acquire. No problem, as my aircraft GPS would take us there. Or so it would have done if it had not failed at that point! Even then, we would have been fine if ATC had allowed us to start our approach. Incidentally, at this stage, the weather deteriorated and we were now in cloud. Still no problems, until the tower informed us that we would have to hold for ten minutes or so as they were busy. So much for our booked approach.

Again, no problem as we could maintain our navigational awareness by reference to the beacon on the airfield and ultimately the ILS ground equipment. A break in the cloud allowed my experienced co-pilot to point out features that he 'definitely' recognised, so all was well. But by then my instrumentation was playing up. It now was giving rubbish information from the ground beacon and the ILS equipment had unlocked. I informed Cranfield that I was temporarily unsure of my position and was told to proceed to a visual reporting point to the north. Difficult if one has little idea where one was to start from, and anyway, we were in cloud. What part of 'in cloud' did they not understand?

So, being smart, we decided to give up and go home. Surely heading westwards would ensure that we picked up major landmarks and arrived home in time for tea and medals. The large town that my chum had positively identified slipped further and further behind us, but amazingly, an identical town appeared in our eleven o'clock. So what was the town we left behind? Luckily, by then, the aircraft equipment picked up another beacon and we thus established a good position fix. The previous town was thus identified and upon informing our destination airfield that we had given up due to equipment failure, we were informed that their beacon on the ground was also now unserviceable. That would explain a few things. Not our day! Whatever, we soon identified a useful landmark and arrived back at base some forty-five minutes after take-off.

Lessons learnt, yet again:

1. Have Plan 'A', Plan 'B', and a Plan 'C'. My standby GPS should have been readily available.
2. Think wind. While we were orbiting in cloud, the strong wind at 3,500 feet was blowing us eastwards fast.
3. Do not fold one's map so that anything east of one's destination is not in view. If we had not done that, we would not have misidentified a major town.
4. Double check that ground beacons are working. Do not just assume it is the equipment in the aeroplane that has failed. If we had known that the ground beacon was unserviceable, we would not have bothered with an instrument approach in cloud in the first place.
5. Do not be complacent! What seems like a simple task may well develop into something far more difficult.
6. Believe the old airman's saying: 'Never let your aeroplane take you to somewhere that your brain did not get to five minutes earlier'.
7. Do not assume, check!

But no harm done and lessons learnt. More wake-up calls!

Actually, a minor incident (lucky it was only minor as it could have had dire consequences) occurred about a year later. Despite my vast experience, I landed on the wrong runway at another airfield. I was given runway 20 as the runway in use, but landed on runway 02. Now I am not dyslexic, but I had been expecting 02, the wind favoured that runway and no other aircraft was in sight (luckily). I felt very ashamed and another lesson learnt. On landing, I telephoned air traffic control to grovel and donate shed loads of loot to the local air ambulance by way of a self-imposed fine. ATC did, however, make me feel a little better by saying 'you are not the first, nor will you be the last to do that'. But hopefully that lesson was yet another learnt and I for one would not do that again.

So what is the moral behind this blunder? Was I complacent? I think not, but I suppose it was a combination of expecting a certain runway and not actually listening to what had been said. I 'heard' what I expected to hear. Certainly the fact that 02 is similar to 20 contributed to the stupid error. All was well that ended well, but it should not have happened. Hopefully never again, for next time I might not get off so lightly.

Obviously the lesson learnt was that even an experienced pilot can (and will) screw up. We should always be vigilant and never ever complacent. Moreover, the saying 'when pilots stop learning, they should stop flying' is very apt.

41

The Final Odyssey

Having purchased and restored my Bulldog, it made sense to join the Beagle Pup and Bulldog Club so I could enjoy events with like-minded pilots and their own Bulldogs. A previous car club, of which I had been a member, ran an annual event known as the 'Weekend of the Year', otherwise known as the WOTY, so I used this as a model for a similar event for our club. The first one I organised for the club was to RAF Llanbedr, an ex-missile testing airfield on the west coast of Wales. Five Pups and Bulldogs met up in at Welshpool, a small airfield in mid-Wales, then some of us flew in formation to Llanbedr. The week there was a bit of a curate's egg; flying round Snowdonia in formation was great, but little to do other than a visit to Portmeirion where we sheltered from the rain in a small café. The last day dawned gloomy and wet, with low clouds rolling in off the sea. Luckily, the weather at my base was fine, so with radar surveillance from nearby RAF Valley, I climbed up to 7,000 feet in cloud and crossed the mountains *en route* to Turweston and home. Job done.

As the WOTY 2016 to Cornwall, which I had also organised, was conclusively rained off, I decided to be just a little more ambitious in 2017. What could be more spectacular than a flying tour of the Hebrides? Having got married for the umpteenth time in May of that year, I had already planned the expedition as a belated honeymoon. Well, my new bride was also a pilot and a darn good one at that. Obviously, we hoped for good weather as bad weather, mountains, and little aeroplanes do not usually mix. Some hope—but more of that later. Subsequently, an offer to join my old squadron, No. 6 Squadron (Typhoons), at RAF Lossiemouth was too good an opportunity to miss, thus I tagged that on to the end of our adventure. Sadly, though, perhaps the odyssey was a bit too arduous for many of our club members as only two Bulldogs accepted the challenge, later to be joined by one other from Perth.

Now you would think that I, as an experienced single-seat fighter pilot, with an additional seventeen years of global aviation as captain of a heavy four-jet, would make short work of flying a wee puddle-jumper around Scotland. Nothing could have been further from the truth. Flying a fast jet allows one to zoom up above the weather when it becomes pants. A jet airliner is always above the weather, unless making an instrument approach to an international airport. Moreover, both enjoy significant mission support.

So it was with some trepidation that the two couples, our friends Mike and Jayne, and myself and my wife Su, set off in our Bulldogs to cross the sea to Mull, Skye, and all points west. In the past, I would have carried a dinghy, worn an immersion suit, and worried when down to just three engines. Now I had just one engine and a cheap lifesaving jacket. I even had to pay for the petrol.

It started badly with me leaving my cold weather jacket at home and my Bulldog's GPS failing on take-off (shades of the usual navigation failure of the Jaguar avionics). Mike and Jayne were initially weathered in at Audley End; however, both Bulldogs made it to Halfpenny Green, where we were to meet up, and the adventure commenced. Then a short hop saw us through the shark-infested custard that is the Manchester Control Zone, landing at RAF Woodvale for fuel. This refuelling stop was specifically planned, as it was where my Bulldog had spent most of its life as the steed of the Officer Commanding the University Air Squadron. An hour later, initially with Mike leading, and after passing Blackpool Tower (the scene of a previous Bluntie Blunder), we ploughed into totally unexpected heavy weather in the Solway Firth. Despite a good forecast, the good old British climate had turned incredibly sour and, with cloud almost on the deck and visibility down to 2 feet 6 inches, I took the lead. Initially, I thought the problem might just be a large shower so we flew on. Trouble was, the weather continued to deteriorate and though we were over the sea and with three independent GPSs (thus knew our exact position) and with unfriendly mountains on the nose, I reluctantly initiated a diversion to the nearest suitable aerodrome. Despite knowing that it would screw our day, I prudently decided that tea and medals in a warm hotel would be more acceptable to all. This resulted in an unplanned landing at Carlisle airport, but a somewhat agreeable night in a local hostelry. At the airport, the handling agent royally looked us after, provided fuel, hangars, and even a taxi to take us to our lodgings.

The following morning dawned crystal clear and, following a man-sized breakfast, the two-ship launched for Glenforsa on the Isle of Mull. The route would take us across the highlands and fiords of South West Scotland, past Prestwick where my little aeroplane had been manufactured and onwards abeam the islands of Arran, Islay, and Jura. Under a bright blue sky, it proved an ideal day for taking some really scenic photographs. The whole flight was simply magnificent: the mountains beneath us shimmered in the morning sun and the water in the lochs twinkled at us as we flew by. It was just a truly wonderful day. This was definitely something that the majority of mankind never get to experience. Finally, as we rounded Sgùrr Dearg, we got our first view of the Sound of Mull and Glenforsa itself. For those who have not been to that lovely little airfield, it is a little 700-metre grass strip sandwiched between large mountains and the sea. The hotel next to the runway is great, but in need of a little refurbishment. Not that I minded, as the view from my window was to die for: mountains, sea, Stearman biplanes, Super Cubs, and our own Bulldogs.

The next day, two other club members, Kerr and Fiona from Perth in their Bulldog, joined us. So as a three-ship, we took advantage of rare wonderful weather and planned a tour of the islands culminating with a landing at a short strip near Plockton. Being cautious, I earlier had concerns at flying over the sea in a single-engined aeroplane, as if we had ditched, it would have resulted in almost certain death. But I soon put those worries aside as the three Bulldogs flew over vast swathes of sea and lochs. Maybe it was the perfect weather, the fact that we were three Bulldogs in formation or the sunlight glinting off the calm sea that made me forget the consequences of engine failure. Anyway, the engine did

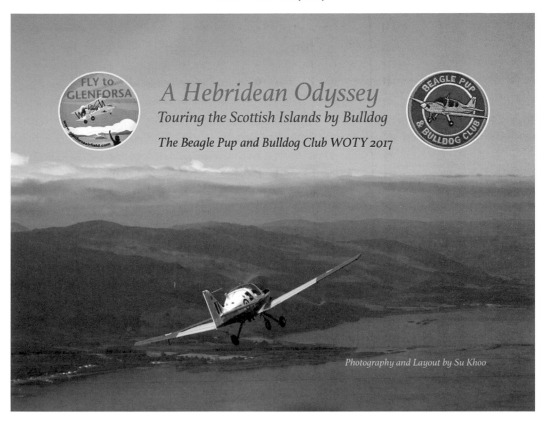

The cover of the book *A Hebridean Odyssey* adventure 2017. (*Su Khoo*)

not know it was over the sea. Onwards we flew, past Lismore lighthouse, up Loch Linnhe, over the famous Glenfinnan monument, past the misty Isle of Skye, and down over Loch Alsh. Finally, we landed on the small 500-metre strip at Plockton for lunch. Three Bulldogs flying low down the runway in Vic formation must have woken up the locals.

After a cracking seafood lunch, Kerr and Fiona headed back to Perth via Oban and the remaining two Bulldogs returned to Glenforsa for even yet more mega Langoustines.

Following two days of pretending to be tourists, with of course the mandatory distillery visit, seal watching, and the obligatory café stop in the pouring rain, having refuelled for the second time at Oban, the two remaining Bulldogs set off for Lossie, way up north in Morayshire. This is where my previous Jaguar experience paid dividends, as even in really atrocious weather, the Great Glen was easy to navigate at a quarter of the speed of my Big Cat. However, we could not deviate right or left because of the rock faces, or even climb as that would turn the aeroplane into an ice cube. In short, we flew the entire length of the Great Glen as though through a tunnel: rocks on both sides, water perilously close under our wheels, and rather nasty storm clouds just above our fins. So it was not surprising that without possessing my military experience, Mike decided that discretion was the better part of valour and returned to Oban. After another distillery visit and more seafood, he and Jayne later went home by train, returning the following week to collect their aeroplane. But the Great Glen had few problems for me. I knew exactly where I was, I knew that unlike some Scottish valleys, no cables were strung across the loch and the forecast was for better weather the more we made progress up the loch. I also suspected that no other idiot would be flying down Loch Ness in such bad weather, so it would be unlikely that I met anyone going the other way. Thus XX614 naturally made it in fine style to Lossie, though we were rather disappointed not to be escorted in by a 6 Squadron Typhoon on each wing. Perhaps they could not keep up with me. That night, XX614 was tucked up nice and warm in a hangar full of very expensive jet fighters, while I enjoyed mess life at Lossie for the first time in probably forty years. It was good to see that the young bucks were just as frolicsome as I was all those years ago.

Following a superb 6 Squadron weekend (more distilleries, a dining-night, BBQ, etc.), we departed south over the mountains, dodging the thunderstorms for Perth and yet another night stop. Here we were well hosted by Kerr and Fiona, which was especially appreciated given that we were billeted in the 'YMCA' (well, the hotel where we stayed was little better). At least XX614 got better accommodation as Kerr parked it next to his Bulldog in the club hangar. In fact, it was only at Glenforsa that the Bulldogs had to sit outside in the rain.

The weather on the following day proved to be no better than on the previous day, so discretion yet again being the better part of valour, we ditched our plan to fly down the west coast route to Carlisle and thus high-tailed it all the way down the opposite side of the UK to Church Fenton in Yorkshire, my old QFI aerodrome. It was good to observe that little had changed, though sad to see just how deserted it was. Perhaps the ghosts of pilots past sat in my aeroplane that night as it slept in the empty hangar. This would be a great base for another flying club tour as they have vast hangar space, the Yorkshire atmosphere is a welcoming one, and there are all the delights of York to see. More importantly, it is not as far as the extreme wilds of northern Scotland and I could reach it without risking a water crossing. Already my mind was planning the next adventure.

The next day dawned fairly bright and clear, but with a promise of thunder-bumper clouds later in the afternoon. So I brought the take-off time forward, cancelled my intermediate stop at Turweston airfield, and flew direct back to my base in Gloucestershire. Dodging controlled airspace and the occasional rain shower, I flew more or less the length on England back to the old Red Arrows hangar at Kemble. The Dog was now safely back in its kennel again and I breathed a huge sigh of relief at surviving what was quite an experience and definitely not what most couples opt for as a honeymoon.

Will this be my last ever mega adventure? Possibly as there are no 'old bold pilots', and perhaps I was becoming a little too bold once again. I think I should quit while I am winning.

42

Twilight

Now I have plenty of time to look back on my life: what mattered to me and what did not. Did I get my priorities right? No, not all of the time, but my motto was 'plan for the worst, hope for the best'. Not a bad motto and I kept to it, most of the time. Did I make mistakes? Yes, of course, I did, in the air and on the ground. Was I a good man? Well, that is for others to judge, but I think I was. I was also flawed.

Was I a good pilot? Well I like to think I was one of the best, but unlike Uncle Derek, I was never really judged in genuine combat. I saw some, but not much. I had my moments, least of which was my episode with the duck, which others judged to be my finest hour.

Was I a good fighter pilot? No, I was not. They do say that good pilots, like good F1 drivers, are risk-averse (though good risk managers), but I was far too careful, too cautious. I started this book by quoting from Brig.-Gen. Robin Olds: 'There are pilots and there are pilots; with the good ones, it is inborn. You can't teach it. If you are a fighter pilot, you have to be willing to take risks'. Everybody takes risks. It just depends on your personal safety level. I also suggested that 'there are old pilots and there are bold pilots, but there are no old pilots'. I was a good pilot, but I was far too cautious to be the greatest fighter pilot. I was never a big risk taker. However, that made me a good VC10 pilot—probably one of the best. At least it said so on paper.

So, in the twilight of my days, do I like myself? Well, yes I do, and that, dear reader, is perhaps something I can be proud of.

Well there you have it, the whole story. Well just about what I am prepared to divulge, warts and all.

Uncle Derek never did return from his mission to 'Happy Valley'. Neither did any of his crew, but the tale has an interesting twist. Years later, I was sitting in the foyer of the Hotel Intercontinental in Nairobi with my navigator who was reading a three-day-old copy of the *Daily Mail*. He had just got to the bit entitled 'Every Picture Tells a Story'. A Second World War veteran had sent in a newspaper article about an RAF pilot called Derek Sharp who had experienced an incredibly lucky escape while training in Tuscaloosa Alabama. My navigator said: 'This bloke's got the same name as you and he looks just like you'. I looked at the photo and immediately recognised it as my Uncle Derek. He must have been in his twenties when the photo was taken. The letter told part of an amazing story and, for the very first time, I learnt of Uncle Derek's daring exploits in the air.

Uncle Derek was one of many young men in the Second World War who were trained to fly in America under the Arnold Scheme, named after the head of the USAF.

Flying magazine of November 1948 told of an amazing story regarding my uncle. Apparently, he was a boisterous young man (a bit like me really when I was young). It was these high spirits that led to an almost unbelievable incident on 14 January 1942 (almost forty-one years to the day to my own amazing incident). On a training flight in a two-seater Stearman biplane, due to turbulence, the aeroplane suffered negative-*g*. Having forgotten to fasten his seatbelt, the turbulence catapulted my uncle out of the plane and high into the sky, many hundreds of feet above the ground. He flailed in the air for a few horrifying seconds and then started to plunge towards earth. But by some astonishing chance, he landed on the aeroplane's tail!

As he clung on for dear life, his horrified instructor signalled my uncle to jump off. Unfortunately, our wretched student, who had received rather a large bump on his head, considered his parachute had been damaged in the ejection so declined the instruction to jump. Thus the instructor, a Mr Jay A. McCausland, was forced to make an emergency landing with Derek Sharp Snr clinging to the rear of the aircraft for his dear life.

This was not the end of his adventures in the USA. Six days after his amazing escapade, on 20 January, my uncle almost lost his life again when his aircraft, with him at the controls, was struck by a landing aeroplane while he was waiting to take-off at an auxiliary airfield just 5 miles south of Tuscaloosa. This is the report of an eyewitness:

> He was preparing for takeoff when Cadet Sidney Sims in another plane, decided that Sharp looked most inviting for a soft landing. The plane came down and the wheels hit the wing about six inches from Sharp's head, actually cutting off a portion of the wing itself. Sims flew around again and made a perfect landing, whilst Sharp descended and looking resignedly at his ship said, 'I wonder just how long this can last'. Personally I think that if Sharp fell into the river fully dressed, he would come out washed, shaved, and with clothes cleaned and neatly pressed.

A newspaper article of the time concurred: 'When a plane lands on top of another sitting on the ground, someone is usually killed. But not in this case. Derek Sharp and his golden horseshoe cheated old Mr Death just as he had cheated him not six days before'. His instructor stated afterwards that he was certain that this second escape, so soon after the first, must be due to the fact that Sharp was blessed with some sort of supernatural protection. Reports of these incredible incidents made national headlines across the USA and for a brief period my uncle was a celebrity. Famous for five minutes!

Sadly, we now know that his luck was to finally run out just over one year later. Like so many of his generation, he paid the ultimate sacrifice and gave his life for his country. I always find it interesting that in 2012 we, quite rightly, were agonising over a single death of a British soldier in Afghanistan. Then I remember that the RAF lost hundreds of young aircrew every single night during the Second World War.

But was Derek's life in vain? Was I reincarnated from the ashes of my uncle? We are more than just alike. Of course, I carry most of his genes. But uncannily we are so similar. Who knows, perhaps he was there outside my cockpit that fateful day in February 1983, guiding me and my stricken craft to an unbelievable safe landing.

What other rationalisation have you got to explain how a pilot, bleeding and blind, could restart an aeroplane's sole engine and fly it to a perfect landing? How else did I, as a very slow, below average pilot, go solo, well ahead of my colleagues? I still remember that flight in a Jet Provost XN 465 on 15 July 1965. Spooky or just an incredible coincidence?

From almost that day, I have kept a fridge magnet that reads 'Never drive faster than your Guardian Angel can fly'. Good advice. Good advice indeed! From early days, I have dreamed of flying: it was a passion—it still is. I started this journey with a lovely song from ABBA. I will finish it with this one:

> I had a dream, a plane to fly,
> I saw the wonder of the fairy tale.
> I took the future knowing I wouldn't fail.
> I believe in angels, something good in everything I did
> I believe in angels, I knew the time was right for me.
> I took to the sky, I had that dream.

I served Her Majesty for thirty-nine years. When I joined, fighting for my country was nothing further from my mind. Senior officers did not possess medals and we had been at peace for over fifteen years. I joined a 'flying club' merely to fly. I had a great time and did see active service. Sadly, many of my friends were killed, though mainly as a result of aircraft accidents—I survived. I am no longer that silly spotty youth all those years ago who longed to be a pilot who just only wanted to fly. I now have feelings, thoughts, and principles. My lasting impression is that war is inherently bad and that politicians, not military men, make war. Some wars are justified and indeed necessary; certainly the one that my father and uncle fought in was. The last two I 'fought' in were, in own opinion, completely unethical. The First Gulf War was fought on a lie and the whole world still suffers from it. I apologise for the sermon, but as one gets older, one gets wiser. Sadly, not everyone does, as the song says: 'When will they ever learn?'

So there it is warts and all. I had a vision and it all came true. As the song says, 'Regrets, I've had a few; but then again, too few to mention'. I have had a magnificent time and have a fantastic kaleidoscope of memories. Finally, I remember the uncle I never met; at the going down of the sun, and in the morning, I will remember him. I really do wonder if his spirit lives on in my guardian angel.

Epilogue

Many years from now, there will be no such thing as pilots who drive aeroplanes while sitting in them. Already the RAF operates pilotless drones over Afghanistan, while their pilots sit in comfy armchairs back in the UK drinking coffee. Computers rule the world and I have no doubt that very soon they will fly aeroplanes without pilots even remotely operating the controls from a distance. Whether Joe Public will accept a passenger plane without crew is another thing, but pilotless offensive support aircraft are here to stay.

Consequently, this book will serve as a reminder of how things were. Moreover, my descendants in the twenty-second century and beyond may well be fascinated by how primitive human beings actually sat in aeroplanes and went to war! So this is for those who come after me, a long time in the future. They will not believe what we did—I can hardly believe it now! However, for today, I am off to fly my Scottish Aviation Bulldog, to slip the surly bonds of earth, dance the skies of laughter-silvered wings, and do things that you in the future will never even dream of.

APPENDIX I
Aircraft Qualified to Fly

1. Slingsby T 38 Grasshopper
2. Slingsby Tutor T21
3. Slingsby T31
4. Slingsby Kirby Tutor
5. Slingsby Swallow
6. Schleicher K7
7. EON Olympia 2b
8. DH Chipmunk T10
9. Scottish Aviation Bulldog T Mk1
10. Beagle Pup 100, 150
11. Cessna 150, 152
12. Piper PA 28 140, 161
13. EV 97 Eurostar
14. Breezer
15. Flight Design CT
16. Aquila A210
17. Tecnam P2002
18. Cirrus SR20, G1, G2 & G3, SR22 GTS
19. Jet Provost Mk 3, 4, 5A
20. Folland Gnat T.1
21. BAe Hawk T Mk1
22. English Electric Canberra B2, T4, B15, B16, B(I)8
23. Hawker Hunter F6, F6A, T7, FGA9
24. Sepecat Jaguar GR1, T2
25. Scottish Aviation Jetstream T Mk1
26. Boeing 737 200
27. Vickers VC10 C1, C1K, K3, K4

APPENDIX II
Record of Service

Unit	From	To
No. 1 ITS RAF South Cerney	7 December 1964	1 April 1965
SPHU RAF Dishforth	20 April 1965	14 June 1965
3 FTS RAF Leeming	15 June 1965	25 June 1966
4 FTS RAF Valley	26 June 1966	14 November 1966
6 AEF White Waltham	15 November 1966	11 December 1966
231 OCU RAF Bassingbourn	12 December 1966	15 May 1967
73 Sqn RAF Akrotiri, Cyprus	16 May 1967	24 March 1969
14 Sqn RAF Wildenrath, Germany	25 March 1969	3 October 1970
CFS RAF Little Rissington	4 October 1970	18 April 1971
HSP RAF Church Fenton	19 April 1971	19 April 1972
RNEFTS RAF Church Fenton	20 April 1972	18 April 1974
Jaguar OCU RAF Lossiemouth	19 April 1974	9 January 1977
SRF RAF Leeming	10 January 1977	25 February 1977
234 Sqn TWU RAF Brawdy	26 February 1977	19 June 1977
226 OCU RAF Lossiemouth	20 June 1977	3 November 1977
6 Sqn RAF Coltishall	4 November 1977	8 June 1980
79 Sqn RAF Brawdy	9 June 1980	7 August 1980
Standards Sqn RAF Brawdy	8 August 1980	9 September 1980
63 Sqn RAF Chivenor	10 September 1980	1 February 1980
151(F) Sqn RAF Chivenor	2 February 1980	24 April 1983
Ops Wing RAF Coltishall	25 April 1983	9 March 1986
METS RAF Finningley	10 March 1986	20 July 1986
241 OCU RAF Brize Norton	21 July 1986	10 January 1987
10 Sqn RAF Brize Norton	11 January 1987	30 January 1994
55 ® Sqn RAF Brize Norton	31 January 1994	25 June 1995
10 Sqn RAF Brize Norton	26 June 1995	23 October 2003

APPENDIX III

Record of Jaguar Crashes

The first production Jaguar T2, XX136, was lost on 22 November 1974 after an engine caught fire on its 236th flight. The aircraft crashed near Wimborne St Giles, Dorset. Both crew on board, Wg Cdr Rustin and Flt Lt Cruickshanks, ejected successfully.

T2 XX831/W of 226 OCU, flown by my chum Flt Lt Whitney Griffiths, crashed at Lossiemouth on 30 April 1975 after loss of control during an inverted run over the airfield while doing a display practice. The pilot ejected and was slightly injured. I actually watched this. The root cause was that the rear seat was unoccupied and the projected map display ill fitted. During the manoeuvre, it slid backwards, pushing the control column backwards. As the aircraft was inverted at the time, at a mere 500 feet, the aeroplane nose-dived into the ground.

On 6 February 1976, T2 XX137/A, allocated to 226 OCU, crashed into the Moray Firth after it ran out of fuel owing to a leak in the low-pressure system. The pilot ejected.

The first Jaguar fatality occurred on 2 July 1976 when GR1 XX822 of No. 14 Squadron crashed 15 miles west of Aldorn, West Germany. The pilot, Flt Lt T. M. Bushnell, was killed. Terry and I joined the RAF together in 1964.

NATO exercise Teamwork 76 saw the loss of two more Jaguars and their pilots. On 15 September 1976, GR1 XX735 from No. 6 Squadron crashed near Eggebek, West Germany, killing Flt Lt G. L. Sheppard. Two days later, GR1 XX120 from No. 54 Squadron crashed into the Kattegat off Samsoe Island, Denmark, killing Flt Lt P. S. West.

GR.1 XZ102/H of No. II(AC) squadron crashed 10 miles north-east of Laarbruch, West Germany, on 14 December 1976. The aircraft went into an uncontrolled roll immediately after take-off, and the pilot (Bill Langworthy) decided to eject when he could see light above his head. The cause of the crash was a tailplane powered feedback control unit that had not been connected, which meant that once the tailplane moved, it just kept going with nothing to tell it to stop—hence the uncontrolled roll.

On 25 February 1977, GR1 XZ120 of No. II(AC) Squadron crashed into the North Sea off Nordholm, Denmark, after losing contact during a formation join-up. The pilot, Flt Lt D. G. Stein, was killed.

On 14 June 1977, GR1 XX978/DM, assigned to No. 31 Squadron, struck a house at Verden, West Germany. The pilot, Fg Off. T. V. Penn, was killed.

On 29 July 1977, both 226 OCU crew on board T2 XX148/M were killed when the aircraft crashed near Whittingham, Northumberland. They were Flt Lt Hinchcliffe and Fg

Off. R. F. Graham. I knew Taff very well as I had previously served with him on 3 Squadron, 226 OCU. I was the effects officer assigned to assist Dee, his widow, and attended his funeral on a dank Scottish afternoon. I was to return to Craigellachie, where he is buried, some forty years later.

On 21 March 1978, GR1 XX971/DE of No. 31 Squadron crashed shortly after take-off from CFB Lahr, West Germany, after the No. 2 engine failed. Despite jettisoning external stores and attempting an emergency landing, the pilot ejected successfully after speed and height had decayed such that he did not anticipate being able to make the airfield.

On 27 April 1978, T2 XX149/N from 226 OCU emerged from cloud in a steep inverted dive and crashed into a mountain near Banff, Scotland. The crew (Flt Lt C. Everett and Flt Lt J. Rigby) ejected just before the impact, but were both killed.

On 6 June 1978, GR1 XX761 from the OCU was destroyed in a ground fire after an engine explosion. The cockpit was salvaged as 8600M.

On 25 July 1978, GR1 XX823 of No. 17 Squadron flew into a hill near Cagliari, Sardinia, while on an APC sortie from Decimomannu, killing the pilot, Flt Lt R. J. West.

On 1 November 1978, GR1 XX759 from 226 OCU crashed near Selkirk, Scotland. The Ecuadorian Air Force pilot was killed.

On 18 July 1978, GR1 XX960/AK of No. 14 Squadron crashed at Islehorn, West Germany. The pilot ejected.

On 26 March 1979, T2 XX147/BY from No. 17 Squadron crashed near Südlohn, Borken, West Germany, after suffering a bird strike. Both crew ejected.

On 22 June 1979, XX142/G of 226 OCU crashed into the Moray Firth 10 nmi north of Lossiemouth. This was caused by loss of control while in inverted flight carrying out a loose article check. Unfortunately, the check was carried out at low level instead of the prescribed 7,000 feet. With full external tanks, the C of G rapidly shifted forward, and the crew could not recover in time. The front-seat student (Capt. Rasmussen RDAF) initiated the ejection sequence but the aircraft struck the sea before the seat fired. The backseat staff pilot, Flt Lt John Skinner, ejected but drowned. This accident caused the introduction of a front canopy Liner Cutting Charge on T2s to speed up the ejection sequence.

On 23 November 1979, GR1 XX762 of 226 OCU crashed 2,000 feet up Beinn a'Chleibh mountain near Dalmally, Argyle, Scotland. The staff pilot, Flt Lt Al Proctor, ejected. Unfortunately, the weather made it impossible to find the crash site. When the site was located, it was discovered that the pilot had survived the ejection but his parachute had been caught by the wind, which dragged him down the mountain. During this, he sustained a head trauma, which rendered him unconscious. As a result, he froze to death on the mountain.

On 10 December 1979, GR1s XX749 and XX755 of the OCU collided during formation training over Lumsden, Aberdeenshire, Scotland. The pilot of XX755, Flt Lt N. Brown, was killed. The student pilot in XX749 ejected. The canopy failed to jettison because the firing link was not connected, so the seat passed through the canopy, injuring the pilot.

On 25 May 1980, there was another mid-air collision, this time between XX961 and XX964, both from No. 17 Squadron, during a break for landing at RAF Brüggen. The pilot of XX961, Flt Lt J. Cathie, was killed. The wreckage landed on the airfield. XX961 caught fire, but the pilot was able to eject, the aircraft landing just outside the airfield.

On 17 July 1980, GR1 XX817 of No. 17 Squadron crashed at Mönchengladbach in West Germany after a reheat fire caused by a fuel leak from the port LP fuel system. The pilot ejected and the wreckage landed close to houses at the edge of a wood.

RAF Germany Jaguars took part in exercise Red Flag 81/2, which started at Nellis AFB on 17 January 1981 and lasted for six weeks. During this exercise, GR1 XX827/BM of No. 17 Squadron crashed on the Nellis ranges on 12 February. The aircraft was observed to pull up sharply, roll inverted, and strike the ground with the engines in reheat. The pilot, Flt Lt D. Plumbe, was killed.

On 14 April 1981, GR1 XX973 of No. 31 Squadron crashed 4 miles north-west of Gütersloh, West Germany, after the aircraft entered an unrecoverable spin during an air-combat training sortie. The pilot ejected safely and the wreckage hit the ground 50 metres from a farmhouse.

On 1 June 1981, T2 XX828/P of 226 OCU crashed 8 miles east of Kirriemuir, Tayside, Scotland, after a bird strike shattered the canopy. Fragments of the canopy were ingested by both engines, causing both to fail. The crew ejected successfully.

On 17 July 1981, GR1 XX113 launched from RAF Abingdon on an air test following a major service. The aircraft carried out an un-commanded flight control movement (UFCM) when the port spoiler powered flying control unit (PFCU) extended to full travel caused by a loose object jammed in the PFCU feedback mechanism. The OCU staff pilot lost control and ejected near Malvern, breaking his ankle during the process. The loose object was never identified or recovered.

On 24 July 1981, T2 XX916 operated by the ETPS was carrying out a NAVWASS assessment when it suffered a bird strike, which damaged both engines, and crashed into the sea. The pilot ejected safely. The back-seater (Flt Lt S. Sparks) ejected but mistakenly detached his personal survival pack (PSP) lanyard instead of the PSP's single-handed release connectors (SHRC), became tangled in rigging lines on landing in the sea and drowned.

On 6 August 1981, GR1 XX972 of 31 Squadron flew into the ground near Barnard's Castle, Northumberland. The pilot, Sqn Ldr R. Matthews, did not attempt to eject.

On 21 October 1981, GR1 XX957 of No. 20 Squadron crashed on approach to landing at Brüggen after the aircraft was struck by lightning. The port engine failed, but the pilot inadvertently shut off fuel to the starboard engine, causing that engine to fail as well. The pilot ejected but suffered a spinal crush fracture.

Jaguar GR1 XX758/18 belonging to No. 226 OCU crashed 14 miles north-west of Dingwall, Ross and Cromarty, on 18 November 1981. The pilot, Fg Off. A. Crowther, was killed when the aircraft flew into a hillside during a snowstorm.

On 2 April 1982, GR1 XX122 of No. 54 Squadron crashed into the Wash, killing the pilot, Capt. Bjornstad RNoAF. Unbelievably, the aircraft's low height audio warning had been set to zero feet.

Jaguar GR1 XX963/AL of No. 14 Squadron was shot down on 25 May 1982, 35 miles north-east of RAF Brüggen, West Germany, by a live AIM-9L Sidewinder accidentally fired from Phantom FGR.2 XV422 of No. 92 squadron during a simulated combat exercise. The pilot (Steve Griggs) ejected safely. The Board of Inquiry determined that the master armament switch in the Phantom had not been taped in the 'safe' position and the pilot inadvertently rendered one of the two main safely switches 'live'. The Phantom's pilot and navigator were court-martialled and found guilty of offences of neglect, for which they received severe reprimands.

On 11 July 1982, GR1 XX820 of No. 31 Squadron crashed on approach to RAF Brüggen after engines failure caused by the ingestion of the intake auxiliary air door hinge bolt. The pilot ejected successfully.

On 13 September 1982, Jaguar GR1 XX760/AA of No. 14 Squadron crashed 11 miles north of Bonar Bridge, Sutherland. The pilot ejected after an engine caught fire.

Jaguar GR1 XX768/BA of No. 17 Squadron crashed on 29 September 1982 near Heinsberg-Rauderath, West Germany, while on approach to RAF Brüggen. An engine caught fire, possibly the result of a failure of the LP compressor. The pilot ejected.

On 7 March 1983, Jaguar GR1 XZ376/BE of No. 17 Squadron crashed at RAF Tain, Ross and Cromarty, after the pilot lost control during a bomb toss manoeuvre. He ejected at 325 feet. The canopy jettisoned but did not clear the aircraft. The seat passed through the canopy rendering the pilot unconscious. The aircraft was carrying two inert 1,000-lb bombs. The aircraft's drop tanks broke up in mid-air.

On 19 April 1983, GR1 XX742 of No. 6 Squadron crashed into the North Sea 25 nmi from the coast after an un-commanded flight control movement. The pilot ejected but sustained a wedge fracture of the vertebrae. The aircraft's wreckage was not recovered. As a result of this accident, a sonar location beacon was fitted to RAF Jaguars.

On 16 June 1983, GR1s XZ105 and XZ110, both of No. II(AC) Squadron, collided at Goose Bay, Canada, during a break to land. Both pilots ejected.

On 22 June 1983, GR1 XX721 of No. 54 Squadron crashed 8 nmi south of Hahn AB, West Germany, while on a weapon training sortie. Both engines flamed out after apparent fuel starvation, but the cause was never positively determined. The pilot ejected but sustained a wedge fracture of the vertebrae.

On 19 September 1983, Jaguar GR1 XX114/02 of No. 226 OCU crashed at RAF Lossiemouth after a bird strike caused double engine failure. The pilot ejected.

T2 XX915 operated by the ETPS crashed near Porton Down, Wiltshire, on 17 January 1984. After an engine failure, the pilot was attempting an emergency landing at Boscombe Down, but the second engine ignited leaking fuel from the No. 1 engine and the aircraft crashed. The pilot ejected safely.

On 7 February 1984, GR1 XX750 of No. 6 Squadron crashed on the Nellis ranges during a Red Flag exercise. The aircraft struck a desert ridge during a harsh threat evasion manoeuvre. The pilot, Flt Lt Jackson, did not attempt to eject.

Jaguar GR1A XZ393 of No. 54 Squadron was written-off on 12 July 1984, when it crashed into the North Sea off Cromer after colliding with Tornado GR.1 ZA408. The pilot, Sqn Ldr Dim Jones, ejected. I watched this from the RAF Coltishall tower in my position as SLOPs. The Jaguar pilot was on the wrong radio frequency and did not hear warnings of the approaching Tornado.

On 22 August, another GR1A went down in the North Sea, this time it was XZ395, also from No. 54 Squadron. The pilot lost control after an un-commanded flying control movement during an ACT sortie, and ejected.

On 1 April 1985, GR1 XZ388 of No. 14 Squadron flew into the ground near Celle, West Germany, after the pilot became distracted tuning the radio. The pilot ejected, the canopy jettisoned as normal but shattered, the drogue gun fired, but the bullet passed through the canopy frame, which swung round and struck the pilot on the helmet, rendering him unconscious. He also sustained a broken ankle, bitten through tongue and crushed vertebrae.

On 19 July 1985, GR1A XZ365 of No. II(AC) Squadron crashed on Bastenberg Hill, West Germany. The pilot continued VFR into IFR conditions. The aircraft struck the top of the hill, the pilot ejected and aircraft wreckage landed on a road in the valley floor beyond. The pilot was found negligent and removed from flying single-seat fast jets.

On 7 October 1985, GR1A XX731 and GR1 XX728, both from No. 6 Squadron, collided in mid-air over the Hartside Pass in Cumbria. The pilot of XX731 (Flt Lt L. Stovin) did not attempt to eject and was killed. XX728's pilot managed to eject despite there being flames in the cockpit and the parachute withdrawal line being almost burnt through. Flt Lt Stovin's wife was on duty that day at an Air Traffic Control officer at RAF Coltishall. I was SLOPs. She arrived in my office quite distressed and reported the loss of two of our Jaguars and one pilot possible killed. I asked her who, and she replied, 'My husband.' Like a true professional she insisted on returning to her watch.

The only loss during 1986 was of GR1A XX732/03 of 226 OCU, which crashed on Stock Hill, 11 miles south-west of Hawick on 27 November. The USAF exchange pilot, Capt. Bateau, was killed.

In 1987, there were two losses within six days. GR1 XZ116/D of No. 41 Squadron went down on 17 June after colliding with Tornado GR1 ZA493 of No. 20 Squadron in the Borrowdale Valley 6 miles south of Keswick, Cumbria. The Jaguar pilot, Flt Lt Andrew Mannheim, was killed. The subsequent enquiry was able to establish that from the relative routes of each aircraft and terrain masking, it would have been very unlikely that either crew would have seen each other before the accident and in time to take avoiding action.

GR1A XZ386/05 of 226 OCU went down on 24 June 3 miles south-east of Builth Wells, Powys, after the pilot, Flt Lt I. Hill, lost control. He was killed.

Jaguar T2A XX834 of No. 6 Squadron crashed near Hahn AFB, West Germany, on 7 September 1988, when it struck power lines. The back-seater, a USAFE F-16 exchange pilot, successfully ejected, but the pilot, Flt Lt S. P. Nelson, was killed when his seat hit the steep side of the valley.

On 16 April 1989, GR1A XZ359 was destroyed when it crashed into cliffs at Lumsdaine Beach, 2.5 nmi west-north-west of St Abb's Head. The pilot had continued VFR into IFR conditions. The aircraft impacted 100 feet from the top of 500-foot cliffs and the pilot was killed instantly.

On 9 January 1990, Jaguar GR1A XZ108 collided with Tornado GR.1 ZA394 over the Spadeadam weapons range in Northumberland. Despite losing 2 feet of its port wing tip, the Jaguar was recovered to RAF Leeming. The Tornado crashed near Hexham, and both crew-members sustained major injuries when they ejected.

Jaguar GR1A XZ387 crashed into the Solway Firth 5 miles off Southerness Point on 12 September 1990, killing the pilot, Flt Lt J. Marsden.

Jaguar GR.1A XX754 flown by Flt Lt Keith Collister crashed in Qatar on 13 November 1990. The pilot was killed when the aircraft hit a ridge in the desert.

On 29 August 1991, Jaguar T2A XX843/GT was destroyed following a mid-air collision with Cessna 152 G-BMHI over Carno, Powys. The Cessna pilot and Jaguar pilot Wg Cdr